TO
Hear
AND *Obey*

TO HEAR AND Obey

Essays in Honor of
FREDRICK CARLSON HOLMGREN

Edited by
BRADLEY J. BERGFALK AND PAUL E. KOPTAK

COVENANT PUBLICATIONS

ISBN 910452-83-0, book edition
ISSN 0361-0934, *The Covenant Quarterly*, Vol. LV, Nos. 2-3,
    May and August 1997
Copyright © 1997 by Covenant Publications
3200 West Foster Avenue, Chicago, Illinois 60625
Production: Jane K. Swanson-Nystrom, Sally Johnson,
    Sandra C. Escontrias, David R.Westerfield, Ann-Marie Olson

Fredrick Carlson Holmgren

Tabula Gratulatoria

Marlene and Paul Bramer, *Chicago, Illinois*
Arthur A.R. and Laurel F. Nelson, *Chicago, Illinois*
F. Burton and L. Grace Nelson, *Chicago, Illinois*
Glenn and Sharon Palmberg, *Bellevue, Washington*
Philip Stenberg and Evonne Peterson-Stenberg, *Mendota Heights, Minnesota*
James V. Sundholm, *Minneapolis, Minnesota*
Norma S. Sutton, *Chicago, Illinois*
Wayne C. and Mary Anne Weld, *Des Plaines, Illinois*

Contents

CHRISTIAN CANON

BIBLIOGRAPHY

Foreword

Over his long career of teaching, preaching, and writing, Fred Holmgren has reminded us over and over again that the Hebrew Scriptures are and remain thoroughly Jewish. He has also reminded us that Christianity, for all its departures from its elder brother, still has its roots in, still draws it sustenance from, its original Jewish soil. In this he is saying exactly what the Apostle Paul did in Romans 11. Gentile Christians, Paul insists, are "wild olive shoots" grafted onto the ancient living olive tree of Israel. For this reason both Paul and Fred warn us, "Do not be arrogant" (Romans 11:17-21).

Fred has insisted that texts from Isaiah and Amos, 1 Samuel and 1 Chronicles, Ezra and Esther, must be as much a part of Christian teaching and preaching as texts from Matthew, Ephesians, and 1 Peter. God gave us the *whole* Bible for the instruction and edification of the church. To use an image from Robert Farrar Capon, the Bible is like a wonderful art gallery full of paintings from various artists of varying eras and styles. God wants us to visit, to study, to seek to understand *every* wing of that gallery, *every* picture on the walls. *All* are part of his gallery, not just the pretty ones, not just the ones we like and understand. If we leave anything out, we have falsified God and the Scriptures. He wants us to ponder the dark, painful, and difficult as well as the bright, joyful, and clear.

Thank you, Fred, for your insistence that we view the *whole* gallery, that we see the *whole* story. Your colleagues, both at North Park and in the wider scholarly community, your former students, your fellow Covenant pastors, and many friends salute you and wish you many more fruitful years of scholarship, writing, and friendship.

JOHN E. PHELAN JR.
President and Dean
North Park Theological Seminary

Preface

This collection of essays has been gathered to honor the faithful ministry of Fredrick Carlson Holmgren in the service of his church. Fred taught Old Testament at North Park Theological Seminary for nearly thirty-five years. During that time a generation of pastors, teachers, and lay leaders in the Evangelical Covenant Church, as well as in the larger Church and community, have come under his tutelage.

We have been challenged by Fred's careful attention to the biblical story and its enduring relationship to church and synagogue. In addition, we have recognized Fred's passion for listening to, and obeying, the sacred Scripture in our contemporary context. For that reason, then, we joyfully present this collection of essays to our friend and mentor, Fredrick Holmgren. May they reflect the best of what he has taught us, and furthermore demonstrate that biblical scholarship can address both the head and the heart at the same time.

These exegetical and theological essays are the work of friends, colleagues, and former students. The first group of studies is centered on the Hebrew Scriptures. Erhard Gerstenberger explains the dynamic of complaint and confession at work in the complex prayer of Psalm 69. Robert Johnston asks why wisdom psalms are not considered prayers as well. Jack Lundbom shows how scribal editing and juxtaposition shapes and communicates theology in texts from Genesis, Isaiah, and Jeremiah, while Patrick Miller examines geographical movement and command-response structures as signs of faith and faithlessness in Deuteronomy. Herman Schaalman offers a study of the names Israel and Judah as they are used for the people of God in the Hebrew Bible. As an expression of Israelite wisdom, the book of Job makes many references to creation, and Bradley Bergfalk draws out their theological significance for contemporary environmental concerns. Paul Koptak shows how Kenneth Burke's rhetorical approach to reading can provide clues for understanding and preaching the story of Judah and Tamar in Genesis.

The second group of essays examines the relationship between the testaments in the Christian canon, again through thematic and exegetical study. James Bruckner uses the debate over law-keeping in the intertestamental literature to shed light on Jesus' citation of the law against covetousness in Mark 10. Peter Fieldler explains the citation in Matthew

12 of the Servant Song in Isaiah 42 as part of an inner-Jewish debate on the identity of Jesus. After reviewing the characteristics of apocalyptic writing in the Hebrew Bible and intertestamental literature, David Freedholm argues that Mark 13 offers an "apocalyptic timetable" that is intended to encourage Christians who suffer hard times. Lothar Ruppert shows that the Old and New Testaments both speak to how one treats strangers, while Klyne Snodgrass looks to the Old Testament to find the inspiration and model for Jesus' parables.

Finally, Norma Sutton presents a comprehensive bibliography of Fred's published works. It is offered as a testimony to Fred's continuing influence on the larger community of faith and his concern for biblical scholarship that is both inclusive and directed to the ministry of preaching and teaching.

A bibliography is but one way of summarizing a life of accomplishment and service. Fredrick Holmgren joined the faculty of North Park Theological Seminary in 1960. Before coming to teach at North Park, Fred earned an associate of arts degree from North Park College and a bachelor of arts at Calvin College. He received a diploma from North Park Theological Seminary and served for five years as pastor of the Evangelical Covenant Church of New Rochelle, New York. While at New Rochelle, he began his studies at Union Theological Seminary in New York. He earned a bachelor of divinity (magna cum laude), a master of sacred theology (summa cum laude), and a doctor of theology from Union. Postdoctoral research has taken him to Ruprecht-Karl Universität in Heidelberg and Hebrew Union College in Cincinatti as a visiting scholar, and to the university libraries of Tübingen, Freiburg, Marburg, Göttingen, and Oxford.

In addition to his regular teaching at North Park, Fred has also taught courses at Garrett-Evangelical Seminary, McCormick Theological Seminary, and Spertus College of Judaica. He lectured in German at the Theologisches Seminar in Ewersbach, Germany, as a visiting professor. He has spoken often to lay and ministerial groups on themes relating to the Bible, ministry, and preaching from the Hebrew Scriptures. A longtime participant in the Jewish-Christian conversation, Fred was asked to give the Charles Rosenstock Memorial Lectures sponsored by Temple Israel in Omaha, Nebraska. He was the second Christian scholar invited to speak to this gathering of rabbis and Christian pastors in the first forty years of its history.

Many members of the Covenant ministerium will remember Fred for his teaching. In his classes students were treated to the challenge of looking at the text from new angles, continually being asked to consider how the text demonstrates God's love and kindness. Lectures and discussions were always seasoned with a good dash of humor, Holmgren style.

Fred retired from teaching in December 1994 and continues to work as research professor at North Park Theological Seminary.

The editors would like to express their appreciation to the contributors for their thoughtful essays and to Thomas Luchsinger for compiling the list of abbreviations. We especially want to thank John Phelan for his encouragement and support of the project, Wayne Weld, editor of the *The Covenant Quarterly*, for his guidance and attention to detail, and the editorial staff at Covenant Publications for producing an attractive volume. Together we offer this collection to Fred, his wife, Betty, and their son, Mark, and daughter, Margaret, in the hope that it will express our appreciation for Fred's teaching, scholarship, and friendship.

BRADLEY J. BERGFALK
Concord, New Hampshire

PAUL E. KOPTAK
Chicago, Illinois

Abbreviations

AB	Anchor Bible
ANET	*Ancient Near Eastern Texts Relating to the Old Testament*
ANRW	*Aufstieg und Niedergang der römischen Welt*
AOAT	Alter Orient und Altes Testament
ATANT	Abhandlungen zur Theologie des Alten und Neuen Testaments
ATD	Das Alte Testament Deutsch
BA	*Biblical Archaeologist*
B.C.	Before Christ
B.C.E.	Before the Common Era
Bib	*Biblica*
BJRL	*Bulletin of the John Rylands University Library of Manchester*
BK	*Bibel und Kirche*
BK	Biblische Kommentar
BThW	*Bibeltheologisches Wörterbuch*
BZ N.F.	*Biblische Zeitschrift Neue Folge*
BZAW	Beihefte zur Zeitschrift für die altestamentliche Wissenschaft
CB	*Cultura biblica*
CBQ	*Catholic Biblical Quarterly*
CBQMS	Catholic Biblical Quarterly Monograph Series
C.E.	Common Era
EKK	Evangelisch-katholischer Kommentar zum Neuen Testament
ET	English Translation
ETL	*Ephemerides Theologicae Lovanienses*
EvQ	*Evangelical Quarterly*
FOTL	Forms of the Old Testament Literature
FRLANT	Forschungen zur Religion und Literatur des Alten und Neuen Testaments
GHK	Göttinger Handkommentar
HAT	Handbuch zum Alten Testament
HSS	Harvard Semitic Studies
HTKNT	Herders theologischer Kommentar zum Neuen Testament
HUCA	*Hebrew Union College Annual*
IB	*Interpreter's Bible*
ICC	International Critical Commentary

IDB	*Interpreter's Dictionary of the Bible*
IEJ	*Israel Exploration Journal*
Int	*Interpretation*
JAOS	*Journal of the American Oriental Society*
JBL	*Journal of Biblical Literature*
JCS	*Journal of Cuneiform Studies*
JJS	*Journal of Jewish Studies*
JNES	*Journal of Near Eastern Studies*
JQR	*Jewish Quarterly Review*
JSNTSup	Journal for the Study of the New Testament Supplement Series
JSOT	*Journal for the Study of the Old Testament*
JSPSup	Journal for the Study of the Pseudepigrapha Supplement
JTS	*Journal of Theological Studies*
LXX	Septuagint
MTZ	*Münchner theologische Zeitschrift*
NBL	Neues Bibel-Lexikon
NICNT	New International Commentary on the New Testament
NRSV	New Revised Standard Version
NTD	Das Neue Testament Deutsch
NTS	*New Testament Studies*
RevQ	*Revue de Qumran*
RSV	Revised Standard Version
SBL	Society of Biblical Literature
SBLDS	Society of Biblical Literature Dissertation Series
SBLMS	Society of Biblical Literature Monograph Series
SBM	Stuttgarter biblische Monographien
SBS	Stuttgarter Bibelstudien
SBT	Studies in Biblical Theology
SJT	*Scottish Journal of Theology*
SNT	Studien zum Neuen Testament
TDOT	*Theological Dictionary of the Old Testament*
THAT	*Theologisches Handwörterbuch zum Alten Testament*
THKNT	Theologischer Handkommentar zum Neuen Testament
TTZ	*Trierer theologische Zeitschrift*
TWAT	*Theologisches Wörterbuch zum Alten Testament*
TZ	*Theologische Zeitschrift*
VT	*Vetus Testamentum*
VTSup	Vetus Testamentum Supplements
WBC	Word Biblical Commentary
WD N.F.	*Wort und Dienst Neue Folge*
WMANT	Wissenschaftliche Monographien zum Alten und Neuen Testament
ZNW	*Zeitschrift für die neutestamentliche Wissenschaft*

HEBREW SCRIPTURES

Psalm 69:
Complaint and Confession

ERHARD S. GERSTENBERGER

Working towards a commentary on the Book of Psalms,[1] I thought that as I offer my contribution to a *Festschrift* I would also ask my honored friend to partake in my labor. Fredrick Holmgren, respected colleague and dear visitor at Marburg University, will appreciate the general topic and will offer his judicious critique of my exegesis, thus helping me in my interpretive efforts.

The Psalm

Psalm 69 has always received much attention from Bible readers and interpreters. There are connections to the New Testament passion narratives, as well as to other writings within and without the New Testament and the early Jewish communities. It is possible that the Jeremianic tradition was linked to our psalm, and the history of exegesis through the Christian era has given it special recognition as a powerful song of suffering and salvation.[2] Form critical exegesis unanimously has labeled the psalm a clear example of "individual complaint," with its main elements of complaint, petition, imprecation, and vow.[3]

Besides the force of language and imagery, daring metaphors, and theological depth, modern observers will note the unusual length of this prayer. Individual complaints are the most frequent genre within the Psalter, comprising about thirty to forty texts.[4] Psalm 69 is one of the largest of its kind, extending over forty-four poetic lines, in comparison to an average length of between ten and twenty lines for the bulk of the Psalter's individual complaints.[5] If we consider the original *Sitz im Leben* of such complaint-psalms, the normal size of the text becomes quite plausible. Individual complaints were part and parcel of prayer services for sufferers. They used to be recited by the "patient" under professional supervision of a "man of God" (or perhaps a prophet, Levite, singer, healer, etc.), as Akkadian ritual texts of Mesopotamia indicate.[6] These prayers, preserved in healing liturgies of Israel's older neighbors, are quite similar in content, form, and size to the Old Testament ones.[7] Because these prayers are similar in purpose, one may conclude that the patient was obliged to recite a limited text only, never approaching the extent of our Psalm 69. Moreover, no matter how far the Old Testament prayers for suffering persons were removed from the familial service or ritual, they preserved, as a rule, the old structure and size. Why, then, did Psalm 69 outgrow this traditional mold and attain this double size?

The Elements

CLOSING LINES. Form critical analysis of the Psalms starts out from the presupposition that complaint psalms do consist of specific form-elements that correspond to certain liturgical necessities. There should be an invocation, because no suppliant may approach his or her God without preparing for the appearance before the deity by such a preliminary appeal. There should be a statement of the sufferer's case, be it complaint, lament, or protestation, as well as a formal petition. There also should be some kind of response to divine exigencies in terms of loyalty and faith. All these expectations are fully met in Psalm 69; we find also some identification of evildoers and enemies, as well as imprecations against them (this element corresponds negatively to the petition for one's own cause). The opening part being typical, what immediately calls our attention is the closing lines (vv. 33-37 [Eng. 32-36]). Extending well-wishes to the poor, more specifically to "distressed, miserable, and captives" (vv. 33-34 [Eng. 32-33]), and summoning to praise—a hymnic element[8]—a whole universe and a whole people (vv. 35-37 [Eng. 34-36]), seems to exceed by far the concerns for an individual sufferer within his primary group. These observations lead us to suspect that the individual complaint has been reworked in a wider, communal setting. Such a reworking of older psalms becomes obvious to the scrutinizing eye of interpreters, as for example in Psalms 12, 31, and 102.[9]

COMPLAINTS. If we next look at the structure of Psalm 69 to determine the liturgical nature of each element, we soon find out that there indeed has been a thorough reworking of the text. We see that a quite different psalm of individual complaint has been brought into an older text.

The first compact element of our psalm is found in verses 2-5 (Eng. 1-4). Invocation is, as in some parallel texts (cf. Psalms. 7:2 [Eng. 1]; 54:3 [Eng. 1]; 86:2), combined with an urgent cry for help. This sense of emergency alone justifies such a modification in word order and etiquette: "Help me, God!" (v. 2a [Eng. 1a]). Perhaps we may assume that preparatory liturgical elements, when recited before the complaint proper, furnished a more adequate appellation of God and a proper initial plea to be heard (cf. Psalms 4:2 [Eng. 1]; 5:2-3 [Eng. 1-2]). In our text, anyway, the complaint element begins right away with strong expressions of despair in tight, extremely short phrases of three and two stressed syllables, which occasionally dwindle to breathless two and two accented shouts (vv. 4-5 [Eng. 3-4]). The imagery is rich and shifts rapidly: the chaos-waters are rising, and the mire of the netherworld is ensnaring the feet of the supplicant. Dangers of this mythical dimension were ordinarily seen in all kinds of threats to life and well-being (cf. the Psalm of Jonah, Jonah 2; but also Psalms 6 and 88, and the general picture of the netherworld in Isaiah 14:4-21).[10]

A sordid description of crying and pleading to God follows the initial outburst of anguish. It is a standard motif of complaint-psalms (cf. Psalms 17:1; 28:2; 38:9 [Eng. 8]; 61:3 [Eng. 2]; 88:2, 10 [Eng. 1, 9]; 130:1; 142:2-3 [Eng. 1-2]), intended, liturgically, to move the heart of the deity. What a demonstration of tearful and helpless suffering! The three concluding lines of the complaint (v. 5 [Eng. 4]) are reserved for an intense complaint against the enemies. Naturally, as ancient Hebrews took it, suffering and the danger of losing one's life had to be attributed to some malevolent entity, whether it be human, demonic, or divine. Certain identification in naming those evil-mongers possibly could be won in those days by ordeal or oracle. Several times we read in the Hebrew Scriptures that people in distress would consult God, trying to clarify the root and the outcome of a personal crisis (cf. 1 Kings 14:1-3; 2 Kings 1:1-2; 4:21-25). Asking God for guidance had a long tradition in the ancient Near East; there were many professionals involved in these inquiries. Israel took part in general divination practices, even if the deuteronomic movement tried to interdict popular inquiries (Deuteronomy 18:9-13). In our case, some enemies who slanderously raise accusations against the supplicant have been identified as the sources of his bad state. The (false) charge is a criminal one, as reflected in civil laws and customs (cf. Exodus 21:37-22:8; Leviticus 19:13; Proverbs 22:22). The Psalms treat this type of false suing for criminal offenses in various places: Psalm 7:4-6 (Eng. 3-5) is a protestation of innocence and a conditional curse in this kind of situation. In Psalm 26:6, 11, an accused refutes the charges against him in a more general way and does not hesitate to denounce his opponents as totally corrupt (Psalm 26:9-10).[11] It is important to realize that these charges are leveled against the sufferer on the basis of alleged criminal conduct.

This very horizon changes drastically in the next liturgical section (vv. 6-14a [Eng. 5-13a]). Now a definite moment of loyalty to Yahweh alone and to his congregation enters the scene. Religious faith becomes the central problem now, not criminal offense. Formally as well as in regard to contents and theological motivation, verses 6-7 (Eng. 5-6) are different from the introductory complaint. The poetic lines are fuller; verse 6 (Eng. 5) seems even overcrowded with words (4 + 3 stresses).

There is also a new invocation, and its wording, "God, you know my stupidity" (*'iwwelet* and its derivates are typical wisdom jargon), derives from prophetic or sapiential dialogue rather than from formal, cultic prayer language.[12] Or, to put it differently, the old rituals of worship apparently did not use the expression very much, although it was used more frequently in later times. The first stichos (v. 6a [Eng. 5a]) already admits, in sapiential terminology, faulty existence, but the formal confession of guilt is articulated in verse 6b (Eng. 5b). Terms related to *'āšām*, "guilt," however, are very rare in the Psalter (only Psalms 68:22 [Eng. 21] and 69:6b [Eng. 5b]); they strictly belong to Priestly layers of the Hebrew Scriptures (cf. Leviticus 5, etc.). The whole line, therefore, comes close to becoming a rather exquisite confession of sin. (For contrasts in the line of old complaint songs, cf. Psalms 38:5 [Eng. 4] and 51:5-8 [Eng. 3-6].) These last-mentioned passages straightforwardly employ the regular words for "sin," "error," and "guilt," placing the supplicant directly before his God.[13] "I have erred" is a recognized confessional formula (Psalm 51:6a [Eng. 5a]; cf. Joshua 7:20; 1 Samuel 15:24, 30; 2 Samuel 12:13; 19:21; 24:10, 17; etc.).

Just as the beginning line of the actual section does not fit well into the linguistic and theological patterns of the old complaints, the other two lines (v. 7 [Eng. 6]) have their own peculiarities, which make them look a little strange in the context of the initial complaint. The phrases are formulated as negative wishes, and each of them ends up with a weighty invocation first, "Yahweh Sebaoth," and second, "God of Israel." While the double negative (an almost apotropaeic imploration with concomitant appellation of God) does have some parallels in other prayers (cf. Psalms 6:2 [Eng. 1]; 27:9; 35:22, 25; 38:22 [Eng. 21]; 83:2 [Eng. 1]), the specific affirmations of our two lines are unique in the Psalter. Instead of asking God to keep the supplicant from shame, that is, the impending disgrace of being sentenced and ostracized by society, and instead of trying to put the full blame on the "enemies" (cf. Psalms 31:2b, 18 [Eng. 1b, 17]; 35:26), our text pleads that those who "hope for you" and "seek you" "will not be put to shame on my account." The "I" of the supplicant suddenly takes on a different quality or character. He becomes the intermediary—the messenger, or servant, of the Lord—whose existence is bound up with the message to the faithful. "Shame" now does not simply mean the destruction of human existence under the onslaught of false or right condemnation. Shame is a consequence not of unethical actions committed but of attitudes taken over against a person of Yahweh's confidence (or at least a person who thinks him- or herself in line with the ordinances of God). Theoretically, this can be only persons of very special standing in the community, figures like Moses, Jeremiah, or Ezra, who are portrayed in the Scriptures as special representatives of their

God. Still, it is needless to say that all successors of crucial leaders tend to step into the footprints of their masters and think of themselves as equally important.

The remaining lines of the section under discussion, verses 8-14a (Eng. 7-13a), spell out in greater detail that peculiar relationship between the supplicant and God which makes the main difference over against the older complaint pattern. Because of God, the sufferer is being despised (v. 8 [Eng. 7]); or, more precisely, he fell into disgrace with (some of?) his brothers because of his zeal for the "house of God," that is, the temple (v. 10 [Eng. v. 9]). Alienation from his compatriots is the result (v. 9 [Eng. 8]). This latter motif, alienation from kinfolk and neighbors, is a standard theme in complaint (cf. Psalm 88, Job 19:13-22). However, the reasons recognizable in the common model are either suspicion of criminal record or "evidence" of divine castigation because of some grave aberration (cf. Job). In our case, the alienation is caused by religious zeal in favor of God Yahweh and in support of the sanctity and integrity of his temple. The only way to make sense of these statements is to visualize a religious rift in the community which makes for vicious animosity among its members. What for some may be considered zealous endeavor for the God of Israel and his holy dwelling place, for others is unnecessary or even detrimental fanaticism.

We note the difference between the two complaint sections. The first one (vv. 1-7 [Eng. 1-6]) deals with serious dangers threatening from slander and false accusation within a political and social community. The second complaint (vv. 8-14a [Eng. 7-13a]) tells us about religious hatred within a religious congregation. The passage uses traditional imagery and metaphors to voice the lament. For instance, going in sack and ashes in order to demonstrate solidarity with mourners or people practicing penitence (vv. 11-12 [Eng. 10-11]) is well attested also in Psalm 35:13-14 or in Job 1-2. Likewise, being scorned by those sitting in the gate (v. 13 [Eng. 12]), that is, by people in a public place, has its counterpart in other texts (Job 30:9; Lamentations 3:14; Isaiah 28:7-10). In our second complaint section, however, the traditional motifs and expressions of dissonance are all subjugated to the general claim: "For your sake am I being disdained." The supplicant is suffering because of his loyalty to Yahweh. Wearing clothes of mourning, then, would also have some religious or confessional connotations that escape our knowledge. A concluding line wants to ascertain the prayer of frustrated zeal for the Lord (v. 14a [Eng. 13a]). Reference to one's own prayer more likely than not is a matter of introductory or concluding words (cf. Psalms 4:2 [Eng. 1]; 6:10 [Eng. 9]; 17:1; 39:13 [Eng. 12]; 88:3, 14 [Eng. 2, 13]; 109:4; 141:2, 5; etc.).

PETITIONS AND IMPRECATIONS. The petitionary section of verses 14b-19 (Eng. 13b-18) apparently has two distinct parts. The first unit,

verses 14b-16 (Eng. 13b-15), is intimately linked to the opening complaints of verses 2-5 (Eng. 1-4) in its vocabulary and style. After renewed
invocation ("God . . . hear me," v. 14b), the supplication is precisely for
rescue from the waters and the mire in which the sufferer is drowning.
Thus there can be no doubt about the original linkage between the passages.[14] On the other hand, verses 17-19 (Eng. 16-18) turn to Yahweh
only in the most general way, pleading for recognition and acceptance of
the supplicant for the sake of God's graciousness and mercy. The words
used for God's hoped-for closeness and deliverance are partly traditional
(for example, in vv. 17-18 [Eng. 16-17]), partly unusual and rare; "Be
close to me and redeem me" (v. 19a [Eng. 18a]) does not have an exact
counterpart in the Hebrew Scriptures. Therefore, neither vocabulary nor
style will easily reveal anything about the literary affiliation of the lines
in question. Perhaps, however, the lone auto-designation "your servant"
in verse 18a (Eng. 17a) has some significance. It does not occur verbatim
in verses 6-14a (Eng. 5-13a), but the concept of God's mediator and servant, as pointed out, is there. Also, the pointed use of "Yahweh" in verse
17 over against "Elohim" in verse 14b would support the literary analysis
linking the first segment of petition to the old complaint, and the second
one (vv. 17-19 [Eng. 16-18]) to the "confessional lament" of verses 6-14a
(Eng. 5-13a).

Looking for cross-connections of this type, we have to ask, however, what about the "enemies" and "persecutors," which are so important in both complaint sections already discussed? This may be a test case
for our analysis. The petition, so far, is hardly concerned about these
dangerous adversaries. Our present petitionary passage, verses 14b-19 (Eng.
13b-18), briefly touches the opponents in verses 15 (Eng. 14) and 19
(Eng. 18). The first reference is in the middle of demands for help and
deliverance from deadly mire and wild waters; "from my haters" seems
misplaced in this context, and some exegetes suggest a textual emenda-
tion. The second reference to "my enemies" (v. 19 [Eng. 18]) moves the
supplicant to ask God for nearness and intervention. In other words, the
formulation "because of my enemies"—please help me!—does possibly
suggest a special relationship of the supplicant to Yahweh, and a special
situation with regard to Israel and her neighbors.[15]

Our psalm does not end, as we might expect, with petition and
possibly a vow, but starts another round of complaint, this time joined to
extended imprecations of enemies (vv. 20-29 [Eng. 19-28]). Are we able
to continue the work of bi-partitioning the prayer to find two distinct
layers of tradition in it? The section again begins with that ominous formula, "You [God] know" what trouble I have seen, namely, three kinds of
shame (in Hebrew: *ḥerpāh, bōšet, kelimmâ*[16] The formula itself, as well as
the suspicious accumulation of shame words, suggests that this line had

some connection with the confessional version of complaint.[17] The next line (v. 21 [Eng. 20]) also talks about *ḥerpâ*, "shame," but lacks the usual reinforcement with synonyms. It also paints a rather typical kind of alienation between supplicant and villagers. The supplicant is counting on neighborly solidarity, but does not receive it, just as in Psalms 35 and 41. Neighbors and friends have turned hostile for practical reasons; you have to steer clear of a person punished by God so as not to be caught in the same castigation. The expression "give vinegar for water" probably is proverbial for "to recompense evil for good" (cf. Psalms 35:12; 41:10 [Eng. 9]). The metaphor at this point does not have a cultic meaning, but comes from everyday experience. Most probably, then, the renewed complaint fits the pattern of traditional articulations. No specific reference is made, either, to the precarious existence of a messenger of God, nor is there any hint as to actual persecution for the sake of Yahweh or any conflict or rift between factions of the Jewish community.

Instead of positive petitions for one's own cause, this new round of liturgy presents a series of imprecations. Form critical study long has recognized that petition and imprecations in ritual practice are but two sides of the same coin. Both actively deal with overcoming evil, imprecation choosing direct action (via the deity appealed to) against the evil-mongers and sources of all suffering. Thus, imprecations belong to the basic structure of those complaint-psalms that deal with personalized enemies.[18] Destructive prayer-wishes, to be executed by God himself, are flung against those who cause mischief (vv. 23-26 [Eng. 22-25]; cf. Psalm 109). The evil-mongers are to be hit in their religious practice; their very sacrifice is to be perverted, producing nothing but bad luck (v. 23 [Eng. 22]). Their physical health is to be impaired and their homes destroyed (vv. 24, 26 [Eng. 23, 25]). All these bad effects on the evildoers are to flow out of God's wrath (v. 25 [Eng. 24]). Up to this point, there is no sign of any specific condemnation of internal opponents based on true or false worship of Yahweh. The motive clause in verse 27 (Eng. 26), the only line legitimating the brutal punishment of the wicked, sums up, in a way, the whole scenario: they "persecute" the sufferer who has been castigated by God. Now, is the concept of "persecution" to be understood in a religious or confessional way? Hardly so. Many individual complaints use the term for "regular" harassment of suspects who are considered punished by God and therefore are being treated as outcasts (cf. Psalms 7:2, 6 [Eng. 1, 5]; 31:16 [Eng. 15]; 35:3; 109:16). The tenor of the two cola (which again seem "overstretched," with altogether nine lexems, but regular three and three accented syllables) goes in the same direction. God himself has hit the sufferer, and he is not—like Jeremiah—a messenger zealously engaged in the work of the Lord.

In fact, verse 27 (Eng. 26) closes the liturgical set-up. The motive

clause gives the reason for the preceding imprecations. The two lines
that follow (vv. 28-29 [Eng. 27-28]) are imprecative in the same style
(imperatives and jussives directed to God), but they do employ a different vocabulary and betray a very distinct purpose. No longer does the
supplicant demand the destruction of physical conditions and the frus-
tration of religious endeavors of his adversaries. Instead, he clearly moves
within the community of the "just" and is trying to expel the others from
the ranks of the *ṣaddîqîm*. The "book of the living" is a late concept used
to symbolize the loyalty and homogeneity of the true faith community.[19]
The request to blot out enemies from this book can only refer to acts of
purification within this community. For all these reasons, verses 28-29
(Eng. 27-28) are to be considered a new layer of imprecation corresponding to a different life-setting.

VOW AND THE REST. Having studied the complaint and petition
blocks of Psalm 69, we once more must look briefly at the closing units of
this prayer. Form critical research from the beginning has held petition
to be the most essential and climactic element of complaint-songs. Theoretically and liturgically, a prayer may end at this high point (cf. Psalms
36:11-13 [Eng. 10-12]; 44:27 [Eng. 26]). As a rule, however, complaint-
songs close with some praising affirmation or a vow to offer thanks to the
helpful deity. This liturgical feature is quite natural and in line with general human behavior.[20] The benevolent God who will rescue the sufferer
is to receive laudations and even a certain recompense.

The vow of praise appears at the close of Psalm 69. The distribution of the closing elements is problematic due to the two layers of psalmic
tradition. Verses 30-32 (Eng. 29-31) sound like old affirmations of hu-
mility and anxiety (30a; cf. formulaic expressions of this type in Psalms
40:18 [Eng. 17]; 70:6 [Eng. 5]; 86:1; 109:22), a final plea for help (30b),
and a vow to sing praises if God's help will materialize (31). In both lines
'elohim is either addressed directly or mentioned in the third person. The
next line (32), however, appeals to Yahweh and seems to add a second
thought on the value of thanksgiving *songs* in contrast to thanksgiving
sacrifice. The term *tôdâ*, "thanksgiving offer," at the end of verse 31 thus
is being reinterpreted in the light of non-temple worship (cf. Psalms 40:7
[Eng. 6]; 50:8-13; 51:18-21 [Eng. 16-19]). Therefore, the verse may not
be an original part of the first closing passage, but neither is it to be
linked with the confessional psalm, in which the temple plays such a
central role.

All the rest of this long prayer (vv. 33-37 [Eng. 32-36]), as stated in
the beginning, goes beyond the boundaries of special worship for some
patient seeking help because of sickness or social ostracism. Well wishes
for "oppressed ones" and frequent references to Zion, the Zion community, the cities of Judah, and the cosmic universe[21] are significant indica-

tors of the place of origin for this final part of Psalm 69. Delimitation of the congregation of the faithful implicitly wards off those traitors who persecute people for their zeal in regard to Yahweh and his holy abode.

LIFE-SITUATIONS. At various points we have hinted at the *Sitz im Leben* of the two layers of our rich and lengthy text. This diachronic view has to be systematized briefly, so that we may draw some theological conclusions afterwards.

We identified a first and traditional individual complaint that possibly comprises verses 2-5, 14b-16, 21-27, and 30-32 (Eng. 1-4, 13b-15, 20-26, 29-31). Speaking in general terms and not insisting on locating every single word, we estimate that about twenty-three of the forty-four lines may have constituted the basic layer of an independent complaint song for the individual sufferer. The essential form elements are present in a liturgical sequence: invocation and complaint, petition, complaint, imprecation, final plea, and vow. This original complaint is concerned with the individual in his or her primary group. Life is in great danger, threatened by abysmal forces of destruction and personal enemies raising false accusations. The only possible salvation is with the personal God who is able to help against powers of death and deadly calumny. Significantly, most parts of the traditional prayer are oriented towards *'elohim*, "God," and not to Yahweh. Thus *'elohim* appears in verses 2, 14b, 30, and 31 (Eng. 1, 13b, 29, and 30), that is, four out of seven times within the traditional prayer. The only use of YHWH (out of five occurrences) within this older text is in verse 32 (Eng. 31). But, as discussed above, the line in question may be a later addition to the text. If our analysis is correct, the traditional prayer, coming out of the older family religion in Israel,[22] was oriented towards *'elohim*, most likely the deity of family or clan. The widespread belief that a so-called "Elohistic Psalter" (Psalms 42-83) originally was composed of Yahweh psalms that at some indefinite point suffered an "elohistic redaction" is hardly tenable.[23] Especially in the case of Psalm 69, it proves absurd. Five uses of YHWH compare to seven occurrences of *'elohim* in this prayer.

To test our identification of a younger or "confessional" layer, extending over verses 6-14a, 17-20, 28-29, and 33-37 (Eng. 5-13a, 16-19, 27-28, and 32-36), at this point we observe that the younger part of Psalm 69 does use YHWH in a demonstrative way throughout. Verse 7b (Eng. 6b) has the first emphatic appearance, after verse 6 (Eng. 5) named the deity (by mistake? Scribal error?) *'elohim* in its invocation. Verse 7d continues with *'elohim yisra'el*, "God of Israel," which is, of course, equivalent to YHWH. Next, verses 14a and 17a (Eng. 13a and 16a) are prominent lines, closing and opening a liturgical section. Both carry the name of YHWH and no other designation of divinity. Lastly, verse 34 (Eng. 33) has YHWH in a prominent place, the difficulty being that twice in this last section *'elohim* appears in contexts where one would expect YHWH. The verb *drš*, "seek"(v. 33 [Eng. 32]), can be linked to *'elohim* (cf. Psalm 14:2; the psalm in general does not discriminate between the two designations) or to YHWH (cf. Psalms 22:27 [Eng. 26]; 34:5, 11 [Eng. 4, 10]; 105:4; the latter has no *'elohim* as independent name but three times uncontested YHWH). Even worse, *'elohim* is attested even in connection with Zion in verse 36 (Eng. 35). This means that the evidence is not as clear as one would wish; therefore, the only plausible answer would be that the younger prayer uses YHWH pointedly in some parts, but obviously does not attribute much weight to it in the closing section.

We should still examine the "confessional" prayer in Psalm 69 to answer the question whether or not it may have been an autonomous liturgical text at one time. We tried to understand the opening element in verses 6-7 (Eng. 5-6) as a plaintive petition with a peculiar, Jeremianic twist to it. In the Psalter there is no comparable introductory statement. The four parallels from Jeremiah do not lend much force to the hypothesis that "God, you know my stupidity" could have been used as a first line of a prayer. (Jeremiah 12:3, 17:16, and 18:23 place the formula "you know" into a larger context; only in Jeremiah 15:15 does it open a new section.) The complaint of verses 8-13, ending with a petition in verse 14a (Eng. 7-12, 13a), is a full-fledged liturgical element. Similarly, the petition in verses 17-19 (Eng. 16-18) qualifies as an autonomous part of a complaint-song. Verses 20 and 28-29 (Eng. 19, 27-28), however, are most likely redactional accretions that interpret the older text at hand. The final section, verses 33-37 (Eng. 32-36), then, places the whole prayer into the context of a congregation of poor and righteous believers, the so-called "community of the oppressed"[24] (extant in some psalms, for example, Psalms 9/10, 37, 49, and 73), without mentioning explicitly the internal split between warring factions.[25] In that the closing section by itself transcends the border of complaint service for individuals, it cannot be a trustworthy witness to our question. To summarize, the younger layer, identified as confessional in nature, most probably never existed as an independent, liturgical text, but most likely does consist of redactional additions to the standard complaint song pointed out earlier.

Therefore, Psalm 69 derives from earlier family traditions where prayer rituals in support of ailing members of the intimate group were performed, usually under the auspices of expert healers and liturgists. The treasure of this old family religion was handed down to the exilic and post-exilic communities of Yahweh-believers. They expanded the old texts. In the case of Psalm 69, emphasis shifted from the individual sufferer towards a whole community of persons struggling to survive in a foreign-dominated world. The early Jewish congregations in Palestine as well as in Babylonia, Persia, Egypt, and Syria had to rally around their traditional faith. In doing so, it was natural that schisms arose on confessional and social grounds. Quite early, some groups were more zealous than others in defending the traditional values. The community of the "poor" and "oppressed" seems to have developed not only a strong conscience of justice and equity for Israelites, but also a keen sense of temple-orientation. The heated discussion in Haggai 1 about reconstructing the temple could be an example of two opposing positions on this issue. As a consequence of that particular zeal for Yahweh, those who would not join the active confessors were viewed with suspicion and sometimes banished from the community. Or, perhaps more frequently, the internal distribution of power worked the other way around. As we have seen, the poor and oppressed complain very succinctly in the Psalter (cf. Psalms 9/10, 37, 49, and 73). In any case, the redactional or "confessional" layer in Psalm 69 poses the problem of survival for each member of the Jewish community in the sixth and fifth centuries. Apparently, the details and degrees of allegiance to Yahweh were at stake at the time, as happened again and again in succeeding centuries.

Incentives

Considering diachronic developments of biblical texts which are clearly distinguishable through critical analysis, I cannot see a theological justification to evaluate only the very last or canonical stage of Scripture when asking for theological significance.[26] This means with regard to Psalm 69 that we have to acknowledge at least two different levels of interpretation in this composite complaint-song.

The first level is that of primary group relationships, and in particular the way of dealing with extreme situations of threats to life and social ostracism. No matter how grave the deviation, guilt, or abnormality of a person, we may judge, in the light of Old Testament concern for the marginalized and powerless, that the "outcast" always had to get a chance for rehabilitation.[27] The traditional complaint-prayers and their concomitant worship services are witnesses to this effect. Even in cases when family solidarity already had broken down, there still existed the possibility of performing rehabilitation rituals (cf. Psalms 41, 88).

Another point needs clarification. In antiquity the family or clan was the last resort for persons suffering from any deficits, losses, or disorientations. If these primary groups failed to provide help, chances were slight of finding outside sponsors, counselors, ritual experts, or priests who would venture salvatory action. When all these options were exhausted, the afflicted person was left alone and lost in the wilderness like those "embittered" and "distressed" men whom David collected (1 Samuel 22:2). In our own industrial and urban societies, primary and natural groups long have lost their financial and emotional capacities to take care of their marginalized members. The worst cases in question are children and elderly persons.[28] To whom are we addressing ourselves if we try to preach the gospel of the complaint genres in the Old Testament? Certainly we need to address the church community, which already in ancient times took over some of the social responsibilities, as the second layer of Psalm 69 attests (cf. also Psalms 12, 37, 102, 146, etc.). But unfortunately, churches cannot possibly heal all the ills of any given society. Millions and millions of poor people nowadays are not able to benefit from church aid and engagement. Therefore, we have to sensitize our political and economic entities to the discrepancies of our own society. Human fallout in social terms is alarmingly high and increasing rapidly, and there "should not be any poor in your midst" (Deuteronomy 15: 4).[29] Eventually our Christian or Jewish communities must reflect about the social, political, and economic structures that produce all the typical miseries of this world.

But what kind of rehabilitation do the needy of our time want? And what kind of assistance should be supplied according to the will of God today? Needless to say, protection from evil spirits does not rank high in our day, nor does help against calumny or the evil eye. But the basic demands are very elementary. The needy have to be freed from the worldwide slander that they cause all the evils on this planet by multiplying too fast, by being idle and living on the income of innocent working people, by not adapting to the rules of honest labor. Next, the millions of marginalized are in desperate need of food, clothing, housing, health care, education, and (most of all) real job opportunities. Millions of abandoned children, millions of hopelessly overburdened women, and again millions of persons discriminated against on account of their color, ethnic identity, minority position, or quantity and special situation probably are the groups most exploited and abused on this earth.

Of course, there is a whole category of poor and despised who are suffering on a different level. They do not lack so much the physical means to lead decent lives, but they are deficient in psychic stability, moral orientation, and personal posture. They too are clamoring for attention and rehabilitation in our days. Again, congregations and churches cannot possibly provide all the psychological and spiritual assistance necessary. We should do what is possible, and alert others to the necessity of integrating efforts and social structures. God wants those who believe in him or her to be open to the supplicants of our times and their specific complaint-songs. In front of the cathedral of the city of Cologne there has been, these past decades, a "wailing wall." Everyone is allowed to publicize his or her lament on a poster right there. Many church officials are working to clear the place of what they think is a nuisance and an insult to the harmonious world of the well-to-do Christians. They may prevail in the courts—a bad omen for Christian witness, which should proclaim the gospel to the poor.

On the second plane of our psalm, the problem of the needy shifts from basic needs for a decent human life towards the survival of the individual and the community in the face of external oppression and injustice on the one hand and internal rifts and parties on the other. Just as happened in early Jewish antiquity, our Christian existence today is overshadowed by innumerable conflicts among believers, brought about by exaggerated confessionalism and self-centered fundamentalism. Christianity (and for that matter also Judaism, but in this regard I am not able to evaluate the situation), in spite of all efforts to come together and live in brother- and sisterhood according to John 17:21 and the love of Christ, still represents a torn body of believers in the one and undivided Savior. This is an extremely sad picture which constantly defies the preaching of the proper gospel.

What are we to make out of this dreary reality? How could we demonstrate that believed and confessed unity in Christ? What are possible ways to assist those who are feeling maltreated for their zeal in regard to God and the correct faith? Again, we are living in different times and circumstances from those psalmists who complained about wicked persecutors among their own people. For most of us there is no place to defend that could be declared the "holiest of holy," no particular church to protect that considers itself exclusively correct and absolutely unique in this world. We have to rethink the essence of zeal and zealousness in matters of faith and religious community.

Some critical observers of Western culture have noted that in our days Christian faith has lost most of its ground, but Christian zeal is surviving in secularized forms. In fact, nowadays we are witnessing many active Christian militants who have few scruples as to the means available to achieve their ultimate ends. They are rivaled only by some Muslim, Hindu, or other religious fundamentalists. Such zealousness for the cause of others (preferably helpless persons or the altogether defenseless nature) may be entirely justified. Zeal means identification with a lost cause and sacrifice of one's own self for others. In this sense, Jesus may be considered a zealous preacher, and some interpreters of his life actually link the narrative about his cleaning the temple with Psalm 69:10 (Eng. 9). John 2:17 reports that his disciples remembered that passage of our psalm. So there is, from the beginning, a legitimate holy wrath in our tradition which even implies a degree of violence (cf. Exodus 32:19, Judges 14:6, 1 Samuel 11:6-7, etc.). Still, no zeal should become in any way arbitrary and authoritarian; it must be controlled by justice and love. We constantly need to discuss the goals and methods of full engagement for "holy" causes in our own time. To go to war and slaughter innocents in order to achieve supremacy of one's own ethnic or religious group does not qualify as legitimate zeal, in my opinion. On the other hand, to join a liberation movement of oppressed, dehumanized classes or minority groups and fight for their rights might be a direct consequence of preaching the gospel of love. The ends of zeal and the methods of actualizing zealousness are decisive in evaluating its legitimacy before God and Christ.

The existence of assemblies of poor and oppressed that also claim to represent true faith in God is another challenge to Christian convictions. During centuries of ecclesiastic tradition, the well-to-do churches, often intimately aligned with political powers, have become the dominant force in the Western world. Poor congregations or movements, exercising full solidarity with the exploited, mostly survived (if at all) in niches and undercurrents of official religion. Today, so-called underdeveloped countries and some ghettos or slums of our big cities shelter authentic congregations of disenfranchised people, while a few groups within the academic world and the mainstream of middle-class religion try to maintain sympathetic connections with the outcasts of our system. In the light of heavy biblical evidence that God and Christ side with the poor, we should be aware of the consequences of our social standing. After all, truth and the practice of truth have something to do with plain property rights, as Jesus pointed out succinctly: "How hard is it for those who have riches to enter the kingdom of God" (Luke 18:24).

To sum up, by using the diachronic method to study the Bible and the Psalter as a highly important part in it, we discover layers of communal life, each with their different articulations of theological problems and answers. Although our world has changed greatly over the centuries, basic insights of our spiritual ancestors remain active and challenging for us because human beings do not change much in their different environments. The parameters of our times have to be brought into account, however, to get down to that theological orientation for which we are legitimated by Christ to be zealous.

Endnotes

1. The second volume of *Psalms, with an Introduction to Cultic Poetry*, FOTL XIV, 2 (Grand Rapids: Eerdmans), long overdue, is in its nascent stage.

2. To my knowledge, there has not yet been written an extensive, book-sized study about this psalm, but treatment in commentaries and articles has been intensive; also, in past centuries see Aurelius Augustinus, *Enarrationes in Psalmos* (Corpus Christianorum X, 2; Series Latina 38.39.40; 1956), 930-39; and D. Martin Luther's *Psalmenauslegung*, ed. Erwin Mühlhaupt, vol. 2 (Göttingen: Vandenhoeck & Ruprecht: 1962), 349-61.

3. For a brief discussion of this genre, cf. Erhard S. Gerstenberger, *Psalms,*

FOTL XIV, 1 (Grand Rapids: Eerdmans, 1988): 11-14.

4. Cf. Hermann Gunkel and Joachim Begrich, *Einleitung in die Psalmen* (Göttingen: Vandenhoeck, 1933), sec. 6, 172-265; Sigmund Mowinckel, *The Psalms in Israel's Worship*, 2 vols. (New York and Nashville: Abingdon Press, 1962).

5. Statistics about size of individual complaints can be found in Gerstenberger, *Der bittende Mensch*, WMANT 51 (Neukirchen: Neukirchener Verlag, 1980): 123-27.

6. Text editions of these rituals containing outright prescriptions of cultic procedure, prayers, and incantations include R. J. Caplice, *The Akkadian Namburbi Texts*, Sources from the Ancient Near East 1/1 (Los Angeles: Undena Publications, 1974); Erich Ebeling, *Die akkadische Serie 'Handerhebung'* (Berlin: Akademie, 1953); James B. Pritchard, ed., *Ancient Near Eastern Texts Relating to the Old Testament*, 3rd ed. (Princeton: University Press, 1969).

7. Cf. Gerstenberger, *Der bittende Mensch*, 64-72.

8. Typical for one type of hymn is a call to praise issued by the leader of the assembly; cf. Psalms 105:1-6; 136:1-26; Frank Crusemann, *Studien zur Formgeschichte Hymnus und Danklied in Israel*, WMANT 32 (Neukirchen: Neukirchener Verlag, 1969); Gerstenberger, *Psalms*, vol. 1, 16-19.

9. Cf. Joachim Becker, *Israel deutet seine Psalmen*, 2nd ed., SBS 18 (Stuttgart: Katholisches Bibelwerk, 2nd ed. 1967); Erich Zenger and Frank-Lothar Hossfeld, *Die Psalmen*, vol. 1, Die Neue Echter Bibel (Würzburg: Echter Verlag, 1993).

10. Cf. Christoph Barth, *Die Errettung vom Tode in den individuellen Klage-und Dankliedern des Alten Testaments* (Zollikon: Evangelischer Verlag, 1947).

11. Hans Schmidt designated a subgroup of individual complaints as "Psalms of falsely accused persons": idem, *Das Gebet des Angeklagten im Alten Testament*, BZAW 49 (Giessen: Töpelmann, 1928).

12. "You know," as an affirmation made about God himself, occurs with some frequency in the Book of Jeremiah (cf. Jeremiah 12:3; 15:15; 17:16; 18:23) and rarely elsewhere: for example, 2 Samuel 7:20; 1 Kings 8:39; Ezekiel 37:3; Psalms 31:8 (Eng. 7); 40:10 (Eng. 9); 139:2, 4; 142:4 (Eng. 3); 144:3; Nehemiah 9:10; 1 Chronicles 17:18; 2 Chronicles 6:30 (all passages cited). The formula in most cases conveys a feeling of deep personal piety.

13. The very traditional triad of terms (*pešaʿ*; *ḥaṭṭāʾt*; *ʿāwōn*) has been studied by Rolf Knierim, *Die Hauptbegriffe für Sünde im Alten Testament* (Gütersloh: Gütersloher Verlagshaus, 1965); cf. also the relevant articles in the TDOT.

14. Cf. L. C. Allen, "The Value of Rhetorical Criticism in Psalm 69," *JBL* 105 (1986): 577-89.

15. "Because of" (*lemaʿan*) in this context means "in order to refute the adversaries, to silence them and put them to shame." Exilic and post-exilic preaching characteristically has dwelled on this motif for asking divine help (cf. Psalm 83; Exodus 32:12; Leviticus 18:24-25; Deuteronomy 7:17-26; etc.), but there also may have been an older variant in liturgical practice: Psalms 5:9-11 (Eng. 8-10); 143:11-12.

16. The words really are synonymous; cf. Martin Klopfenstein, *Scham und Schande nach dem Alten Testament*, ATANT 62 (Zürich: Theologischer Verlag, 1972).

17. Cf. Saul M. Olyan, "Honor, Shame, and Covenant Relations in Ancient Israel and Its Environment," *JBL* 115 (1996): 201-18.

18. There are many special studies about the problem; cf. Othmar Keel, *Feinde und Gottesleugner*, SBM 7 (Stuttgart: Katholisches Bibelwerk, 1969); Erhard S. Gerstenberger, "Enemies and Evildoers in the Psalms: A Challenge to Christian

Preaching," *Horizons of Biblical Theology* 4/5 (1982/83): 61-77.

19. All occurrences of the term seem to be late, even the one in Exodus 32:32-33. Being a list of the recognized "righteous" in Israel (Isaiah 4:3; Jeremiah 17:13; Ezekiel 13:9; Malachi 3:16; Daniel 7:10; 10:21; 12:1; Psalms 87:6; 139:16), it must come out of those periods in which the confessional state became decisive in evaluating membership in Israel.

20. Anthropological, cultural, historical research has long discovered a subtle system of exchanging gifts as a kind of fundamental constant; cf. Marcel Mauss, *The Gift: Form and Reason for Exchange in Archaic Societies* (New York: W. W. Norton & Company, 1990).

21. Self-descriptive terms are used abundantly in verses 33-34 (Eng. 32-33); and Zion, the cities of Judah, and the congregation of faithful ("descendants of his servants," "those who love his name") are repeatedly referred to in verses 36-37 (Eng. 35-36). The line in the middle between these two subunits bursts out in universal praise (v. 35 [Eng. 34]).

22. Family religion should be recognized as a distinct reality in Israel, in the ancient Near East, and even in modern societies; cf. Hermann Vorländer, *Mein Gott. Die Vorstellungen vom persönlichen Gott im Alten Orient und im Alten Testament* AOAT 23 (Neukirchen and Kevelaer: Neukirchenr and Butzon, 1975); Gerstenberger, *Der bittende Mensch; idem, Jahwe—ein patriarchaler Gott?* (Stuttgart: Kohlhammer, 1988), English translation published in 1996 by Fortress Press, entitled *Yahweh the Partriarch*); Ranier Albertz, *A History of Israelite Religion in the Old Testament Periods*, 2 vols, (Louisville: Westminster John Knox Press, 1994).

23. I raised that suspicion already in my commentary (cf. Gerstenberger, *Psalms*, vol. 1, 37); it has been getting stronger ever since.

24. Cf. Norbert Lohfink, *Option for the Poor: The Basic Principle of Liberation Theology in the Light of the Bible* (Berkeley: BIBAL Press, 1987); idem, *Lobgesänge der Armen* SBS 143 (Stuttgart: Katholisches Bibelwerk, 1990). Also Erich Zenger, *Die Psalmen*, and Latin-American liberation theologians highlight the presence of autonomous congregations of poor people.

25. This aspect has been little treated so far; cf. Morton Smith, *Palestinian Parties and Politics That Shaped the Old Testament*, 2nd. ed. (London: SCM Press, 1987).

26. The discussion about "canonical interpretation" has been held for some time already; cf. Brevard S. Childs, *Old Testament Theology in a Canonical Context* (London/Philadelphia: SCM Press/Fortress, 1985). To "canonize" the final text is in itself an illusion, because there never has been one definite, final text, as the Greek tradition proves beyond any doubts. Furthermore, the freezing of one particular text, trying to make it normative, absolutizes one particular historical and social structure, which in itself is an affront against the living and ever concrete word of God. Cf. Erhard S. Gerstenberger, "Canon Criticism and the Meaning of 'Sitz im Leben,' " in *Canon, Theology, and Old Testament Interpretation*, ed. Gene M. Tucker et. al. (Philadelphia: Fortress Press, 1988), 20-31; Klaus Seybold and Erich Zenger, eds., *Neue Wege der Psalmenforschung*, Herders Biblische Studien 1 (Freiburg: Herder Verlag, 1994).

27. Of course, Hebrew Scriptures also let us know about circumstances of official banishment of culprits or sick off-kin, perhaps the worst example being the exclusion from social solidarity of persons stigmatized by a certain skin disease (Leviticus 13:45-46; 2 Kings 7:3-10; Matthew 8:1-4); cf. Erhard S. Gerstenberger, *Leviticus*, ATD 6 (Göttingen: Vandenhoeck, 1993), English translation forthcoming from Westminster Press, Old Testament Library. But the overwhelming impression from Old Testament texts is this: Our spiritual forebears

went to the limit of their knowledge and capabilities to incorporate those at the margins, and Jesus, under different cultural conditions, did the best in his time to overcome exclusivistic barriers.

28. We hear about substandard living conditions of large numbers of young and elderly persons all over the world; cf. key words in the news: "abused children," "abandoned children or older persons," "child prostitution," "child gangs," etc.

29. Read and discuss the latest UN report on world social conditions. Also, national statistics on economic growth and incomes, unemployment and welfare, the situation of children and school opportunities, single mothers and old-age poverty, and many more areas should inform us.

Practicing the Presence of God: The Wisdom Psalms as Prayer

ROBERT K. JOHNSTON

I t is easy to be swept along by the dominant tradition, whether in church life or in scholarship. However, there is always "another side to the story." Fredrick Holmgren knows this better than most. Thus, his scholarship has often been concerned with neglected or problematic aspects of the Christian faith. How should Christians relate to Jews? What of the biblical texts that are never read in the lectionary? What about a Third World perspective for a commentary series on the Old Testament? I have learned much from Fred's probing and pastoral scholarship, just as I have benefitted from his warm and caring friendship.

This essay is written to honor Fredrick Holmgren for his ongoing contribution to the scholarship of the church. It does so by asking one of those "neglected" questions that Fred himself might have asked: Why are the wisdom psalms that appear in Judaism's and Christianity's prayerbook not read as prayers?

Instruction and/or Prayer?

In his 1992 article "The Psalms as Instruction," J. Clinton McCann concludes that "the shape and shaping of the Psalter indicates that Psalms are to be received as the instruction of the Lord to the faithful."[1] That is, when readers look closely at how the various prayers of the Psalter were brought together to form the one book of the Psalms, they note the strong place given to teaching, not least of all the placing of Psalm 1 at the beginning of the collection as an introduction. The Psalms would *teach* us how to approach God. McCann would have us read all the psalms, even the laments and hymns, for the lessons they teach.

But if *all* of the prayers of the Psalter are now to be understood as instruction, is it also the case that *some* of the instruction in the Psalter— namely, the wisdom psalms—can also be received as prayer? This question has not often been addressed.

The starting point for this essay is an understanding of the entire Book of Psalms as the prayerbook of Israel and of the church. To view the majority of the psalms as prayers is to recognize a truism. But seldom in contemporary scholarship is the term *prayer* applied to a small group of the psalms, the wisdom psalms. If this were done, would our interpretation and understanding of these psalms be affected? How seriously should we take the canonical place of these psalms as being within Israel's prayerbook? What difference does it make that these wisdom pieces are included in the Psalms and not in Proverbs, or as a companion to Ecclesiastes or Job? Can you pray these psalms—psalms that do not usually address God directly?

The Psalms are "tools for prayer." So says Eugene Peterson in his book *Answering God*.[2] In saying this, Peterson simply gives voice to the understanding of the Psalter that Jews and Christians have had down through the ages. Prayer, he says, "is language used in personal relation to God. It gives utterance to what we sense or want or respond to before God. God speaks to us; our answers are our prayers." Peterson's threefold depiction of prayer as utterance about what we 1) sense, 2) want, or 3) respond to is suggestive. For just as we often limit prayer to being only that conversation with God in which we say "Help" (our wants) and "Thank you" (our response), so commentators on the Psalms have tended to focus on the psalms of lament and thanksgiving.[3] In the process, we have forgotten that prayer can also be an expression of what we sense, or understand, about Creator and creation. It can be more communion with, and not one-way communication to, God.

No doubt much of the reason for ignoring the wisdom psalms as prayer centers around prayer's usual dialogical character. Biblical prayer is most often experiential and personal. Walter Brueggemann has expressed it well: The psalms are "prayers addressed to a known, named, identifiable You. This is the most stunning and decisive factor in the prayers of the Psalter."[4]

Granting this primary, more "conversational" model of biblical prayer, can it *also* be said biblically—and do the wisdom psalms not suggest this—that prayer can *also* take other forms? Can prayer also be communion? Are there nonconversational, nondialogical prayers that also seek to understand Creator and creation? Must all prayer have a direct address to God? In what sense can reflection on one's life with God be thought of as a prayer, for example?

It is to a consideration of such questions that the wisdom psalms draw us. For these psalms often fit Peterson's first category, one otherwise largely neglected in Scripture. They speak of what we sense before God. What are we to make of these nontraditional prayers? What can we learn from them for our own day?

Previous Wisdom Psalm Research

Psalms research, since the ground-breaking work of Hermann Gunkel and Sigmund Mowinckel, has focused on questions of the form of individual psalms and the life-situation that gave birth to them.[5] Individual psalms have been understood to reflect a variety of *literary* genres and a common (though not univocal), ill-defined *liturgical* setting. More recently, research has turned from a focus upon the individual psalms to a consideration of the *canonical* shape of the Psalter, that is, to a consideration of the book as a whole. Is there an editorial shape to the whole of the Psalter that is discernible?[6]

But although research on literary forms, liturgical settings, and canonical shape is critical for an understanding of the Psalms, these approaches have risked losing sight of the Psalms as a book of prayers to be prayed even today. Nowhere is this more evident than when one turns to a consideration of the wisdom psalms. There, questions of classification have been the center of what little scholarship there has been, and the question of these psalms' function as ongoing prayers has been largely ignored or dismissed.

Research on the identification of wisdom psalms can be said to have begun with Hermann Gunkel (1862-1932). Gunkel understood the Psalms to fall into certain genres, that possessed given characteristics. Typical themes and literary structures were seen to characterize hymns, psalms of individual and communal lament, and those of thanksgiving. But Gunkel also noted that the Book of Psalms contained a small number of psalms that did not fit his categorizations. Included in these were some simple proverbs (Psalm 127 and Psalm 133) and a few longer wisdom poems (Psalms 1, 37, 49, 73, 112, and 128). Gunkel's listing of these psalms was not altogether clear, and he refrained from naming "wisdom" as a major genre. Nevertheless, modern scholarship on the wisdom psalms can be referenced to Gunkel's pioneering work.

Sigmund Mowinckel, one of Gunkel's pupils, accepted his form critical approach but struggled to understand the wisdom psalms from a different vantage point. (He labeled them "learned psalmography.") The larger focus of his scholarship on the Psalms had been on the liturgical origin of most psalms. With respect to learned psalmography, however, because a life-setting within the temple liturgy did not seem to fit, Mowinckel tried to make sense of these prayers as noncultic. Rather than being oriented toward public worship, the wisdom psalms were thought to be more private compositions that both praised God and instructed the youth. When analyzed in terms of style and content, the Psalms were seen by Mowinckel as containing the following wisdom psalms: 1, 34, 37, 49, 78, 105, 106, 111, 112, and 127.

The form critical and cult-functional work of Gunkel and

Mowinckel lies behind all modern Psalms research, including that on the wisdom psalms. Their struggle to understand these psalms that did not fit well into their respective systems set the tone for subsequent work. It should not be surprising, then, that no clear-cut characterization of the wisdom psalms has emerged. They remain a critical problem, on the boundaries of form critical and cult functional analysis.

Perhaps the most recognized effort to date that has attempted clarification concerning these wisdom psalms has been that of Roland Murphy. In his article "A Consideration of the Classification 'Wisdom Psalms,' " he sought to distinguish "pure" wisdom psalms from other wisdom-related psalms that could be fit into a cultic setting. Murphy used as his criteria "a certain uniformity of style . . . structure and recurrence of motifs (content), as well as the life-setting."[7] Arguing that only a cumulative approach would suffice, Murphy concluded that seven poems could be assigned to this category: 1, 32, 34, 37, 49, 112, and 128.

Following Murphy, most would agree that there is a group of psalms that have a sufficient commonality of stylistic, structural, thematic, and contextual characteristics to justify their label as wisdom psalms. But the exact number remains debated. Kenneth Kuntz, for example, would add to Murphy's list Psalms 127 and 133.[8] I would add the later Torah-wisdom psalms, Psalms 19 and 119, as well as Psalm 73. Gerhard von Rad lists Psalms 1, 34, 37, 49, 73, 111, 112, 119, 127, 128, and 139.[9] Thus, while there is much overlap, lists continue to be debated.

The lack of precision regarding which psalms to include as wisdom is based in the fact that "there is no general agreement on the exact criteria for determining a wisdom psalm."[10] Although wisdom characteristics can be found in many psalms, when are these to be considered "sufficient" within Murphy's "cumulative" approach so they might allow a psalm to be labeled "wisdom"? Perhaps the best one can say is the *predominance* of a wisdom style, content, and possible context is *usually* thought sufficient to label *some* psalms as wisdom. Examples of such style, content, and situation-in-life can be given:

1) With regard to style, wisdom features are found scattered throughout the Psalter, but they are typical of certain wisdom psalms. A) The use of the *'ašrê* formula (blessed) is found in such wisdom psalms as Psalms 1, 32, 34, 112, 119, 127, and 128. In all but Psalm 127, this blessedness is related to one being in right relationship with God. B) The use of acrostic poems both to guide the person in prayer and to reflect a wholeness or completeness in life is evident in the wisdom of Psalms 34, 37, 111-112, and 119. C) The use of simple comparisons, or similes, is by no means the exclusive domain of the wisdom writers. Nonetheless, they are often used by them (cf. 49:15; 1:3-4; 32:9). D) One can also add typical wisdom forms of address (cf. 78:1), proverbial sayings (cf. 37:16), and nu-

merical sayings (cf. 62:11).

2) With regard to content, such themes as the contrast between the ways of the righteous and the wicked (cf. Psalms 1, 34, 37, 49, 73, 111-112, and 119), the centrality of the fear of the Lord (cf. Psalms 19, 34, 111, 112, and 128), the importance of meditating on the Torah (that is, on God's instruction, cf. Psalms 1, 19, and 119), the problems of retribution and the suffering of the righteous (cf. Psalms 34, 37, 49, 73, and 112), and practical advice regarding conduct (cf. Psalms 32, 112, and 127) may be highlighted.

3) As to life-setting, little can be said definitively except that, as Murphy notes, these poems "spring from the *milieu sapientiel*."[11] No precise life-setting for this type of psalms can be offered. To posit a "school" context would be conjectural, but some influence is apparent. Given their location within the Psalter, a final setting for these psalms in the cult seems probable. Perhaps the sage's teaching has simply been adapted and adopted for Israel's worship (and now, a "word from the wise"). The question remains, however, was it also adapted as an indirect form of prayer?

The Wisdom Psalms Reconsidered

A focus upon the particular characteristics of a wisdom psalm, or a consideration of the possible life-settings for these psalms, has brought scholars largely to an impasse. What can be said has been said. Relegated to the edges of discussion by form critics, wisdom psalms have been largely neglected. A new set of questions is needed. Chief among these surely is this: if the wisdom psalms are situated in the Psalter, why are they not interpreted as prayers like the rest?

In discussing these psalms, a few have said simply that they are not to be interpreted as prayers because they are *not prayers*. R. B. Y. Scott, for example, believed that "the most important formal feature" of wisdom psalms was that they were "not addressed to Yahweh in prayer or praise but to men, and especially to the less instructed and less devout."[12] Typical of the interpretation of Psalm 1 is the judgment by Roland Murphy that it "is not a prayer." Instead, "it provides a definite perspective for the entire Psalter. It summarizes the ideal follower of the Lord, one who obeys the divine will and becomes a model for all those who read and pray *the rest* of the book."[13] Murphy makes a similar judgment about Psalm 37: "Moreover, the psalm is not a prayer, but an exhortation not to give up on God's ways with humans."[14]

James Mays argues similarly to Murphy, labeling the wisdom psalms "psalms of instruction" and contrasting them with psalms of prayer and praise. Mays notes that it would be wrong to place the life-setting for these psalms in the "school" rather than in the individual and corporate worship of the people. The wisdom psalms are for Mays "the harvest of a phase in the history of psalmody when the strategies and styles of the literature of teaching were combined with those of prayer and praise *to teach* a people at worship."[15] The context is worship, but the content is teaching, not prayer. While helpful, Mays's analysis, like Murphy's, reinforces the dichotomy between teaching and prayer. The use of a psalm seems to be limited to one or the other.

A clue as to how we might move beyond the present critical impasse comes, not untypically, from Gerhard von Rad in his *Wisdom in Israel*. Commenting on the relation between wisdom and cult, he notes that "the connections between wisdom and the hymn are numerous. Here, it was the wise men who did the borrowing." Von Rad then goes on to comment, "But the connection with the individual psalm of thanksgiving is also striking."[16] In this brief but provocative aside, von Rad provides a perspective for understanding the wisdom psalms as the prayers that they are. One need not say that the prayers in the psalms have become teaching. Rather, one can look for connections between wisdom and both the hymn and thanksgiving psalms. What we have in the wisdom psalms is a joining of instruction with prayer, prayer with instruction.

Understanding wisdom psalms in this "both/and," not "either/or," mode—that is, recognizing that even psalmic instructions are in some sense still psalms, or prayers to God—we can indeed note that some of the wisdom psalms seem more oriented to prayers of thanksgiving (cf. Psalms 32, 34, 37, 49, and 73). Their focus is often on the enigma and suffering of life. And their "solution"? It is found in the presence of the Lord (cf. 32:5; 34:22; 37:23; 49:15; 73:23). These psalms are spoken to others (to a congregation?), but they have the quality, or at least the potential, of being concurrently voiced to God. Some of these psalms are usually classified by form critics as thanksgiving psalms (Psalm 73), some as wisdom psalms (Psalm 37). In reality, they are on a continuum and might best be seen as of a piece—as both.

Other wisdom psalms might best be correlated with hymnic prayers (cf. Psalms 1, 19, 111-112, 119, and 127-128). But rather than addressing God directly in praise, they are more indirect. They are reflective prayers, meditations on what God has done and on how life with God is to be characterized. It is this latter group of psalms that has caused scholars particular problems, as we have seen. How could these psalms be prayers? But if they are perceived as meditations upon God, now transformed into reflections on God's gifts of creation, life, and law, then they become alternate forms of "hymns." In their indirection, they are nonetheless to be lifted up as praise to the Creator and Redeemer.

WISDOM PSALMS AND THANKSGIVING. The recognition that wisdom psalms are sometimes linked with thanksgiving is commonplace. Yet viewed from the perspective of classification, such overlapping of interest has been more of a problem than a help. Put most simply, should a particular psalm be viewed as wisdom or as thanksgiving when evidence of both is present?[17] Roland Murphy has written,

> And it is not apparent why the wisdom psalms should be excluded from the cult. One argument in favor of their cultic use is their relationship to the testimony or *Bekenntnis* of the Thanksgiving Psalms. As the testimony took on more and more a didactic character, the role of wisdom within the cult would have been secured, and with it the independence of the wisdom psalm form.[18]

Murphy therefore posits that, while Psalm 34 has become an independent wisdom psalm, this is not to be seen as the case in Psalm 73.

Psalm 73 is still so strongly linked to the genre of thanksgiving psalms, thinks Murphy, that its wisdom elements cannot be said to determine its form. Rather, a cultic setting is clearly evident (v. 17). But, while Psalm 73 is not a "pure" wisdom psalm, to allow the issue of classification to be framed in this way confuses as much as it clarifies. For Psalm 73 is also a wisdom composition. It is linked thematically both with Psalm 1 and with Psalms 37 and 49. Following upon Psalm 72:20, where the editor of the Psalter announces that the prayers of David are ended, Psalm 73 begins a second time, verse 1 repeating the theme of Psalm 1 ("Truly God is good to the upright, to those who are pure in heart.").[19] What follows in verses 2-16, however, is a description of the dislocation when life doesn't work out that way. Why are the evil prospering (v. 3)? Given the goodness of God (v. 1), how is the pain and suffering of one of God's people to be understood (v. 14), especially in light of the pride and violence of the wicked (v. 6)? The sage narrates his own pilgrimage, much like other wisdom writers. Like Job, he seeks to "understand" his predicament: "It seemed to me a wearisome task" (v. 16).

The pivotal verse in the psalm is verse 17. It is in the "sanctuary of God" (v. 17) that the psalmist discovers his perspective on living. Despite evidence to the contrary, God's order still prevailed. Overcome by the presence of his God, he realizes that he has been "stupid and ignorant" (v. 22). All he now wants is to be "continually" with his Lord:

> Nevertheless I am continually with *you*;
>   *you* hold my right hand.
> *You* guide me with *your* counsel,
>   and afterward *you* will receive me with honor. (vv. 23b-24)

Here is a prayer to the Lord. The address is clear. Yet this psalm has also been a recapitulation of experience much like the Book of Job. Wisdom has been put into prayer language, as the psalmist experiences a personal, mysterious resolution to the question of theodicy. Thanksgiving is called for:

> But for me it is good to be near God;
>   I have made the Lord God my refuge,
>   to tell of all your works. (v. 28)

The psalmist has no answer for his anguish until he enters the sanctuary to worship his God. And, having met God, he rejoices as he relates his experience to others in the congregation. Right to the end of this psalm, the psalmist praises God. He says he will "tell of all *your* works." His instruction and his prayer have become one and the same.

In Psalm 49 the psalmist again mixes wisdom and thanksgiving, instruction and prayer. He writes/sings:

> My mouth shall speak wisdom;
>   the meditation of my heart shall be understanding.
> I will incline my ear to a proverb;
>   I will solve my riddle to the music of the harp. (vv. 3-4)

As he sings to his Lord, the psalmist will also be teaching the congregation.

Much like the opening chapters of Ecclesiastes, the psalmist critiques those who trust in their wealth (v. 6) or their wisdom (v. 10). They are in reality poor and foolish, for death is the great leveler. It is not from life as it presents itself that its enigma will be solved. Instead, in a song of prayer to God, the psalmist concurrently reminds those who are listening:

> But God will ransom my soul from the power of Sheol,
>   for he will receive me. (v. 15)

Just as in Psalm 73, it is in the presence of God that the psalmist finds meaning.

Many have found Psalm 37 problematic.[20] It speaks with the confidence of the Book of Proverbs. But its simple trust in God seems naive, given the experience of life:

> Trust in the Lord and do good;
>   so you will live in the land, and enjoy security.
> Take delight in the Lord,
>   and he will give you the desires of your heart. (vv. 3-4)

Where is the pain, the passion, the anguish? It is not the case that wrongdoers "will soon fade like the grass" (v. 2). How can the psalmist sing concerning the blameless, "In the days of famine they have abundance" (v. 19)? The psalmist says he is now old, "yet I have not seen the righteous forsaken or their children begging bread" (v. 25). Where has he been? Is this life?

The key to understanding this psalm is found in verse 7: "Be still before the Lord, and wait patiently for him." The psalmist looks at life not only as it is (verse 1 recognizes the presence and power of the wicked): he would have us consider life as it *really* is—from and unto God. The psalmist is not naively precritical, to use modern terminology. His calm is instead postcritical, on the other side of worry. He would have us reside with him with God.[21]

Psalm 32 narrates its psalmist's experience. He had concealed his faults and was wasting away (v. 3). Only through the confession of his sin to the Lord did he experience relief and new joy (vv. 5-7). Here is a recurring theme in wisdom literature—one thinks of the counsel of Job's friends. In this psalm, the *'ašrê* formula, so typical of wisdom, is used in the opening two verses to generalize out from the psalmist's experience. Only as people experience the Lord's forgiveness, only as the Lord judges us "not guilty," can we be "happy," or "blessed" (vv. 1-2). Davidson points out that here, atypically of other *'ašrê* sayings in the Old Testament, the focus is not on what we must do (for example, fear the Lord), but on what God can do and has done.[22]

Yet this psalm is not simply instruction. Having told his story, the psalmist is carried off in prayerful praise of his Redeemer:

> You are a hiding place for me;
>   you preserve me from trouble;
>   you surround me with glad cries of deliverance. (v. 7)

What follows in verse 8 has been variously interpreted. Having just focused on his Savior, the psalmist sings:

> I will instruct you and teach you the way you should go;
>   I will counsel you with my eye upon you.

Some have thought the psalmist has continued his preoccupation with his God, now speaking prophetically in his name to the people through a divine oracle. Others think that the psalmist has simply assumed again the role of a teacher. The text is ambiguous—and this is as it should be, for the line between wisdom and worship need not always be clear. Psalmist and wisdom teacher have come together in this psalm in ways that are not always fully explicable.

WISDOM PSALMS AND MEDITATION. Gerhard von Rad has said with regard to didactic, or wisdom, prayers:

Obviously we are dealing here with a type of school poetry which, in the post-exilic period, was delivered to an audience of pupils. It is possible that the wise men wrote down such prayers also for their own edification. The impression of a certain dichotomy—prayers to God and instruction for pupils—is awakened only in the modern observer. At any rate, they are genuine prayers, and the often sublime pathos of these hymns, etc., is pure. The didactic element scarcely obtrudes.[23]

Most will find von Rad to have overstated his point. It is not obvious to many that the *Sitz im Leben* for wisdom psalms is an audience of pupils. It is also not at all the case that in Psalm 127, for example, the didactic element scarcely obtrudes. One might better say that the psalm's "prayer to God" scarcely obtrudes. But Von Rad is no doubt correct in criticizing the false dichotomy that too many would make with regard to the wisdom psalms. Prayers to God and instruction of the faithful need not be tightly separated.

Patrick Miller, in his comprehensive study of the forms and theology of biblical prayer (*They Cried to the Lord*), says little about the wisdom psalms. Seeing the heart of prayer in that twofold movement of seeking the Lord in need and responding to God's help in joy, and emphasizing the conversational and dialogical nature of prayer, Miller speaks only in passing about prayer's meditative function, that is, "seeking direction or instruction from God." But Miller does recognize that in the Psalter there is this mention of an alternate dimension of prayer. Psalms 19 and 119, for example, refer to prayer as a meditation or musing. Writes Miller, "Such meditation is not generalized or empty thinking. While we are not always given an object of meditation, in most cases it is clear. The psalmist meditates on God, on God's wonderful works, or on God's instruction or law."[24]

Like the hymnic psalms, the focus of the wisdom psalms is not on the urgencies of life, but on the God of life. The focus, even when experience is mentioned, is not on responding to life's events, but on resting in God's truths.

In Psalm 1, for example, there is no emphasis on keeping the commandments, on obeying the law, although the Torah is central. Rather, Psalm 1 declares "blessed" (*ašrê*) those whose "*delight* is in the law of the Lord, and on his law they *meditate* day and night" (v. 2). Such *meditation* originally included recitation as well as contemplation. Roland Murphy comments that in ancient Israel, "one knew the key passages by heart and recited them. Thus the command is given in Deuteronomy 6:6-7: 'Take to heart these words which I enjoin on you today, drill them into your children. Speak of them at home and abroad, whether you are busy or at rest.'"[25] For Murphy, this implies that such prayers, which were originally addressed *to* God, became teaching addressed *from* God to the faithful. But such a dichotomous conclusion need not follow. One need not choose between "to" and "from." The vocabulary of *delight* suggests that the readers of the Psalms are to go beyond recitation and study—even oral recitation. That which is addressed from God to the faithful (the wisdom psalms) reflexively becomes that which is also addressed to God—and vice versa. This psalm would have us practice the presence of God.

Such a focus on meditation/prayer is central to Psalm 19, as well. After dwelling on God's work both in creation and in the giving of the Torah, the psalmist concludes: "Let the words of my mouth and the meditation of my heart be acceptable to you, O Lord, my rock and my redeemer" (v. 14). What is it on which he meditates? "The heavens are telling the glory of God" (v. 1). From nature, speech pours forth day and night, though there are, of course, no actual words or voice (vv. 2-4). The psalmist gives an example of such meditation on nature as he compares the coming of the sun to "a bridegroom" coming "from his wedding tent" (vv. 4b-6). One is reminded of the contemporary hymn of praise: "This is my Father's world, / and to my list'ning ears / all nature sings and round me rings / the music of the spheres."[26]

When the meditation of the psalmist in Psalm 19 turns to a reflection upon the law of the Lord (vv. 7-10), the language again centers on delight. He pauses to consider the law, finding it "perfect, reviving the soul," "sure, making wise the simple," "right, rejoicing the heart," "clear, enlightening the eyes," and "pure, enduring forever" (vv. 7-9a). Such language is not meant to communicate, as much as it is to commune. There is content, to be sure, but there is also connection. If the heavens are alive in their silence, the Lord is also present in the Torah, in his "instruction" to us. The psalmist desires to hear the Lord's word more than to have fine gold; God's ordinances are "sweeter also than honey, and drippings of the honeycomb" (vv. 9b-10). In view of what God has done in deed and word, and thus of who God is, the psalmist prays that, as the Lord's servant, he will be kept from proud thoughts and hidden faults (vv. 11-13). He would, instead, meditate on the Lord (v. 14).[27]

The call to meditation takes on a variety of forms within the wisdom psalms. It was a commonplace of Israelite wisdom literature, for example, to recognize that the beginning of wisdom was "the fear of the Lord" (cf. Proverbs 1:7; 9:10; Job 28:28).[28] The sages not only reflected on this reality in their teachings, however. They gave voice to it in their prayers as well. In Psalms 19:9, 34:11, and 111:10 such advice is presented, as also in 112:1 and 128:1, 4. "Happy is everyone who fears the Lord" (Psalm 128:1).

In Psalm 111 it is said that the beginning—the basis, or point of departure—for wisdom is "the fear of the Lord":

> The fear of the Lord is the beginning of wisdom;
> All those who practice it have a good understanding.
> His praise endures forever. (v. 10)

Such "fear" is linked in the text to the Lord being "awesome" and thus worthy of praise. ("Fear" and "awesome" come from the same Hebrew root; cf. v. 9c, "holy and *awesome* is his name.") It is also viewed as synonymous with practicing the Lord's "precepts" (cf. v. 10b, "all those who practice *it*," or in the Hebrew, "all those who practice *them*," referring to the precepts in v. 7b). The psalmist would have us live in the full awareness of the Lord's works (vv. 2a, 3a, 4a, 5a, 6a, 7a, 9a), according to the divine presence and precepts (vv. 3b, 4b, 5b, 6b, 7b, 8, 9b). Wisdom is not for him an abstract concept, not a disembodied practice, not a cerebral activity. It arises from a posture of "praise" (v. 1a), from all who "delight" in the works of the Lord (v. 2b).

To live reverently, to live out of a recognition of the presence of the Lord, to "fear" the Lord, is the essence of wisdom and brings happiness. As he meditated on this truth, the psalmist found his words becoming a hymnic prayer.[29]

In addition to a focus on "the fear of the Lord," other wisdom prayers encouraged listeners and speaker alike to "delight" in the Torah (Psalms 1:2a; 19:7-10; 119:14, 16, 24, 35, 47, 70, 77, 143, 174). Jon Levenson has suggested that the Torah that is in view in such psalms as Psalm 119 is broader than the Mosaic Law. It can mean "instruction" from the received tradition (Psalm 119:99-100), from cosmic or natural law (Psalm 119:89-91), and even from God directly (Psalm 119:26-29).[30] Revelation from God can be received from all of life. We are to delight in opening ourselves to the Lord in and through all that we do, in and through all that the Lord does. Again, the expression of piety is the aim of these psalms. We are to practice the presence of God.

Other wisdom psalms admonish us to "trust in the Lord" (Psalm 32:10; 37:3), to "commit your way to the Lord" (Psalm 37:5), and to "be still before the Lord, and wait patiently for him" (Psalm 37:7; cf. v. 34). Psalm 127 notes the importance of letting it be the Lord who "builds the house" and "guards the city" (v. 1). Such psalms are at one and the same time instruction and prayer. The very act of recital is an act of commitment, an active resting in the Lord.

It is worth noting in this context as well that the wisdom psalms most closely identified with the instructional style of Proverbs (Psalms 127, 128, and 133) lack any explicitly stated admonition. These psalms observe rather than directly admonish.[31] That is, their focus is not simply on direct address to others. They allow for a more reflective gaze. It would be a mistake not to see an indirect admonition here. But there is also a simple observation of what is necessary in life: the importance of living in harmony with the Lord. These psalms are the least obvious in their meditative reflex, but they too invite hearer and speaker alike to trust in the Lord. If there is an admonition characteristic of these psalms, it is that of waiting. "Be still before the Lord, and wait patiently for him; do not fret over those who prosper in their way, over those who carry out evil devices" (Psalm 37:7).

We can observe this close connection between meditation on who God is and meditation on how we are to live as God's creatures by looking at the pair of psalms, Psalms 111 and 112. Just as Yahweh is committed to righteousness, so human life should evidence a care for righteousness. What seems to some merely a reflection on being human, something similar to what might be found in the book of Proverbs, is in reality an extension of the psalmist's reflection on God. Brueggemann, in his discussion of "The Psalms as Prayer," sees such a pattern in Psalm 24. It begins with a doxology ("The earth is the Lord's and all that is in it") and then immediately turns to consider how God would have us live ("Who shall ascend the hill of the Lord? . . . Those who have clean hands and pure hearts"). States Brueggemann, "Praise of God is joined to human obligation and discipline."[32]

A Theology of the Wisdom Psalms

As with wisdom literature more generally, it is a mistake to read the wisdom psalms as being simply pragmatic. Rather, wisdom presents an alternative way of doing theology, a contrapuntal voice that is to complement Israel's more dominant theological melody. The God who acts is also the God who *is*. The God who redeems is also the God who creates. The precepts of the Lord are right and, therefore, to be followed. They also make the heart rejoice (Psalm 19:8). The pragmatic bent of the wisdom writings invites our pietistic gaze. When that becomes evident, the wisdom psalms are allowed to become the prayers they were intended to be.

There are at least three ways that one can understand the wisdom psalms as prayer: 1) These prayers arise from our life of faith when we sense that we are securely oriented, or grounded; 2) these prayers help us to attend to God, even by concentrating upon God's world; and 3) these prayers can be an antidote to our one-sided "race with time."

WISDOM'S PRAYER AS EXPRESSING "ORIENTATION." In his provocative essay "Psalms and the Life of Faith" and his subsequent writings, Walter Brueggemann has sought to rethink the typology that is typical of form critical studies on the Psalms. While accepting the best judgments concerning the Psalms' form and setting in life, Brueggemann has gone beyond them to ask the question, "What has been the function and intention of the Psalms as they were shaped, transmitted, and repeatedly used? That is, what was the purpose of 'doing them,' albeit in highly stylized form?" Making use of the work of Paul Ricoeur, Brueggemann proposes "that the sequence of *orientation-disorientation-reorientation* is a helpful way to understand the use and function of the Psalms."[33] In his book *Praying the Psalms*, Brueggemann says,

> I suggest, in a simple schematic fashion, that our life of faith consists in moving with God in terms of (a) being securely *oriented*, (b) being painfully *disoriented*, and (c) being surprisingly *reoriented*. This general way of speaking can apply to our *self*-acceptance, our relations to significant *others*, our participation in *public issues*. . . . Most of all, it may provide us a way to think about the Psalms in relation to our common human experience, for each of God's children is in transit along the flow of orientation, disorientation, and reorientation.[34]

Brueggemann finds the psalms of disorientation (for example, the laments) and the psalms of reorientation (for example, declarative hymns and songs of thanksgiving—"songs of celebration") more interesting than those of orientation. He believes that they can be correlated respectively with Paul Ricoeur's hermeneutic of suspicion and his hermeneutic of recollection and representation. They speak to the extremities of human experience as known concretely in Israel and by us. These psalms are "limit-expressions" that match our "limit-experiences" of disorientation and reorientation. "It is experiences of being overwhelmed, nearly destroyed, and surprisingly given life which empower us to pray and sing," he believes.[35]

But Brueggemann also recognizes that some psalms function in a third way—they speak to a basic orientation, a givenness in life. In such psalms as Psalm 1, there is no qualification or contingency. There is no real action or agency. Instead, God's being or God's moral order are the focus. The psalmist finds himself to be at home, "in place." Betraying his interest in texts that are rooted in the flow of life, Brueggemann states,

> While we all yearn for it [a situation of equilibrium], it is not very interesting and it does not produce great prayer or powerful song. It consists in being well-settled, knowing that life makes sense and God is well placed in heaven, presiding but not bothering. This is the mood of much of the middle-class Church. In terms of the Bible, this attitude of equilibrium and safe orientation

is best reflected in the teaching of the old Proverbs
which affirm that life is equitable, symmetrical, and
well-proportioned. This mood of humanness is minimal in the Psalms. . . . In order to pray them, we must
locate either in our lives or in the lives of others situations of such confident, buoyant, "successful" living.[36]

Brueggemann believes that "the psalms we include here are not the most
interesting, for there is in them no great movement, no tension to re-
solve."[37] He would have us move "beyond our time of equilibrium."

Brueggemann reads the wisdom psalms as being simply naive. Basic to such a judgment is a reading of these psalms as expressing a largely
inadequate interpretation of life's ebb and flow. But I would submit that
basic to our praying these psalms is not our dubious ability to locate ourselves as "successful" middle-class Christians, but our ability to focus on
life as from God and for God.

In the wisdom psalms, the psalmist's focus is not on himself or herself, but on who God is and what God has done.[38] These prayers of orientation teach a clear, reliable retribution (for example, 1, 32, 34, 37, 49),
or are characterized by a sense of the orderliness of life (for example, 19a,
111, 127, 128, 133), or a delight in the law of the Lord (for example,
19b, 112, 119). There is a genuine gratitude and piety for the rich blessing of life from God. Rather than being seen as unconvincing when judged
by life's standards, these prayers are to be understood as reflections based
upon God's standards. Rather than offering naive, precritical readings of
reality, these psalms of orientation might better be judged as offering
postcritical meditations on reality.[39]

Given his interest in Paul Ricoeur, Brueggemann might have found
in Ricoeur's notion of a "second naiveté" a helpful perspective by which
to value the psalms of orientation as well. In *The Symbolism of Evil*, Ricoeur
describes a first, or primitive, naiveté as the "immediacy of belief" by our
noncritical consciousness. This precritical trust is what Brueggemann finds
uninteresting, even shallow. But Ricoeur also speaks of a second naiveté
that is mediated by means of a critical consciousness. We believe so we
can understand, but we also understand so we can believe. Here is the
postcritical equivalent of a precritical hierophany. "It is by interpretation," says Ricoeur, "that we can hear again."[40]

What form critics have sometimes labeled "descriptive hymns"
(Westermann) can be correlated with these wisdom songs of orientation.
Whether reflecting in the hymns on who God is, or in the wisdom psalms
on what God's world is like, the psalms of orientation turn their hearers
outward toward their God. In this way, the wisdom psalms, like hymns,
are prayers—meditations on who God is and what God expects. Rather

than being structured primarily around the urgent recital of personal event, these psalms are often structured rhetorically. Some are composed as wisdom sentences (Psalms 127, 128, and 133). Others are structured according to an acrostic pattern (Psalms 34, 37, 112, and 119). Even those composed around a certain theme of order and wholeness (Psalms 1 and 49) or in the style of a hymn (Psalm. 111) lack any tension or movement. They simply orient one to life under God.[41]

WISDOM'S PRAYER AS "ATTENTION." Another way of looking at the wisdom psalms as prayers is to consider the *attention* that they both express and evoke. Psalms like Psalm 1 speak of the joy of continually attending not to life's circumstances—certainly not to life's detractors— but to Yahweh's instruction. The blessing of God comes from being rooted in the Lord of life. "Be still before the Lord, and wait patiently for him." So says the psalmist in Psalm 37. Rather than view this psalm as the uninformed utterance of an ostrich, what one finds is a prolonged meditation upon the God of our salvation. To "fear the Lord" is to be oriented toward the divine, to attend to the Lord. "Thy way is a lamp unto my feet, and a light unto my path" (Psalm 119:105). Even psalms like 127 and 128 can be understood in this light. They are prayers, sustained reflection on God. The psalmist would have us know that unless our activity—whether in the family or in the community—seeks the perspective of God, stretching out to God's purpose and presence, it will prove empty. However, when Yahweh is at the ongoing center of our activity, when our focus is on the Lord, then we will see our city prosper, and our children's children.

In his article "Worship as the Orientation of Life to God," Daniel Hardy speaks of the present-day problem of worship as centering in the supposition that life is to be lived in unbridled freedom without thought for the sources and resources of life. "When guided by such suppositions, the practice of life distracts from worship, dissipates it, and leads inexorably away from all the 'universe of unfoldings and enfoldings' which occur in worship." However, Hardy believes that life, in reality, is lived by limiting ourselves through concentrations of various kinds, through "acts of attention and particularization" within the modalities of human existence—of environment, geography and demography, sociality, polity, culture, and the like. These are the conditions through which we are in the world, but they are also the conditions by which we are "both from and with God." Hardy believes that we need "to relearn our participation in the active spiritual truth which is the life of God in the world."[42]

Here is a helpful perspective by which to understand the wisdom psalms. By focusing upon ordinary life as lived—by refusing to impose an interpretation on life, but by recognizing a divine pattern which flows outward from life—the psalmists are both participating in prayer and reflecting on what is constitutive of reality. The psalmist is giving concentrated attention to the blessing of God in and through the particularities of our existence. Hardy quotes Simone Weil approvingly: "Attention, taken to its highest degree, is the same thing as prayer."[43] But where Weil believes that such attention requires an emptying of our thoughts, Hardy argues for the opposite. It is in the particularities of human existence that the life of God is ubiquitous. "Where such particularistic presentations of human existence are incandescent to God's activity, their origin in worship is striking."[44]

A similar concern to attend better to life's holiness has been voiced by David Tracy. Referring to the work of Pierre Hadot, the French thinker whose book was soon to come out under the English title *Spiritual Exercises in Ancient Philosophy*, Tracy argues that moderns have difficulty reading ancient and non-Western texts because we have lost the link "between theological and philosophical theories and spiritual exercises." The modern Western way of separating spiritual practices and theories is new and distancing. Again quoting Simone Weil, Tracy reflects, "She thought 'attention,' the ability to attend to the wider whole, was what we, her rushed contemporaries, most lacked."[45] Again, we must understand in order to believe, and believe in order to understand.

Tracy goes on to note that there is, of course, a genuine distinction between theory and practice (in the context of this paper, between instruction and prayer), but not a separation. What is increasingly being recognized, he believes, is the classic link between the two. Spirituality without theological instruction stands in danger of becoming sentimentality. Theology without its link to spiritual exercises risks becoming rationalistic.

These linkages of instruction and prayer, of theology and spirituality, of doxology and doctrine, are central to the psalms, including the wisdom psalms:

> Great are the works of the Lord,
>   studied by all who delight in them. (Psalm 111:1-2)

> Happy are those who fear the Lord,
>   who greatly delight in his commandments. . . .
> It is well with those who deal generously and lend,
>   who conduct their affairs with justice. (Psalm 112:1, 5)

> Unless the Lord builds the house,
>   those who build it labor in vain. (Psalm127:1)

> Happy is everyone who fears the Lord,
>   who walks in his way. (Psalm 128:1)

> How very good and pleasant it is
>   when kindred live together in unity! . . .
> For there the Lord ordained his blessing,
>   life forevermore. (Psalm 133:1, 3b)

By looking at life as intended by God, the psalmists also find themselves attending to God. Rather than view their attention to life as simply instruction, not prayer, we need to understand this concentrated focus on life before and with God also as prayer. The maxim *lex orandi/lex credendi* holds true. The rule of prayer is the rule of belief. Doctrine and doxology can go hand in hand.

WISDOM PRAYER AND MODERNITY. In his Payton Lectures at Fuller Theological Seminary (1996), Jurgen Moltmann spoke of "Christianity and the Values of the Western World." Noting our fascination with time, with the tempo of life, he contrasted "progress" as the leitmotif of modernity with "equilibrium," the leitmotif of premodern cultures. "What we need for survival," he said, "is a balance between 'progress' and 'equilibrium' if we are to develop . . . the ecological culture that will be the culture of the twenty-first century." Moltmann questioned whether the God of the Bible was really as "one-sidedly and in as modern a fashion" the "God of history" as many assert. In like fashion, are God's people simply to be considered those who have been called out to become strangers in a strange world, nowhere at home until God's promise is fulfilled? Are we simply restless hearts in a restless world before a restless God?

Speaking in part self-critically, Moltmann noted that there are many like his teacher Gerhard von Rad, who, for most of his career, unwittingly denied creation and Creator their rightful place. But just as von Rad "discovered" Israel's wisdom literature late in his career and corrected his overemphasis on the "God of history," so Moltmann spoke of the need for those like himself to offer end-course correctives. In particular, Moltmann spoke of modern human beings (those "always at a loss for time") as needing to discover "slowness." Modernity says that "time is money"; we speak of our "race with time."

> The modern "homo accelerandus" . . . does not really experience anything, since although he wants to see everything, he internalizes nothing and reflects upon nothing. . . . We tourists have been everywhere, but we have arrived nowhere. A person who lives ever faster so as not to miss anything, always lives superficially, and misses the deeper experiences of life.

What is the solution? We need to surrender our finite life to the divine life and then receive it back as a gift. The mature experience of

the presence of God can surround us on all sides, like an ocean that
supports those who swim therein.

> Within this divine presence, we can affirm our limited
> life and become engaged in its limits. We become calm
> and composed, and we begin to live slowly and with
> enjoyment. Only the person who lives slowly gets more
> from life![46]

Here, in Moltmann's prophetic words to those of us who would always be
striving, is the perspective of those who would pray the wisdom psalms,
who would meditate on life with the Lord. Our being should be found in
God—"reposing in this godward, and not merely godlike, life."[47] If we
would discover life, we should

> Trust in the Lord, and do good;
>   so you will live in the land, and enjoy security. . . .
> Be still before the Lord, and wait patiently for him . . .
>   those who wait for the Lord shall inherit the land. . . .
> Better is a little that the righteous person has
>   than the abundance of many wicked. . . .
> I have been young, and now am old. . . .
> Wait for the Lord, and keep to his way,
>   and he will exalt you to inherit the land.
>   (Psalm 37:3, 7, 9, 16, 25, 34)

The psalmist too would have us go slow—to *be* as well as become.
Here is that basic orientation that provides perspective on all else. Rather
than conveying the naive wish fulfillment of youth, here is the wisdom of
experience expressed prayerfully. Only the person who has experienced
contentment on the far side of anxiety can rest so nonchalantly. Rather
than being uninteresting or immature, as some would label such repose,
here is a second naiveté that hopes against hope. The wisdom psalmists
know life from and with God. As such, they can link their reflections on
life to both descriptive and declarative praise of God, the giver and
ordainer of life.

Endnotes

1. J. Clinton McCann, "The Psalms as Instruction," *Interpretation* 42, No.2
(April 1992): 120. Cf. James Mays, "The Place of the Torah Psalms in the Psalter,"
Journal of Biblical Literature 106 (1987): 12.

2. Eugene Peterson, *Answering God* (San Francisco: HarperCollins, 1991),
12.

3. In his comprehensive and helpful book *They Cried to the Lord* (Minneapolis: Fortress, 1994), Patrick Miller describes Scripture's foci with regard to prayer as being on those prayers to God that are based in need or in a response to God's help. Here is the typical pattern. Walter Brueggemann argues similarly in his article "The Psalms as Prayer," speaking of Israel's prayers as characteristically happening at the limits of life, whether in "glad abandonment" (praise) or in "anguished self-insistence" (lament). Cf. Walter Brueggemann, "The Psalms as Prayer," in *The Psalms and the Life of Faith*, Patrick D. Miller, ed. (Minneapolis: Fortress, 1995), 57.

4. Brueggemann, "The Psalms as Prayer," 57, 50, 34.

5. Gunkel's work has never been translated, but his article "The Psalms" has been translated into English and was published as a pamphlet (Philadelphia: Fortress, Facet Books, 1967); Mowinckel's two-volume work is *The Psalms in Israel's Worship* (Nashville: Abingdon, 1962).

6. Gerald Wilson has done the best work to date on this question. Cf. Gerald Wilson, *The Editing of the Hebrew Psalter* (Chico: Scholars Press, 1985); Gerald Wilson, "The Shape of the Book of Psalms," *Interpretation* 46, No.2 (April 1992): 129-42.

7. Roland E. Murphy, "A Consideration of the Classification 'Wisdom Psalms,'" in *Studies in Ancient Israelite Wisdom*, James L. Crenshaw, ed. (New York: KTAV, 1976), 159. Cf. Roland E. Murphy, *The Tree of Life* (New York: Doubleday, The Anchor Bible Reference Library, 1990), 103-4.

8. Kenneth Kuntz, "The Canonical Wisdom Psalms of Ancient Israel—Their Rhetorical, Thematic, and Formal Dimensions," in *Rhetorical Criticism*, Jared Jackson and Martin Kessler, eds. (Pittsburgh: Pickwick, 1974), 217.

9. Gerhard Von Rad, *Wisdom in Israel* (Nashville: Abingdon, 1972), 49.

10. Roland E. Murphy, *Responses to 101 Questions on the Psalms and Other Writings* (New York: Paulist, 1994), 11; cf. Murphy, "A Consideration of the Classification 'Wisdom Psalms,' " 159: "The Gattung of wisdom psalms is subject to no clear-cut characterization."

11. Murphy, "A Consideration of the Classification 'Wisdom Psalm,'" 160.

12. R. B. Y. Scott, *The Way of Wisdom* (New York: Macmillan, 1971), 197.

13. Roland E. Murphy, *The Psalms Are Yours* (New York: Paulist, 1993), 75; Roland E. Murphy, "The Psalms and Worship," *Ex Auditu* 8 (1992): 27 (italics mine).

14. Roland E. Murphy, *Wisdom Literature and Psalms* (Nashville: Abingdon, 1983), 146. Cf. Erhard Gerstenberger, *Psalms, Part 1 with an Introduction to Cultic Poetry* (Grand Rapids: Eerdmans, 1988), 21: "We may assume, therefore, that such psalms to a large extent grew out a communal, liturgical instruction, which must have constituted a vital part of early Jewish worship (cf. Nehemiah 8:7). The obvious aim was the edification and orientation of the members of the synagogal community." Gerstenberger goes on to say that the wisdom psalms had the "quality of prayer," but this recognition is left undeveloped as these psalms' instructional focus is emphasized.

15. James Mays, *Psalms* (Louisville: John Knox, Interpretation, 1994), 27, 28. Cf. James Crenshaw, "Psalms," in *Old Testament Form Criticism*, John Hayes, ed. (San Antonio: Trinity, 1974), 219: "Instruction in fact can be surmised to be the driving force behind most of the wisdom poems."

16. Von Rad, *Wisdom in Israel*, 189. Cf. Sigmund Mowinckel, *The Psalms in Israel's Worship*, 108: "In spite of the didactic character of the 'learned psalmography,' it has one characteristic in common with genuine [!] psalmography:

these poems are, and must be considered as, *prayers*. Like every real psalm, they address God, even though they often address men as well." Unfortunately, Mowinckel's insight has been largely ignored.

17. Bentzen might be viewed as one extreme, believing that there were only three psalms that were pure wisdom psalms (Psalms 1, 112, and 127). Others often included in this classification (for example, Psalms 32, 37, and 49) were in reality psalms of thanksgiving. Bentzen has surely understated the presence of wisdom within some psalms, but he has perceptively noted the presence of thanksgiving in some psalms not often interpreted as such. There is in a number of psalms a natural linkage between wisdom and thanksgiving. Here is one reason such psalms were included in Israel's (and our) prayerbook. Cf. Aage Bentzen, *Introduction to the Old Testament* (Copenhagen: Gad, 1958), vol. 1, 161, quoted in Kuntz, "The Canonical Wisdom Psalms," 190.

18. Murphy, "A Consideration of the Classification 'Wisdom Psalms,' " 161.

19. Cf. Walter Brueggemann, "Bounded by Obedience and Praise: the Psalms as Canon," in Miller, ed., *The Psalms and the Life of Faith*, 204.

20. Cf. Walter Brueggemann in *Israel's Praise* (Philadelphia: Fortress, 1988), 115: "Psalm 37 is a clear example of a perception of the world that is skewed by supreme and uncritical confidence in the system. . . . This voice is untroubled by the problems of the real world."

21. An analogous situation might come in giving the advice "Honesty is the best policy." We know that honesty can also get one in trouble. But though honesty doesn't always "work," it remains God's intention for humankind. It is the best policy, for it reflects God's ways for humankind.

22. Robert Davidson, *Wisdom and Worship* (London: SCM, 1990), 33.

23. Von Rad, *Wisdom in Israel*, 48.

24. Miller, *They Cried to the Lord*, 47, 46.

25. Murphy, *Responses to 101 Questions*, 125.

26. Maltbie Babcock, "This Is My Father's World."

27. James Mays comments, "This psalm is composed for oral recitation in an act of worship. The words express the musing of the heart, the seat of consciousness in which thoughts are formed. Through the words the heart finds voice and the self is presented to God. . . . In the intention of the psalmist, this prayer poem is such an offering." Mays, *Psalms*, 100.

28. Cf. von Rad, *Wisdom in Israel*, 53-73. In his chapter "Knowledge and the Fear of God," von Rad speaks of only one world of experience in Israel which "was apperceived by means of a perceptive apparatus in which rational perceptions and religious perceptions were not differentiated" (61). There was, in other words, no rationality "which was independent of faith." For the wisdom writers, all human knowledge must be seen as grounded in a commitment to God.

29. Other evidence that Psalm 111 is both instruction *and* prayer, a wisdom piece and a hymn, comes from noting its acrostic structure, its close linkage to Psalm 112, and its announcement of praise (v. 1). The psalmist reflects reverently on God by considering his past works, and calls us to similarly act in faithfulness and justice.

30. Jon D. Levenson, "The Source of Torah: Psalm 119 and the Modes of Revelation in Second Temple Judaism," in *Ancient Israelite Religion*, ed. P. D. Miller, Jr., P. D. Hanson, S. D. McBride, Jr. (Philadelphia: Fortress Press, 1987), 570. Quoted in McCann, "The Psalms as Instruction," 118.

31. Kuntz, "The Canonical Wisdom Psalms," 217.

32. Brueggemann, "The Psalms as Prayer," 63.

33. Walter Brueggemann, "Psalms and the Life of Faith: A Suggested Typol-

ogy of Function," in Miller, ed., *The Psalms and the Life of Faith*, 3, 9.

34. Walter Brueggemann, *Praying the Psalms* (Winona: Saint Mary's, Pace Books, 1982), 16.

35. Ibid., 17.

36. Ibid., 17.

37. Ibid., 10. Cf. Brueggemann, "Bounded by Obedience and Praise," 197: "It is, however, not universally true (as against Psalm 1) that obedient people prosper and wicked people perish. Only the very sheltered, innocent, and unperceptive could embrace such a naive affirmation as that made in Psalm 1 (see also Psalm 37:25-26)." "Psalm 1 does not invite candid protest or hard, probing questions about moral coherence. Psalm 1 does not entertain or even permit the demanding question of theodicy. For that reason, the simple affirmation of Psalm 1 is not adequate to lived experience."

38. To understand the Psalms as focused on God and not on ourselves helps us also to understand the psalms of vengeance. The yearning for vengeance in Psalm 137 or the hatred expressed in Psalm 139 make sense when they are put within the context of worship. Their expressions of extreme emotion are seen then to flow from a concentration on the majesty of their God. Any challenge is repugnant.

39. In a response to Brueggemann's article "Psalms and the Life of Faith," which first appeared in 1980, John Goldingay criticized Brueggemann along similar lines: "Thus, for the ancient or modern user of the Psalms, to affirm the coherence of life in the terms of the psalms of orientation may reflect uncritical equilibrium or post-critical celebration." John Goldingay, "The Dynamic Cycle of Praise and Prayer in the Psalms," *Journal for the Study of Old Testament* 20 (1981): 89.

40. Paul Ricoeur, *The Symbolism of Evil* (New York: Harper & Row, 1967), 351-52.

41. Not all wisdom psalms are psalms of orientation. Those related to psalms of thanksgiving fit more into Brueggemann's schema as psalms of reorientation. Psalm 73, for example, narrates a pilgrimage from orientation (v. 1) through disorientation (vv. 2-16) to a final reorientation (vv. 17-26).

42. Daniel W. Hardy, "Worship as the Orientation of Life to God," *Ex Auditu* 8 (1992): 56, 57, 68-69.

43. Simone Weil, *The Notebooks of Simone Weil* (London: Routledge & Kegan Paul, 1956), 597, quoted in Hardy, "Worship as the Orientation of Life to God," 64.

44. Hardy, "Worship as the Orientation of Life to God," 65.

45. David Tracy, quoted in William R. Burrows, "Reason to Hope for Reform. An Interview with David Tracy," *America* 173, No. 11 (October 14, 1995): 15-16.

46. Jurgen Moltmann, "Christianity and the Values of the Western World," Payton Lectures, Fuller Theological Seminary, April 19, 1996, unpublished manuscript.

47. P. T. Forsyth, *The Soul of Prayer* (Grand Rapids: Eerdmans, nd, reprint of 1916 edition), 60.

Scribal Contributions to Old Testament Theology

JACK R. LUNDBOM

I am happy to join those honoring Professor Fred Holmgren in this collection of essays. Fred was my first teacher in Old Testament, and in the years since he has become a much-appreciated colleague and friend. We pay tribute to thirty-five years of teaching at North Park Theological Seminary; to faithful service as pastor, teacher, and friend to countless people over an even longer period—in the Covenant and in the larger church of Jesus Christ, both Protestant and Catholic; to his participation in the Jewish-Christian dialogue; and above all to his humanity and embodiment of the genuine Christian graces in a world that seldom sees the two in combination.

The scribes who received such sharp criticism from Jesus (Matthew 23:1-39), and from Jeremiah centuries earlier (Jeremiah 8:8), possessed, nevertheless, an enviable position within Judaism and enjoyed great reputation, for which reason, no doubt, they lay open to censure. Because of their ability to read and write, scribes in ancient societies generally were entrusted with important matters of temple and state, handling administrative affairs, facilitating international relations, copying texts from antiquity, and giving counsel to kings. In Judaism and early Christianity their role in preparing and transmitting Scripture was crucial—some would say indispensable—whether we cite Baruch ben Neriah (Jeremiah 36), Matthew the disciple (Matthew 9:9; cf. 13:52), or Tertius, the amanuensis of Paul (Romans 16:22). Nameless others up until the invention of printing in the fifteenth century diligently copied biblical texts by hand—in daylight and by candlelight—so the treasured word of God might survive to the present day.

Scribes were at their craft over five millennia ago, from the time we first begin to see written texts emerge in Mesopotamia and Egypt. Before then—indeed, a long time before—we have but artwork in caves to look at, animal paintings, mainly, from such places as the Altamira caves in northern Spain and the La Mouthe and Chauvet caves in southern France, the last-named discovery coming as recently as 1994. Ancient Sumer had scribes and scribal schools, called "tablet houses," around 3000 B.C.,[1] and we are now reasonably well informed about scribal practices and scribal schools in Old Babylonia,[2] as well as at Ugarit,[3] where the first alphabetic writing occurred two or three centuries before Israel's arrival in Canaan. Here a simplified cuneiform script of twenty-two to thirty letters was developed, a precursor to the Semitic alphabet. Scribal activity is also in evidence in Egypt from the early third millennium B.C., beginning with the development of a complex state in the Old Kingdom.[4]

While writing of some sort existed in early Israel,[5] it was not until the time of David that scribes (Hebrew *sōphĕrîm*) began appearing at the royal court as high officials.[6] A central administration was not possible without writing. According to Lipinski,[7] annalistic activity of royal scribes began in Solomon's reign, with the first complete annals of a king probably being compiled by Rehoboam. Mowinckel believed that Solomon founded a school for scribes in Jerusalem.[8] In subsequent years, scribes were the ones who collected, committed to writing, and copied for themselves and generations to come temple psalms, collections of proverbs (Proverbs 25:1), accounts of the creation and flood, stories about the Patriarchs—in short, all of Israel's history and literature, a select portion of which came to be included in our Old Testament. In collecting oral traditions and committing them to writing, these individuals were not unlike the Brüder Grimm in Germany and the Peter Christen Asbjørnsen-Jørgen Moe team in Norway in modern times.

Scribes are seen functioning in the court of King Hezekiah (2 Kings 18:18=Isaiah 36:3),[9] and the suggestion has been made that possibly Isaiah the prophet was a scribe.[10] Scribes appear as a professional class in the book of Jeremiah (8:8), where we also meet up with individual scribes such as Baruch (called "Baruch, the scribe" in Jeremiah 36:26, 32)[11] and Baruch's brother, Seraiah, the "quartermaster" of Zedekiah (Jeremiah 51:59-64).[12] Both are cited with patronym or double patronym, "son of Neriah (son of Mahseiah)" (Jeremiah 32:12; 36:4; 51:59), which probably indicates that the father and grandfather were also scribes. In Israel, as in neighboring societies, the profession was passed on from generation to generation, resulting in so-called scribal families (cf. 1 Kings 4:3).[13] Seal impressions with the names of both Baruch and Seraiah have turned up in excavations.[14] Other scribes mentioned in the important chapter 36 of Jeremiah are Shaphan and Elishama (vv. 10-11). Shaphan, a major figure when the lawbook was found in the temple in 622 B.C. (2 Kings 22:8-14), was probably head of a scribal school in Jerusalem,[15] connected, as was customary, with the temple.[16] Muilenburg, noting the enormous amount of scribal activity also in Assyria during the same period, calls this "a scribal age."[17]

In the present essay I wish to point out a single contribution that scribes have made to the theology of the Old Testament, one not altogether obvious and one whose discovery falls more under a study of rhetoric and composition than under text criticism, the usual hunting ground for insights into scribal practice. On occasion scribes will be seen deliberately juxtaposing materials in the biblical text in order to set up a contrast, much in the way modern journal, magazine, and newspaper editors run contrasting articles in succession or place them side by side on a page. They do not tell you they are doing this; nevertheless, the editing is intentional and an effect on the readership is expected. When statements are made in this manner, we must be alerted to them and appropriate them into our theological understanding, for such statements are as important as those of an explicit nature. The phenomenon of juxtaposition has not gone unnoticed in Jewish tradition. Rabbi Akiba is reported to have said, "Every section in Scripture is explained by the one that stands next to it" (*Sifre Num.* 131).

Some years ago Robert Gordis[18] pointed out in the book of Proverbs, amidst a collection dealing with "fools" (26:1-12), these two proverbs in immediate succession:

> Answer not a fool according to his folly
> lest you be like him yourself.
> Answer a fool according to his folly
> lest he be wise in his own eyes. (vv. 4-5)

One proverb says not to answer a fool with foolishness; the other advises precisely that. Each has its reason. The scribe responsible for this juxtaposition knew exactly what he was doing, and most likely wanted to teach us something about the limits of wisdom. One can be right doing either. One can also be wrong. It all depends. The contrast takes us beyond the truth embodied in each individual proverb.

In an earlier article[19] I sought to show how the scribe juxtaposing the Tower of Babel story in Genesis 11:1-9 with the call of Abraham in Genesis 12:1-3, before the genealogies of 11:10-32 were added, intended to make an unspoken point about the relative importance of buildings and people to Yahweh. The contrast is embodied in a play on the phrase, "making a name." The men of Babel say, "And *let us make* for ourselves *a name*" (Genesis 11:4), by which they mean, "Let us erect a city within which we will place a grand temple." The word *tower* in the RSV and NRSV is misleading; the building is a temple, or ziggurat, perhaps of the type described in *Enuma elish* VI, 60-66 (ANET³ 68-69).[20] Yahweh, however, says to Abraham, "I *will make* of you a great nation, and I will bless you, and I will make great *your name*" (Genesis 12:2).

The hubris of humanity is set over against the inestimable grace of

Yahweh. But there is more. The men of Babel seek their name by erecting a pretentious temple, whereas Abraham will achieve his name by having a myriad of descendants. The contrast is between imposing, pretentious temples, which Yahweh rejects, and human descendants, which Yahweh promises to give. The same theology—made from a wordplay on house (*bayit*)—occurs in 2 Samuel 7. Both are early versions of "the church is not buildings, but people" theme. In 2 Samuel 7 this theology is embodied in a single narrative. In Genesis 11:1-9 and 12:1-3, however, it is derived from the juxtaposition of the passages, which is the work of a theologically minded scribe.

This same juxtaposition technique can be seen in three additional Old Testament passages, another from Genesis and one each from Isaiah and Jeremiah. In all three the contrast is to moralize, or better, to teach behavior that is pleasing to God and, in two of the cases, behavior that is not.

GENESIS 38-39. Chapter 38 of Genesis is agreed by all to be an interpolation into the Joseph story, which is chapters 37-50 and one of the most homogeneous passages in the entire Bible. At the other end, in chapter 49, the "Blessing of Jacob" poem is inserted. The Joseph story is sometimes called a novella. The insertion of chapter 38 is credited to a scribe called the Yahwist,[21] whose preferred term for God, *Yahweh*, appears only in chapters 38 and 39 of the narrative.[22]

The story begins with Joseph being sold by his brothers into slavery, arriving in Egypt, and being sold a second time to Potiphar, an officer of the Pharaoh. Chapter 38 then interrupts with a report of what was going on in Canaan, a "meanwhile, back at the ranch" type of interlude.[23] Things actually were not going well. Judah has had an affair with Tamar, his daughter-in-law, which resulted in a child. This would have cost Tamar her life, except that she outwitted her father-in-law, exposing his misdeed. The story by itself relates another important fact. The son born to Tamar became a forefather to King David (1 Chronicles 2:4-15, where David descends from Perez).

But why has the Judah episode in chapter 38 been inserted into the Joseph story at precisely this point? The answer, it seems to me, is found by looking ahead to chapter 39. The two chapters juxtaposed set up another contrast. In 38, Judah knowingly commits harlotry and unknowingly is guilty of incest with his daughter-in-law; in 39, Joseph resists the clutches of Potiphar's wife, who, if she had had her way, would have seduced him into an act of adultery. By juxtaposing Judah's affair with Tamar and Joseph's rebuff of Potiphar's wife, this theologically minded scribe quietly moralizes about sexual propriety and impropriety, ironically contrasting Joseph's virtuous behavior in a foreign land with Judah's misadventure back home. The sum is again greater than its individual parts. In the minds of many, things work just the reverse: corruption comes in a foreign land; purity exists at home.

ISAIAH 5-6. In the prophetic books, it is commonplace to say that materials are not always arranged in chronological order. A case in point is the early chapters of Isaiah, where the prophet's call comes not in chapter 1, but in chapter 6. Earlier scholars, assuming chronological order in the book, had to conclude either that the call took place after Isaiah had been preaching for some time or that chapter 6 was a "call of renewal" following an inaugural call not recorded. Tannaitic interpreters wanted the call at the beginning of the book,[24] which is where the calls of Jeremiah and Ezekiel are placed. The consensus now is that chapter 6 is the prophet's inaugural call, and that the preaching in chapters 1-5 came afterwards.[25] The call is commonly explained as a preface to a collection of material reflecting the Syro-Ephraimite crisis, which ends at 9:6.[26] It came earlier than this crisis, for which reason it is written in retrospect, possibly from Isaiah's own memoirs.[27]

Scholars, however, have paid little or no attention to the relationship between chapter 6 and what precedes it. Leon Liebreich connects chapters 1-5—particularly chapter 5—with chapter 6, citing keywords that refer to Yahweh, the "Holy One of Israel."[28] There are other linking terms that connect chapter 5 to chapter 6, suggesting that the scribe who placed the call where he did intended a juxtaposition with the "woe oracles" of 5:8-22, and another contrast as well. In 5:8-22, Isaiah cries "woe" (*hôy*) on the rich, the drunks, the liars, the conceited, and the unjust in Jerusalem's elite. But in 6:5 he turns the spotlight on himself, saying, "Woe is me" ('*ôy lî*). All together we have seven woes, which is probably significant in that the number seven in Hebrew thought signifies completeness.[29]

The combined message of the two passages is obvious, as more than one sermon has pointed out. The prophet who finds himself capable of making judgments on others is seen to render judgment also on himself, which goes some distance, surely, in humanizing the prophet. But more important, it gives Isaiah his warrant to preach. One who recognizes his own uncleanness can then venture forth to point out uncleanness in others (cf. Matthew 7:1-5). And a scribe provides us with this insight by juxtaposing Isaiah's call with a select number of his oracles of woe.

JEREMIAH 34-35. In Jeremiah, a lack of chronological order is documented in the dated prose of chapters 21-45. Incidents from the reign of Jehoiakim are freely interspersed with those occurring during the reign of Zedekiah, a decade later. In chapters 34-35 we have a clear case where Zedekiah prose has been placed ahead of Jehoiakim prose. Since chapter 34 also does not fit into a rhetorical structure taking in other Zedekiah prose,[30] an explanation is required as to why it is placed where it is. One can be given if we see chapter 34 intentionally juxtaposed with chapter 35 for the purpose of setting up a contrast between the Rechabites and Judah's last king.

Chapter 34 reports an incident in which Zedekiah reneges on a covenant made with the people to honor the Year of Release, that is, to release Hebrew slaves (Deuteronomy 15:12-18). For this he receives strong censure from the prophet Jeremiah. Chapter 35 tells about the Rechabites, a marginal group of seminomadic folk presently living in Judah, whom Jeremiah brings into the temple to give people an object lesson on fidelity and obedience. The Rechabites have taken a vow not to drink wine. Jeremiah therefore sets in front of them jars of wine and tells them to drink. They refuse, and in so doing show fidelity to Jonadab, their father, who had given them the command. The juxtaposition shows the Rechabites to be faithful and obedient in a way Zedekiah was not—another contribution to Old Testament theology by a scribe, in this case perhaps Jeremiah's colleague and friend, Baruch.

Old Testament theology comes through many different types of people and in a variety of literary and rhetorical forms. To the list of inspired prophets and faithful priests, gifted kings and the seasoned wise, must be added theologically minded scribes. Actually, the list is greater, including storytellers and a host of plain, ordinary people. We find theology explicitly stated in creeds, liturgies, hymns, stories, wisdom pieces, oracles, narratives, historical writings, and many other genres, but it is present also, less explicitly, in Hebrew rhetoric—in metaphors, similes, repetitions, hyperbole, wordplays, argument, humor, and countless other rhetorical forms. The task of interpretation is therefore varied and complex, and the sensitive biblical interpreter will look not only to what is said in the text, but also to what is not said, for in the latter also are statements that are part and parcel of the revealed word of God.

Endnotes

1. Samuel Noah Kramer, "Schooldays: A Sumerian Composition Relating to the Education of a Scribe," *JAOS* 69 (1949): 199-215.

2. Benno Landsberger, "Babylonian Scribal Craft and Its Terminology," in *Proceedings of the Twenty-Third International Congress of Orientalists*, ed. Denis Sinor (London: Royal Asiatic Society, 1954), 123-26; C. J. Gadd, *Teachers and Students in the Oldest Schools* (London: School of Oriental and African Studies, University of London, 1956); Carl H. Kraeling and Robert M. Adams, eds., *City Invincible*. A symposium on "Urbanization and Cultural Development in the Ancient Near East" held at the Oriental Institute of the University of Chicago, December 4-7, 1958 (Chicago: University of Chicago Press, 1960), 94-123.

3. Anson F. Rainey, "The Scribe at Ugarit," in *Proceedings of the Israel Academy of Sciences and Humanities III* (Jerusalem: Israel Academy of Sciences and Humanities, 1969), 126-47.

4. See Ronald J. Williams, "Scribal Training in Ancient Egypt," *JAOS* 92 (1972): 214-21; Kraeling and Adams, *City Invincible*, 103, mention a government school for scribes existing ca. 1900 B.C.

5. Alan R. Millard, "In Praise of Ancient Scribes," *BA* 45 (1982): 143-53.

6. Eduard Nielsen, *Oral Tradition*, SBT 11 (Chicago: Alec R. Allenson, 1954): 43.

7. E. Lipinski, "Royal and State Scribes in Ancient Jerusalem," *VT Supp* 40 (1988): 157-58.

8. Sigmund Mowinckel, "Psalms and Wisdom," in *Wisdom in Israel and in the Ancient Near East*, ed. Martin Noth and D. Winton Thomas, *VT Supp* 3 (Leiden: E. J. Brill, 1955): 206.

9. James Crenshaw, "Education in Ancient Israel," *JBL* 104 (1985): 601-15.

10. Robert T. Anderson, "Was Isaiah a Scribe?" *JBL* 79 (1960): 57-58.

11. On Baruch, see the article by James Muilenburg, "Baruch the Scribe," in *Proclamation and Presence*, ed. John I. Durham and J. R. Porter (Richmond: John Knox Press, 1970), 215-38.

12. Jack R. Lundbom, "Baruch, Seraiah, and Expanded Colophons in the Book of Jeremiah," *JSOT* 36 (1986): 101-9.

13. W. G. Lambert, "Ancestors, Authors, and Canonicity," *Journal of Cuneiform Studies* 11 (1957): 2-3; Rainey, "The Scribe at Ugarit," 128; Lipinski, "Royal and State Scribes in Ancient Jerusalem," 162.

14. N. Avigad, "Baruch the Scribe and Jerahmeel the King's Son," *IEJ* 28 (1978): 52-56 [=BA 42 (1979), 114-18]; idem., "The Seal of Seraiah (Son of) Neriah" (Hebrew with English summary), *Eretz-Israel* 14 (1978): 86-87, 125.

15. Lundbom, "Baruch, Seraiah, and Expanded Colophons in the Book of Jeremiah," 108.

16. Rainey, "The Scribe at Ugarit," 128.

17. Muilenburg, "Baruch the Scribe," 216-17.

18. Robert Gordis, "Quotations in Wisdom Literature," *JQR* 30 (1939-40): 137.

19. Jack R. Lundbom, "Abraham and David in the Theology of the Yahwist," in *The Word of the Lord Shall Go Forth* (Essays in Honor of David Noel Freedman), ed. Carol L. Meyers and M. O'Connor (Winona Lake: The American Schools of Oriental Research and Eisenbrauns, 1983), 203-9.

20. E. A. Speiser, *Genesis*, AB 1 (Garden City: Doubleday & Co., 1964): 75-76.

21. Gerhard von Rad, *Genesis* (Philadelphia: Westminster Press, 1961), 352.

22. In Genesis 37-50 *'ĕlōhîm* appears thirty-four times, and YHWH twelve times. All twelve occurrences of YHWH, with the single exception of 49:18, which is in Jacob's poem of blessing, are found in chapters 38-39.

23. So Edwin M. Good, *Irony in the Old Testament* (Philadelphia: Westminster Press, 1965), 107. It is recognized also as an interlude by von Rad, *Genesis*, 352, and Speiser, *Genesis*, 299-300.

24. Mordecai Kaplan, "Isaiah 6:1-11," *JBL* 45 (1926): 251.

25. John Skinner, *Isaiah I-XXXIX*, CB (Cambridge: Cambridge University Press, 1930): 44. Kaplan, "Isaiah 6:1-11," argued on other grounds that chapter 6 was not an inaugural vision, but his lead has not been followed.

26. Chapter 6 fits particularly well with chapters 7-8, since all are biographi-

cal prose. B. Duhm, *Das Buch Jesaia*, HAT (Göttingen: Vandenhoeck & Ruprecht, 1902), ix, says, "zuerst die Drohung, zuletzt die Verheissung, in der Mitte die Motivierung der ersteren und die Vermittlung der letzteren."

27. Scholars usually cite the reference to Uzziah's death in 6:1 as an indica-tion that Isaiah's call was seen in retrospect. See Duhm, *Das Buch Jesaia*, 40-41; R. B. Y. Scott, *Isaiah 1-39*, IB 5 (New York and Nashville: Abingdon Press, 1956): 204. Scott is convinced that the call is from Isaiah's memoirs: "If anything in the book can be said clearly to be Isaiah's own composition, it is the narrative of his call in ch. 6," 157.

28. Leon Liebreich, "The Position of Chapter Six in the Book of Isaiah," *HUCA* 25 (1954): 37-40. His argument runs as follows: 1) chapters 1-5 begin and end with verses designating Yahweh as the "Holy One of Israel" (1:4; 5:24), with Yahweh called this also in 6:3; and 2) chapter 5 mentions Yahweh as a "holy" God three times in 5:16, 19, and 24, which Liebreich says provides a "fitting sequel" to the threefold "holy" in 6:3, p. 39.

29. This could also explain what some take to be the separation of the two "woe oracles" beginning in 10:1 and 5 from those in 5:8-22, that is, it was done to make room for Isaiah's "Woe is me." Professor D. N. Freedman has suggested to me in personal communication that these separated woe oracles in their present locations could act as a frame around a center interpolation of 6:1-9:6. Different spellings of "woe"—'ôy in 6:5 and hôy for the others—point to, though certainly do not prove, editorial work in chapters 5 and 6.

30. Jack R. Lundbom, *Jeremiah: A Study in Ancient Hebrew Rhetoric*, SBLDS 18 (Missoula: Society of Biblical Literature and Scholars Press, 1975): 109-11.

The Wilderness Journey in Deuteronomy: Style, Structure, and Theology in Deuteronomy 1-3[1]

Patrick D. Miller Jr.

The Book of Deuteronomy presents itself as a series of four testamentary speeches of Moses, each signaled by an editorial superscription (1:1-5; 4:44-49; 29:1; and 33:1). The first and last of these speeches are often identified with the Deuteronomistic Historian, as part of the process of integrating the Deuteronomic law into the larger history. Whether or not that is the case for the history of the formation of Deuteronomy and the books that follow, it has become increasingly clear that Deuteronomy 1-3, what some have called the "memoir" of Moses, is a rich and unified account of the journey through the wilderness, one that portrays that journey in particular ways and with specific theological perspectives. Some of those perspectives can be discerned by comparison of these chapters with the accounts of the same events in Exodus and Numbers, but that is not the primary aim of this essay. My intention is to look at Deuteronomy 1-3 as a whole, seeing how its style and structure join with content to effect a thoroughly theological account of Israel's earliest experience as the people of Yahweh.[2] Chapter 4, which develops as a hortatory implication of the first three chapters and has its own quite specific point to make, one that anticipates what is to come in the following chapters, can be formally and materially separated from chapters 1-3 even if it has been editorially and structurally joined with the memoir of the wilderness journey.[3]

Geographical Structure

There are at least two explicit ways in which the material in Deuteronomy 1-3 is ordered and the movement of the journey indicated. One is *geographical*, via a system of travel notices. Thus the book begins with an introductory location of the speeches of Moses (1:1-5) that not

only serves to locate the speeches that follow, but also refers to the journey through the wilderness that is about to be recalled by Moses. This
happens in two ways: 1) the parenthetical detail about the length of time
from Horeb to Kadesh-barnea (v. 2), the first stage of the journey that
ends so disastrously (1:6-46); and 2) the summary reference to the defeat
of the kings Sihon and Og (v. 4), which marks the end of the second
stage and indeed of the wilderness journey as a whole (2:16-3:11). The
introduction in 1:1-5 thus serves to mark the wilderness journey as being
from Horeb to Kadesh-barnea to the plain opposite Suph. This three-
point marking of the journey that is evident in the introduction is confirmed in the Moses speech that follows through the repeated use of the
verb *yāšab*, "to dwell" or "to stay": "You have stayed (*šebet*) long enough
at this mountain" (1:6). "After you had stayed (*wattēšĕbû*) at Kadesh as
many days as you did . . . " (1:46). "So we remained (*wannēšeb*) in the
valley opposite Beth-peor"[4] (3:29).

This marking of the journey serves to do two things: First, the most
obvious effect is the emphasis on the movement through the wilderness,
an emphasis provided not only by the use of the verb *yāšab*, but also by
the large number of travel notices with repeated verbs of movement that
occur throughout these three chapters.[5] Moses' memoir is specifically about
the journey from Sinai to the land. The preface to the promulgation and
instruction of the law does not reach back to prior experience—for example, Exodus—though it might, for the Exodus is specifically recalled a
number of times in what follows, and it serves to ground specific laws.
What seems to be necessary to recall, as Moses begins instructing the
people about how to live in the land, is the lessons learned along the way.

A second effect of the geographical structure, and especially the
marking of the stages by the verb *yāšab*, is the identification of the crucial moments of the journey. The starting point is Horeb, and the whole
preaching of the law will begin by taking the community back to Horeb
to recall there the giving of the law. The end point is where Deuteronomy
places the people. Beth-peor is the place, but the particular name is not
as crucial as its location—on the border, on the boundary between wilderness and promised land. But what is very clear from Moses' way of
telling the story is that the movement from Horeb to the land was through
Kadesh-barnea. And there, one may suggest, is much of the reason that a
second law is given to the people. What happened at Kadesh-barnea,
occupying the central part of these three chapters (1:19-46 plus 2:14-
16), created a situation in which the fundamental response of the people
to the direction of the Lord called into question their willingness to live
by the word of the Lord, an issue that surfaces again (see, for example,
8:3). The journey in the wilderness indicates that the Torah that the
Lord set before the people at Horeb was not enough. This people still has

much to learn. Before they enter the land, the teaching of the past must be reiterated and reinforced by further instruction.

Command and Execution

A second structural device for unfolding the movement of these chapters in smaller units is the repeated sequence of *command and execution.*[6] That is, the chapters unfold in a series of divine commands and the reports of their being carried out—or not being carried out—by the people. (At least, that is the case up to 3:12, where the memoir moves to describe the allotment to the Transjordanian tribes.)[7] The first is from 1:6 to 2:1. This section, of course, is consonant with the first of the two major geographical stages, the journey from Horeb to Kadesh-barnea and the events that happened there. The command-execution structure is as follows:

> I. Introductory reference to the divine word 1:6
> >   Command No. 1 1:7
> > >   Extension of the command 1:8
> > >   Consignment of the land   v. 8a
> > >   Conquest command v. 8bc
> >   Execution 1:19-33
> > >   Partial execution 1:19
> > >   Extension of the command reiterated 1:20-21
> > >   Nonexecution 1:26
>
> II.   Command No. 2 1:40
> >   Execution 1:46-2:1
>
> III. Introductory reference to the divine word 1:42a
> >   Command No. 3=Prohibition 1:42b
> >   Nonexecution 1:43

The initial command is carried by a series of verbs—turn (*pānâ*) and set out (*nāsa'*) and go (*bā'*)—and then extended by a second series— see (*ra'a*), go (*ba'*), and take possession (*yāraš*).[8] The partial execution of the command in verse 19 indicates that the first series of commands was carried out: The people set out (*nāsa'*) and went (*bā'*). In verses 20-21, Moses then reiterates the extension of the divine command in verse 8: See (*rā'â*), go up (*'ālâ*), and take possession (*yāraš*). The one change is in the use of the verb *'ālâ* instead of *bā'*. But that change then becomes the key verb in what happens next, that is, in the nonexecution of the reiterated divine command. The rest of the sequence of command/prohibition and execution/nonexecution centers around the command "Go up" and the response of the people to it.

At just this point, however, the movement from command to execution breaks down. The people indicate that they are "unwilling" (*'ābâ*) to "go up" (*'ālâ*), a response that the text calls rebellion (*mārâ*) against the command of God (v. 26). The movement from command to action has a hitch at this point, and that is the significance of the Kadesh-barnea episode. The movement of history, the fulfillment of the promise, and the obedience of the people break down in the unwillingness of the people to do what the Lord commanded.

The breakdown of the command-execution sequence is underscored stylistically in several ways. One is the use of the characteristic Deuteronomic phrase, "just as (*ka'ăšer*) the Lord our God had ordered us" (1:19). While such *ka'ăšer* clauses are frequent in Deuteronomy and serve, as here, to emphasize the consonance of divine command and human action, the presence of the clause in this instance serves to heighten in anticipation the dissonance between divine command and human action that is about to be recalled. The first part of the divine command that began the journey was precisely according to the command. At the point of the extension of the initial command, however, such correspondence disappears in nonexecution or rebellion. Then, at the end of this whole section, the *ka'ăšer* clause appears again to confirm the obedience of the people to the command of God (2:1).

A second way of underscoring the breakdown is in the very separation of the original command into two parts, the second of which is reiterated by Moses, thus emphasizing the command and setting up in more dramatic fashion the failure of the people to obey. Finally, consonant with this shift in the response of the people, what was at first a Mosaic word of assurance in the reiterated divine command, "Do not fear or be dismayed" (v. 21), is turned into a command, "Have no fear or dread of them" (v. 29), after the people have refused to obey the command (see below).[9]

Such rebellion triggers two more sequences of command and execution, though now things become inverted in an ironic way.[10] The first command (v. 40) reverses the movement from Horeb and sends the people back into the wilderness (1:46-2:1). The second command is a prohibition that *nullifies* the original command to go up and take possession of the land (v. 21). Now the Lord commands: "*Do not* go up [*lō' 'ālâ*] and do not fight" (1:42). Then the execution of the command by the people is an execution of the *earlier* command to go up but a *nonexecution* of, and thus a rebellion against, the *immediate* command: "You rebelled . . . and went up" (1:43; *mārâ* + *'ālâ*). What they would not do at first, they should not do; but what they would not do at first, they now are willing to do. What was rebellion is still that, but now it is presumptive rather than fearful rebellion (1:43).

There is a particular consequence of this rebellion that needs to be noted. It is in the introductory references to the divine word. At the beginning, the Lord spoke directly to the people: "The Lord our God spoke to us at Horeb" (1:6; cf. v. 19a). From now on, however, the Lord speaks through Moses. Beginning at 1:42, the introduction of the divine word is regularly "The Lord said/spoke to *me*" (see below for chapters 2-3). The speech of the Lord in 1:35-40 is ambiguous in this regard. It is clearly directed to Moses, but it also has several plural forms that could be understood as addressing the people directly. That this first divine speech after the initial rebellion of the people is in fact addressed to Moses is indicated in 2:1, where the *ka'ăšer* clause that refers back to the concluding command of the divine speech in verses 35-40 reads "as the Lord had told *me*."

There is thus an explicit and an implicit accounting in Deuteronomy for the mediation of Moses. In chapter 5 we are told that, at Horeb, the people received the Ten Words and then asked Moses to receive the rest of the instruction of the Lord, for they were afraid that if the Lord spoke to them again they would surely die. The Mosaic instruction from then on grows out of that request. This account is consistent with—and may be the ground for—the earlier reporting of the Horeb events in Exodus 20:18-21, where the people ask Moses to speak to them rather than God, so that they will not die. For the rest of Exodus through Numbers, the Lord always speaks to the people through Moses (and/or Aaron or his son Eleazar).[11] Deuteronomy, at its beginning, has Moses recall the command of God to go in and take the land as an address to all the people (1:6), and then reiterates that in verse 19. After the rebellion, however, the Lord no longer addresses the people directly. From then on, all the commands and instruction of God are through Moses. An implicit divine rationale is joined with the explicit human one. The God who had led and kept them along the way, from now on speaks to the people only through Moses. The people's improper fear of the inhabitants of the land serves as well as their proper fear of the Lord to set Moses between them and the Lord.

The command and execution sequence continues in 2:1-3:11 in the following series of units[12]: 2:1-8; 2:9-13; [2:14-15]; 2:16-37; 3:1-11. The sequence is complex but repeated, with modifications, in each of the units. Chapter 2:14-15 is outside the structure of command and execution precisely because it is the central transitional note in the journey, fulfilling the divine oath of 1:34-35 (see below). The series may be outlined as follows, the outline showing how each unit follows virtually the same rhetorical movement:

Introductory reference to the divine word   2:2=2:9=2:17=2:31
                                             =3:2

Preliminary command   2:3; cf. 1:6-7

Beginning of command—
announcement of imminent action   2:4=2:18
Command No. 1=prohibition   2:5=2:9=2:19=(3:2a)
     Parenthetical historical note   2:12=2:10-11=2:20-23=3:9,11
Command No. 2 = positive command   2:6=2:13=2:24a=3:2b
     Extension of second command   2:24b-30 (like 1:8)
          Consignment of the land   v. 24b
          Conquest command   vv. 24c-25
          Requests for assistance   vv. 26-30
     Reiteration of second command extension   2:31
Execution   2:8=2:13=2:32-37=3:2-8,10

In chapters 2-3 the command of the Lord, now through Moses, continues to carry the story and the movement of the people into the land. Whereas the response before was nonexecution, now, from Kadesh-barnea on, each time the command is given the people carry it out. As a result, the Israelites successfully move out of the wilderness and capture the Transjordan as a first stage of the taking of the promised land. What is most noticeable about this series of command-execution movements is the *prohibitions* and the *parenthetical historical* notes along the way. That is, the obvious feature of the march of conquest out of the wilderness is the *absence* of conquest for much of the initial part of the journey. The Israelites are commanded not to harass or engage certain peoples in battle, specifically the Edomites, the Moabites, and the Ammonites. They are then commanded to engage Sihon of the Amorites and Og of Bashan with the assurance that they will succeed in battle because the Lord has given these two kings and their peoples into the hands of the Israelites (2:31, 33; 3:2a, 3a).[13]

Already apparent in the command-execution structure of these events, their schematized character is further indicated by comparison with the account of this same journey in the Book of Numbers.[14] There the events are more haphazard and do not parallel each other in the way in which the outline above indicates for Deuteronomy 2-3. In Numbers, the failure of the people to go through Seir is because Edom refuses to allow them and seems to have a large enough army to back up its refusal (Numbers 20:14-21). The story in Numbers of the encounter with Moab first tells of their unobstructed move through that territory (Numbers 21:10-20) and then focuses primarily on the Moabites' fear of the Israelites and the consequent—and unsuccessful—effort of the king of Moab to get the seer Balaam to curse Israel (Numbers 22-24), a series of events that is recounted after the accounts of the conquests of Sihon and Og. The Ammonites do not come into the picture in the Numbers account of the wilderness journey except as it notes that the conquest of the Amorites was "as far as to the Ammonites; for the boundary of the Ammonites was strong" (Numbers 21:24). There is an intimation here that the Ammonites, like the Edomites, were too strong for the Israelites to oppose.

In any event, there is no schema or repetition in these events at all. They are much more haphazard in their unfolding, although particular details are in agreement with the Deuteronomic account, specifically the request by the Israelites to be able to go through Edom and the land of the Amorites peacefully. Other aspects of these two segments of the journey, however, are handled quite differently in Numbers and Deuteronomy.[15] The one structural similarity to the Deuteronomic account is in the report of the battle with Og in Numbers 21:33-35, which does take place according to the command-execution sequence and with the same language as in Deuteronomy, although the Deuteronomic account goes into more detail about the towns captured. In the Numbers account, we find the quasi-legal language for the divine consignment or granting of the land of Sihon to Israel that is characteristic of Deuteronomy (1:8, 21; 2:31; 3:2).

Structure and Theology

The highly schematic and structured Deuteronomic account serves various theological purposes. In the prohibitions and the parenthetical notes, several things are being set forth. One is the different treatment of the Edomites, Moabites, and Ammonites because of *kinship* relations. The word *āḥ*, "brother" or "kin," which is a critical personal and relational category for the Book of Deuteronomy, is used to designate Edom (1:8a; cf. 23:8 [Eng. v. 7]).[16] That word does not appear in the accounts of moving peacefully through the territory of the Moabites and the Ammonites; but the relational connection is clearly indicated there also, as both groups are specifically referred to as "the descendants of Lot" (1:9, 19), even as the Edomites are referred to as "Esau" (1:5) and "the descendants of Esau" (2:8, 12). The identification of the *'āḥ*, "brother/sister," as a moral category properly has its origins in Deuteronomy. It is clear from this book that such kinship, encountering someone as *'āḥ*, places a moral responsibility upon the one to whom the other is an *'āḥ*. Thus special care to provide for and to keep from harm is placed upon the relationship. This is evident from a number of laws, such as those having to do with the sabbatical release of debts and slaves (15:1-18), lost property (22:1-4), usury (23:20-21 [Eng. 19-20]), and Levirate marriage (25:5-10). The point is made explicit in the laws, specifically in reference to the Edomites: "You shall not abhor any of the Edomites, for they are your kin" (*'āḥ*; 23:8 [Eng. v. 7]).[17]

The prohibitions against fighting the Edomites, Moabites, and Ammonites join with the parenthetical notes in chapter 2 to make the point, clearly and repeatedly, that the Lord of Israel has other stories than simply the one with Israel. Other communities from the seed of Abraham have been kept by the providence of the Lord; other communities have been given place to live by the Lord. The same language is used for the Lord's consignment of territory to Edom, Moab, and Ammon as is used for the Lord's consignment of land to Israel. The point is expressly made in the parenthesis of 2:10-12, where the descendants of Esau are said to have done "as Israel has done in the land that the Lord gave them as a possession." In each case, the Lord makes it clear that the land of the Edomites, Moabites, and Ammonites has not been given as a possession to the Israelites, but has been given to the other peoples.

There could not be a clearer or more emphatic way of breaking through the potential hubris and misunderstanding of God's gift of the land to Israel. This is an activity typical of this deity, at least for those who belong to the promise to Abraham and his descendants. There are clearly others who lose the land, and Deuteronomy gives reasons for that (2:30). But the provision of place to live is as sure for these other peoples as for Israel. The same book that makes the strongest case for the particular election of Israel (7:6-8; 9:4-5; 14:2) vigorously resists a misreading of that. Within the election texts themselves, the misreading under attack is the assumption that there is something in Israel that merits or evokes the Lord's favor (7:7; 9:4-5). In chapters 2 and 3, the misreading undermined is the assumption of exclusive benefits accruing from that election. Others have benefited in the same fashion from the Lord's power and grace.[18] Israel thus hears that its story is not the only one going on.

The parenthetical references to the prehistory of these different territories and their inhabitants seem at first glance to be merely historical footnotes.[19] But they are part of the identification of the other stories, and they make another but implicit point that is consistent with the story of Israel and the Lord. To comprehend their place in the whole, one has to look first at the references to the Anaqim, who are mentioned three times in the parentheses of chapter 2 (vv. 10, 11, 21). They are not, in fact, among the prior inhabitants of the lands of the Edomites, the Moabites, and the Ammonites. But most of those earlier groups—Emim, Rephaim, and Zamzummim—are *compared* to the Anaqim to give some impression of their strength or power.[20] The other places where the Anaqim are referred to indicate that they are the inhabitants of the land that has been consigned to Israel, and they are the cause of the fearfulness of the people and their unwillingness to go into the land:

> The people are stronger and taller than we; the cities are large and fortified up to heaven! We actually saw there the Anaqim! (1:28)

> You are about to cross the Jordan today, to go in and
> dispossess nations larger and mightier than you, great
> cities, fortified to the heavens, a strong and tall people,
> the offspring of the Anaqim, whom you know. You have
> heard it said of them, "Who can stand up to the
> Anaqim?" (9:1-2)

The comparison of the other pre-inhabitants to the Anaqim makes
it clear, therefore, that they played the same role for the Edomites, Moabites, and Ammonites in their journeys that the Anaqim did for the Israelites. They were the fearful inhabitants who made the hearts of the entering peoples melt. They were, like the Anaqim, that fearful and dangerous obstacle that had to be overcome in order to receive the promise.
The other stories of Israel's kinfolk—Edomites, Ammonites, and
Moabites—also included difficulties and terrors that had to be overcome.
They also included the Lord's help against greater and mightier forces.
The text is explicit in referring to the Lord's destruction of the pre-inhabitants (2:21-22). Thus in the Deuteronomic view the stories of God's
involvement with these other people parallel in every way the story of
God's dealing with Israel. Even the rather strange note in 3:11 about the
bed of Og still to be seen in Rabbah of the Ammonites contributes to this
overall picture. For he is identified as one of the giant pre-inhabitants,
but all that is left is a memento of him there at the capital of the Ammonites. He was one of those powerful and giant Rephaim whom the Lord
destroyed from before the Ammonites (2:21; cf. Joshua 12:4; 13:21).[21]

There is one piece of these parenthetical notes that does not seem
to fit the analysis above. It is the reference to the Caphtorim in 2:23: "As
for the Avvim, who had lived in settlements in the vicinity of Gaza, the
Caphtorim, who came from Caphtor, destroyed them and settled in their
place." Here it would seem that we have simply a historical footnote. But
there may be more to this than is immediately apparent. First of all, the
language here lacks any reference to the activity of the Lord of Israel, but
it is parallel to sentences about the descendants of Esau, Edom, and the
Ammonites. In 2:21-22 we have the sequence: destroy, dispossess, and
settle in their place. In those instances, the Lord is the one who does the
destroying so that the Edomites and Ammonites can "dispossess" and
"settle in their place." The note on the Caphtorim differs in not ascribing destruction to the Lord and in not speaking about dispossession or
occupation. But otherwise it sounds just like the other notes.[22] Furthermore, in 2:12 there is another note about the descendants of Esau taking
over from the Horim, and there is no reference at all to the involvement
of the Lord:[23] "Moreover, the Horim had formerly inhabited Seir, but the
descendants of Esau dispossessed them, destroying them and settling in

their place."[24] Without the further note in 2:22 about the Lord destroying the Horites, there would be no indication of the Lord's involvement
in the Edomite occupation of their territory either. But the additional
note makes that clear. One may suggest, therefore, that the note on the
Caphtorim, so similar to the others, is meant to be comparable to them,
explicitly suggesting that their story also has to do with the Lord of Israel.
It is possible, of course, that the absence of such an explicit reference to
the Lord vis-à-vis the Caphtorim is an intentional way of indicating that
there was no relationship. But that leaves the presence of the note on the
Caphtorim without explanation. The sense of the sovereignty of the Lord
over all of the territory of Palestine that is so strongly suggested by these
chapters would have to be qualified at this point.[25]

It may be appropriate, therefore, to refer to one of the prophetic
books that, like Deuteronomy, speaks of Edom as "kin" (*'āḥ*), that is, the
Book of Amos. The condemnation of Edom in Amos 1:11-12 is "because
he pursued *his brother* with the sword." Only one other time, outside of
the Numbers-Deuteronomic accounts of the passing through Edom, is
there reference to Edom as brother of Israel/Judah (Obadiah 10). While
the dating of Amos 1, and indeed of many Amos texts, is debated, one
notes that this reference to Edom as "kin/brother" precedes a later reference to Caphtor in Amos 9:7. In that famous text, the hubris of the
Israelites is condemned, precisely at the point of their assumption of an
exclusive salvific relation with the Lord: "Did I not bring Israel up from
the land of Egypt, and the Philistines from Caphtor and the Arameans
from Kir?"

When one considers that there are only two other references to
Caphtor in the whole of the Old Testament, the resonance of the
Deuteronomy text with the word of the Lord in Amos seems rather large.
The reference to Caphtor in Amos is clearly and explicitly an indication
to the (probably astonished) Israelites that the Lord has similar stories of
deliverance and guidance with other peoples, in this case not just with
kinfolk, but with enemies, the Philistines. Deuteronomy would seem to
bear that out, albeit implicitly. But it is quite important to keep this in
mind in reading Deuteronomy. For there are many features that enable
one to read that book quite chauvinistically and exclusively. Its focus on
the taking of the land—one that is carried through in the Deuteronomistic
history—its emphasis on Israel's election, its legal distinctions between
dealing with Israelites (and *gērîm* or "resident aliens") and dealing with
foreigners, and its heavy insistence on Israel's exclusive allegiance to the
Lord all contribute to a hearing of Deuteronomy as intolerant and exclusive, perpetrating a narrow and nationalistic understanding of God's relation to Israel. These early chapters of Deuteronomy, however, serve to
challenge that notion, suggesting in a way equaled only by the prophet

Amos and the Book of Genesis that, all along the way of history, the Lord of Israel has been at work redemptively and providentially with other peoples and nations. In Deuteronomy it is made clear that Israel's relation with these other peoples and their gods cannot be apart from an awareness of the involvement of the Lord in their stories also.

Word, Faith, and Obedience

The journey of Israel as described in Deuteronomy 1-3 is thus fraught with theological dimensions. In the discussion of chapters 2-3 we have emphasized one, the Lord's involvement with other peoples and their stories, but there are others that need to be mentioned also, albeit more briefly.

First, the fundamental command-execution structure of this whole section (1-3) serves to highlight and underline the centrality and effectiveness of the word of the Lord. Nearly everything that happens is by the word or command of the Lord. In that respect, Deuteronomy and the Deuteronomistic History anticipate or echo the theological orientation of the Priestly tradition, which also understands all that happens as brought into being or accomplished by the divine word or speech (for example, Genesis 1). In Deuteronomy, the command-execution style of P, which reports the very creation of the universe as the accomplishment of a sequence of divine commands, moves now into the particular story of Israel, which is effected by the divine word and instruction. Deuteronomy begins, therefore, with a theology of the word of God as the initiating, effective power of God that shapes and determines history.[26] From Genesis through Deuteronomy to the prophets and the Gospel of John, we hear of the word of God that represents God and the power of God at work in the world. Thus Deuteronomy places all that happens under the sovereignty of the Lord of Israel. What may be reported as simply human activity in Numbers (for example, the refusal of Edom to let Israel pass through) is understood by Deuteronomy to be entirely the purpose and accomplishment of God, events that take place because of Israel's proper response to the command of God. And, in reverse fashion, the resistance of Sihon of the Amorites is also and explicitly the work of God because it happens by God hardening the heart of Sihon to effect a resistance on his part to the passage of the Israelites. Here, then, is the rootage of those later doctrines of the word of God as a powerful force in history (Isaiah 55:10-11) and incarnate with equal effectiveness in Jesus of Nazareth, the Word of God made flesh.

It is important to recognize that such insistence on the initiating power of God in Israel's history does not preclude human initiative, intentionality, and planning to carry out the divine intention. That is signaled quite directly in the way in which the whole enterprise of entering the land is understood as both divine gift and human occupation, legal (divine) transference and military takeover (1:8; 2:24, 31-33; 3:2, 18).[27] Of equal significance in this regard, however, is the activity of Moses. His mediating function is signaled throughout the book in his transmission of the statutes and ordinances that the Lord has commanded.[28] But his initiative is not entirely secondary or mediated. For he sets up a judicial system (1:9-18)[29] and works out an appropriate division and allotment of the Transjordanian territory (3:12-17), as well as a plan for getting the men from the Transjordanian tribes to battle while letting their families settle down (3:18-22). Furthermore, here and elsewhere the people themselves propose strategies that are implicitly (1:22-23) and explicitly (5:28) approved by the Lord. There are clearly critical dimensions of this story that can only be understood as effected by the word of the Lord or by some action of the Lord (2:30), but there is still considerable room within such a highly controlled theological understanding of history for human freedom, responsibility, initiative, and strategy. The hardening of Sihon's heart to the point of rebellion should not lead readers to assume that the Deuteronomic understanding of divine power and sovereignty excludes significant moves by human beings within the larger framework of the divine command.

Second, one cannot leave this journey, or Moses' memoir about it, without signaling its character as a journey of faith and faithlessness.[30] We have already noted that the breakdown of the command-execution schema in Deuteronomy 1 is due to the faithlessness of the people. The Kadesh-barnea episode is very much at the center of the narrative. It is about seeing and believing. The language of "seeing" is thematic in 1:26-27, as the people tell of seeing only the fearsome Anaqim (see above), while Moses reminds them of other things they have in fact seen: the Lord's providential guidance in the terrible wilderness, helping them see the way to go (1:19, 30-33). Despite this, they do not trust in the Lord. The technical term for faith or trust, *he'ĕmîn beyhwh*, literally "count the Lord as reliable/trustworthy," appears only twice in the narrative of Deuteronomy.[31] Both times it is in reference to the unwillingness to go into the land (1:32; 9:23). In both instances, such lack of trust is understood as rebellion. Covenantal righteousness is not simply a matter of obedience to the moral, religious, and social commandments or directions of the Lord. It is obedience to the command of God, whatever form it may take. Resistance to that divine purpose violates the fundamental requirement of Israel's life: full allegiance and obedience to its Lord. The call to trust is not rooted in a blind faith. Moses reminded them very specifically of the legitimate ground for their trust in their experience of the care and guidance of the Lord through the many years (1:30-33).

The movement in verses 26-33 is important because it leaves the

door open for the people to respond faithfully. Moses speaks of the people's
unwillingness as grumbling and rebellion, quoting their words, which are
much like the fearful words of the people at the Exodus (Exodus 14:10-
12). But even though the reaction of the people at Kadesh-barnea is
understood to be grumbling and rebellion rather than crying out for help,
Moses responds in a similar fashion as at the Exodus, that is, with an
oracle of salvation, words of assurance that they do not need to fear because the Lord is with them, fights for them, and cares for them.[32]

But there is significant modification of the usual form and effect of
the oracle of salvation. The heart of that oracle is the assurance "Do not
be afraid." That word is given to the people in 1:21 as an assurance as
they set out from Horeb: "*See, the Lord your God has given the land to
you; go up, take possession, as the Lord, the God of your ancestors, has
promised you; do not fear or be dismayed*" (1:21). In this instance, however, the typical *assurance* (the negative particle '*al* with the second person imperfect) has become, in effect, a command—"You shall not be afraid"
(the negative particle *lō'* with the second person imperfect).[33] The grounds
for not being afraid are similar to what they usually are—the Lord's deliv-
ering presence—but the words of assurance are, in light of the rebellious
character of the people's timidity, no longer the assuring words of 1:21,
whose intended effect is to remove the fear, but a firm command to let go
of their fearfulness and see the power of God that has cared for them.

Even then, however, with the command to relinquish their hesi-
tancy and timidity and with the firm reminder of all that they have seen
the Lord do in their behalf, they are still unwilling to treat the Lord's
word as trustworthy. The movement in the passage from describing the
people as "unwilling" (v. 26) to describing them as not "trusting" is important, for it lets us know that the fearfulness of the people is indeed not
an appropriate anxiety in a situation of crisis and trouble, as one encounters again and again in situations of prayer and lament. The people have
not cried out for help. They have refused to trust. The laments of the Old
Testament that seek always to hear the assuring and transforming words
of the oracle of salvation, "Do not be afraid," presume usually the trust of
the one who cries or prays. Not so here. The assurance thus becomes
instead a command. And the unwilling response is deemed a refusal to
trust, even when their eyes have seen the clear grounds for relying on the
Lord's word.

Over against the faithlessness of the people, Moses sets the obedience of Caleb. Only those who trust in the Lord's promise of the gift shall
receive it. So, in one of the most emphatic constructions in Hebrew, the
Lord declares that those who "saw" only the Anaqim (1:28) will not "see"
the good land God has promised to give.[34] Only Caleb will "see" the
land, and that is because of his fidelity (1:36). Joshua, too, will see the

land, but that is because he will take the place of Moses, who, somewhat inexplicably, is joined with the faithless generation in being kept out of the promised land.[35]

It is for this reason that 2:14-15 stands outside the structure of command and execution. Those two verses report the death of the faithless generation of warriors. It is only after the fearful fighters have passed on, by the Lord's judgment, that Israel can go up against the hostile forces of the land. And the memoir of Moses comes to a close as he charges Joshua to exercise the kind of seeing trust, the eyes of faith, that failed once but are the only way into the land (3:21-22).

Conclusion

Finally, one cannot leave an examination of the structure and movement of Deuteronomy 1-3 without some attention to the conclusion of this section, particularly inasmuch as it seems as if there is a reversal of the movement from command to execution, Moses first encouraging Joshua (3:21-22) and only after that receiving the command to do so (3:28). But such is not in fact the case. Rather, 3:21-22 is the execution of the command given in 1:38, while 3:28 takes the command-execution schema and with it creates a framing device around the second and third speeches, the Deuteronomic law and the covenant (4:44-28:68/69 and 29-32), as it gives the command that is then executed in 31:7. Indeed, the double charge of Moses in 3:18-22—to the people and Joshua—is repeated in chapter 31:1-8. The final example of the command-execution scheme and the final framing effect of that system is found in the movement from 3:27 to 34:1. Commanded at the end of the memoir section of the book, chapters 1-3, to "go up to the top of Pisgah," Moses does just that as the book comes to a close.[36] To the end, the divine command shapes the story of Israel.

Endnotes

1. The following essay develops in more extended form some of the ideas about these chapters set forth in my commentary on Deuteronomy (*Deuteronomy* [Louisville: Westminster, 1990]). I am happy to be able to present them to Fredrick Holmgren in honor of his distinguished contribution to the theological interpretation of the Old Testament.

2. For earlier studies of this material, see, in addition to the commentaries, Martin Noth's classic study, *The Deuteronomistic History*, JSOT Supplement Series, 15 (Sheffield: JSOT Press, 1981), 26-35; Norbert Lohfink, "Darstellungskunst und Theologie in Dtn 1,6-3,29," *Biblica* 41 (1960): 105-34 [reprinted in N. Lohfink, *Studien zum Deuteronomium und zur deuteronomistischen Literatur I*, Stuttgarter Biblische Aufsatzbände, 8 (Stuttgart: Verlag Katholisches Bibelwerk,

1990), 15-44]; *idem*, "Wie stellt sich das Problem Individuum-Gemeinschaft in Dtn 1,6-3,29?" *Scholastik* 35 (1960): 403-7 [translated in N. Lohfink, *Theology of the Pentateuch: Themes of the Priestly Narrative and Deuteronomy* (Minneapolis: Fortress, 1994), 227-33]; William Moran, "The End of the Unholy War and the Anti-Exodus," *Biblica* 44 (1963): 333-42; Joseph Plöger, *Literarkritische, formgeschichtliche und stilkritische Untersuchungen zum Deuteronomium*, Bonner Biblische Beiträge, 26 (Bonn: Hanstein, 1967), 1-59; W. A. Sumner, "Israel's Encounter with Edom, Moab, Ammon, Sihon and Og, according to the Deuteronomist," *Vetus Testamentum* 18 (1968): 216-28; A Nicolaas Radjawane, *Israel Zwischen Wüste und Land: Studien zur Theologie von Deuteronomium 1-3* (Mainz, 1972).

3. See 4:1 with its *wĕ'attâ*, indicating a conclusion to be drawn from the preceding chapters, and the call for Israel to heed the statutes and ordinances, all of which lie in the chapters to come. The concluding verses (41-43) serve editorially to integrate chapter 4 with chapters 1-3 by referring to another feature of the East Jordan settlement by the tribes of Reuben, Gad, and Manasseh. On chapter 4 as a profound sermon on the prohibition of the worship of other gods and, more specifically, idols of Yahweh or other gods, see P. Miller, *Deuteronomy* (Louisville: Westminster/John Knox Press, 1990), 57-63.

4. The relationship between the geographical location of Moses' speeches given in 1:1 and that in 3:29 is not altogether clear. Some would locate the places mentioned in 1:1b further south, in the Negeb or even the Sinai wilderness, but there is no reason to assume an intentional discrepancy between the locations given at the beginnning and at the end of this section. See the suggestion of S. D. McBride that the toponyms of 1:1 "may define a natural amphitheater in the valley near Beth-peor." *The Harper Collins Study Bible* (New York: HarperCollins, 1993), 268. The valley opposite Beth-peor is identified as the location again in 4:46.

5. They are as follows:

> 1:7—journey to the land of the Canaanites and the Lebanon (*pānâ* and *nāsa'*)
> 1:19—journey from Horeb to Kadesh-barnea (*nāsa'*)
> 1:40—journey back into the wilderness toward the Red Sea (*pānâ* and *nāsa'*)
> 2:1—journey back into the wilderness and skirting around Mount Seir (*pānâ* and *nāsa'* + *sābab*)
> (2:3—enough skirting around Mount Seir [*sābab*]; cf. 1:6b and below)
> 2:8a—passing by Seir-Edom ('*ābar*)
> 2:8b—journey to Moab (*pānâ* and '*ābar*)
> 2:13a—command to cross the Wadi Zered ('*ābar*)
> 2:13b—crossing the Wadi Zered ('*ābar*)
> 2:24—command to journey across the Wadi Arnon (*nāsa'* and '*ābar*)
> (2:28-32—no passing through or crossing over ['*ābar*, 3x], so battle at Yahaz)
> 3:1—journey up to Bashan and battle at Edrei (*pānâ* and '*ālâ*)

N. Lohfink has argued, on cogent philological grounds, that the expression *sābab* + '*et* in Deuteronomy 2:1, 3 does not mean to "skirt around" but to "go around" or "surround," which may or may not have a threatening sense, depending on the circumstances ("sbb't in Dtn 2,1.3," *Zeitschrift fur Katholische Theologie* 116 [1994]: 435-39; reprinted in N. Lohfink, *Studien zum Deuteronomium und zur deuteronomistischen Literatur III*, Stuttgarter Biblische Aufsatzbände, 20 [Stuttgart:

Verlag Katholisches Bibelwerk, 1995], 263-68).

6. For a broad treatment of the command-execution sequence as a common feature of Hebraic narrative style, see W. Baumgartner, "Ein Kapitel vom hebräischen Erzahlungstil," *Eucharisterion. Studien zur Religion und Literatur des Alten und Neuen Testaments. Hermann Gunkel zum 60. Geburtstage,* Teil 1, ed. H. Schmidt (Göttingen: Vandenhoeck und Ruprecht, 1923), 145-57.

7. On the ending of Deuteronomy 1-3, see the conclusion of this essay.

8. Cf. 2:24b-25 below.

9. The negatives with *'al* in v. 21 can be understood as prohibitive, but the switch to *lō'* in v. 29 suggests a distinction in the function of the two sets of commands from encouragement to prohibition.

10. William Moran has accentuated the irony in this section with his reference to an "Anti-Exodus" and an "Unholy War" in this sequence of events ("The End of the Unholy War and the Anti-Exodus").

11. For example, Numbers 18:1, 8; 19:1; 26:1.

12. Cf. Lohfink, "Darstellungskunst," in *Studium zur Deuteronomium,* 38-42. Lohfink sees a ring or concentric kind of structure operating in chapter 1.

13. For careful analysis of these differences, see Sumner, "Israel's Encounters."

14. Cf. ibid., for analysis of the differences between Numbers and Deuteronomy accounts.

15. For example, the Edomites are said to be afraid of Israel in Deuteronomy, while in Numbers they have a strong army and are able to stop Israel's movement through. The offer to buy food from the Edomites is refused in Numbers, but the Deuteronomic account is mute at that point. The account of the battle with Sihon gives no indication of the fact that both his opposition and his defeat were ordained by the Lord.

16. On the significance of the term "brother" in Deuteronomy, see L. Perlitt, "'Ein einzig Volk von Brüdern': Zur deuteronomischen Herkunft der biblischen Bezeichnung 'Brüder,'" *Kirche: Festschrift für Gunther Bornkamm zum 75. Geburtstag,* ed. Dieter Luhrmann and Georg Strecker (Tübingen: J. C. B. Mohr [Paul Siebeck], 1980), 27-52 [reprinted in Perlitt, *Deuteronomium-Studien,* Forschungen zum Alten Testament, 8 (Tübingen: J. C. B. Mohr, 1994), 50-73]. Cf. Bert Dicou, *Edom, Israel's Brother and Antagonist: The Role of Edom in Biblical Prophecy and Story,* JSOT Supplement Series, 169 (Sheffield: JSOT Press, 1994), 167-81. Dicou discusses there the suggestion of M. Rose and J. R. Bartlett that the Edomites at some stage may have been worshipers of Yahweh. The primary god of the Edomites, of course, was Qaus, but this may have been a later development in the history of Edomite religion. The evidence for making judgments on the matter is all very indirect.

17. Cf. the summary statement of Perlittt, "'Ein einzig Volk Brüdern,'" 42.

> "Your brother" is therefore a religiously central and thoroughly emotionally colored closer definition of the traditional expression "your brother." This accentuation is to be understood precisely not out of an ethnic or nationalistic design but out of the intent to deepen the humanity (*Mitmenschlichkeit*) of those who live totally out of the liberating love of God; thus Deuteronomy 15 stands quite programmatically at the beginning of this Deuteronomic stream [translation mine].

18. The same point is scored in a somewhat different fashion elsewhere in

Deuteronomy. As the election of Israel does not mean that the Lord is not doing other things with other nations, so also the exclusive claim on Israel's allegiance that is carried in the First Commandments and the Shema and is a fundamental theme of Deuteronomy does not mean that the Lord is not at work among the worship of other gods by the other nations (4:19; 29:25 [Eng. v. 26]; 32:8-9).

19. Thus von Rad speaks of these as "various antiquarian notes about the earliest inhabitants of these regions" and sees "these learned notes" as bearing witness to "Israel's astonishing interest in history and in individual historical moments, even in those which did not in any way touch directly its immediate surroundings" (G. von Rad, *Deuteronomy*, The Old Testament Library [Philadelphia: Westminster, 1966], 42-43). This view of the notices was already set forth by C. Steuernagel, who speaks of 2:10-12 as "sicher Zusatz eines antiquarisch interessierten Lesers" (*Deuteronomium und Josua*, Handkommentar zum Alten Testament, I/3, 1 [Göttengen: Vendenhoeck & Ruprect, 1900], 8). Such an understanding largely continues in much of the German commentary on these passages. See, for example, L. Perlitt, *Deuteronomium*, Biblischer Kommentar Altes Testament (Neukirchen-Vluyn: Neukirchener Verlag, 1990-), 145-46 and 174-89; and S. Mittmann, *Deuteronomium 1,1-6,3 literarkritisch und traditionsgeschichtlich untersucht*, Beihefte zur Zeitschrift fur Alttestamentliche Wissenschaft, 139 (Berlin: Walter de Gruyter, 1993). Sumner, "Israel's Encounters," sees the way in which these notices "provide the logic behind Yahweh's instructions not to take the lands" (220). The comments here are designed to open up that logic in more detail. More recently, Paul J. Kissling has identified several functions of these notes in the narratives (*Reliable Characters in the Primary History: Profiles of Moses, Joshua, Elijah and Elisha*, JSOT Supplement Series, 224 [Sheffield: Sheffield Academic Press, 1996], 37). The analysis in this essay differs at several points from the understanding or the emphasis of Kissling, but shares his sense of the strong role the "parentheses" play in the story.

20. Perlitt gives a rather extended discussion of the Anaqim and the other pre-inhabitants mentioned here in a lengthy essay on giants in the Old Testament. His interest, however, is in demonstrating the nonhistorical character of these references rather than in looking at the role they play in the theological shape of the narrative (see L. Perlitt, "Riesen im Alten Testament. Ein literarisches Motiv im Wirkungsfeld des Deuteronomismus," *Deuteronomium-Studien*, 205-46).

21. There is, of course, an inconsistency here in that Og is represented both as an Amorite and as a Rephaim. And his bed in Rabbah of the Ammonites would suggest that he was among the group that they destroyed to take the land, while the biblical accounts tell in detail of Israel's destruction of Og.

22. It is shortened further by the omission of the "from before them/the Ammonites" that appears in 2:12, 21, 22.

23. Note that the Samaritan text inserts YHWH and changes the verbal form of *šāmad*, "destroy," to singular, making the text conform to the notices in 2:21-22: "The Lord destroyed them from before them and they dispossessed them."

24. There is a textual problem in this verse. One notes that the sequence of "destroy" (*šāmad*), "dispossess" (*yāraš*), and "settle" (*yāšab*) that we find in 2:21-22 is modified here with the verb *yāraš* coming first. But the verbal form there is quite anomalous. It is an imperfect or *yqtl* form that does not fit the context, which requires either perfect *qtl* forms of the verb or the use of the *waw* consecutive. One explanation for the anomaly could be that the original text had the shortened form, exactly like the note about the Caphtorim, that is, omitting the verb *yāraš*. In other words, there were two forms of this stereotyped note, one with three verbs and one with two verbs. A later editor would then have added

the verb *yāraš*, placing it out of sequence and without the consecutive *waw*. That would make the note about the descendants virtually the same as the one about the Caphtorim. There are other possible explanations, of course. It may be that a *qtl* form of *yāraš* has been inadvertently written as a *yqtl*.

25. On Deuteronomy 2-3 as a testimony to the sovereignty of Yahweh over the land and the peoples of Palestine, see Radjawane, *Israel Zwischen Wüste und Land*, 183-85.

26. "What the Deuteronomist presents is really a history of the creative word of Jahweh. What fascinated him was, we might say, the functioning of the divine word in history" (Gerhard von Rad, *Studies in Deuteronomy*, Studies in Biblical Theology, 9 [Chicago: Henry Regnery, 1953]), 91. Von Rad is referring here specifically to the promise and fulfillment schema in the books of Kings. What operates in Deuteronomy 1-3 is related to that but not the same. Here it is the word initiating and evoking human activity—or not, as the case may be. The accumulation of the whole of the instances of command and execution makes it clear that the word or command of the Lord will be accomplished, even if temporarily thwarted by human rebellion (for example, 1:26-45). Even the rebellion may be the work of the Lord (2:30). Thus Lohfink is correct in seeing that the command-execution schema brings what von Rad is talking about to expression, with the important qualification he makes, that is, "in its own way" (Lohfink, "Darstellungskunst," in *Studien zum Deuteronomium*, 38, n. 92.).

27. Cf. Miller, *Deuteronomy*, 45-46.

28. Note how often the expression "[which] I am commanding you" appears on the lips of Moses in the rest of the book (for example, 4:40; 6:2; 7:11; 8:1; etc.). In the movement and structure of the whole book, chapters 4-6 function both to set forth the fundamental principles and guidelines of the Lord's instruction and also to identify the commandments, statutes, and ordinances as coming from the Lord ("his statutes and his commandments"), though presented and taught to the people by Moses ("I am commanding you").

29. The account of the creation of this judicial system in Exodus 18 also attributes it to human ingenuity and common sense rather than to divine command. In that case, however, it is Moses' father-in-law, Jethro, who makes the proposal.

30. For further discussion of these matters, see Miller, *Deuteronomy*, 31-36.

31. It does occur one other time in the curses of Deuteronomy 28:66 in quite a different and nontheological fashion.

32. For extensive discussion of the oracle of salvation and its many Near Eastern and biblical forms, see P. D. Miller, *They Cried to the Lord: The Form and Theology of Biblical Prayer* (Minneapolis: Fortress, 1994), 135-77.

33. Cf. the similar command forms to the judges in 1:17, "You must not be partial . . . you shall not be intimidated."

34. In 1:36-40 there are at least ten emphatic Hebrew words or syntactical constructions to make this point. Cf. ibid, 34.

35. A later Priestly editor will overcome this bothersome blot on the rationality of the deity by ascribing the exclusion of Moses to his actions by the waters of Meribath-kadesh. The resolution, however, then creates an inconsistency in the reasoning, for three times in the first half of the book, the anger of the Lord at Moses is simply said to be "on your account" (1:37; 3:26; 4:21). For extended discussion of the matter of Moses' death outside the land, see Miller, *Deuteronomy*, 42-44, 241-45; and P. D. Miller, "Moses, My Servant: A Deuteronomic Portrait of Moses," *Interpretation* 41 (1987): 245-55.

36. Not surprisingly, these are the only two places where "the top of Pisgah"

appears in the Book of Deuteronomy. The double report in Deuteronomy 1-3 of God's angry refusal to allow Moses to enter the promised land may be explained by the movement of this section. In 1:34-39, the anger of the Lord against Moses is reported—without his prayer—to account for the inclusion of Joshua, along with Caleb, among the survivors of the Lord's judgment on the fearful warriors (2:14-15). Whereas the Numbers account includes Joshua among the faithful spies, nothing is said about that in Deuteronomy. He is allowed to go into the land because, as Moses' servant, he is the one to take Moses' place as the leader of the people (cf. M. Weinfeld, *Deuteronomy 1-11*, The Anchor Bible, 5 [New York: Doubleday, 1991], 150). The first report of God's refusal to Moses is thus anticipatory of the final one, which gives the full story. In 3:23-28, therefore, the prayer of Moses is included, for this report is to account for Moses' not entering the land and to create the framing effect between the end of the Moses "memoir" and the end of the book, that is, the movement from command (3:27) to execution (34:1ff.) that concludes the book of Deuteronomy.

What's in a Name?

HERMAN E. SCHAALMAN

Most individuals, most communities, and surely most nations have little difficulty in telling us what they are called and who they are. This is not the case with Jews. Aside from slanderous appellations, we have been called Hebrews, Israelites, and Jews. And, to no one's surprise, these different names have been applied not only from the outside, but from within as well. Strictly speaking, *Hebrew* ought to be used only as a designation for a language. And while there are a few references in Holy Writ to *'ibrî* (Hebrew) and also the plural *'ibrîm* in various forms, this designation was used as a name of a people primarily and perhaps significantly by Jeremiah, Nehemiah, and the Scroll of Esther.

Origins of a Name

Overwhelmingly, the main designation applied to the biblical nation was *Israel*, in such combinations as *'am yiśrā'ēl* (the people of Israel), *běnê yiśrā'ēl* (the children of Israel), *bêt yiśrā'ēl* (the house of Israel), and the *šibtê yisrā'ēl* (the tribes of Israel). Not suprisingly, the overwhelming use of such terms occurred biblically in those books that traditionally are considered pre-exilic, with far fewer such uses in writings during and after the Babylonian Exile. Technically, or more precisely, the designation *Israel* is, of course, attached to the ten northern tribes, who, after their secession from Rehoboam's rule, founded their distinct kingdom centered in Samaria. Prior to this event, the term *Israel* could be and was applied as the prevailing name for the "Israelites."

The term *yěhûdî* (Jew), with its plural *yěhûdîm*, is used biblically far less frequently. A few references in the book of Jeremiah aside, it appears primarily in the Scroll of Esther and the Book of Nehemiah.

Extraordinary developments of history caused the disappearance of the kingdom of Israel under the hammer blows of the Assyrian empire in the eighth century B.C.E., leaving only a slim remnant, the Samaritans, not subsequently specifically identified with the kingdom of Israel. In effect, it was the southern kingdom, composed primarily of the tribes of Judah and Benjamin, that survived and thus became what we now refer to as the "Jewish" people. The Greek *ioudaios*, by way of the Latin *Iudaeus* and the French *Juive*, penetrated into English as "Jew," an etymological permutation not shared by the German *Jude* or the Polish *Zid*.

Israel in Liturgical Context

To the extent that Jewish tradition never forgot the "lost tribes of Israel," the term *Israel* was retained in part through biblical quotations, especially in liturgical use. Thus we find in the last verse of the *kaddish*, first found in the liturgy of Amram Gaon of the Sura Academy in Babylonia, who died in 875 C.E., the addition to the Jobian passage "He Who makes peace in His heights" to read "shall make peace for us *and all Israel*." While it is possible to dismiss "and all Israel" as poetic exuberance, it is legitimate to consider "all Israel" to be a deliberate reference to the lost Ten Tribes. Read this way, this concluding sentence, found in one of the most frequently recited liturgical utterances, clearly has Messianic overtones. One could cite additional liturgical uses of *Israel*, such as in *šĕma' yiśrā'ēl* ("Hear O Israel," taken from Deuteronomy 6), which is the center point of the biblical section of the liturgy, to indicate that the designation *Israel* never died out despite the disappearance of the ancient kingdom that bore its name.

Astounding for many was the choice of the name *Israel* for the reborn nation whose founders so declared it in 1948. Hence, today the citizens of that state are known as Israelites; its flag, laws, army, and postage all now bear that revived name. This is so without the slightest infringement on or damage to the terms *Jew, Jewish,* or *Judaism*. In fact, Jews are all over the world, including, of course, in Israel. These different terms are firmly established in contemporary usage and valid beyond any reasonable challange.

The Problem of Benjamin

And yet, there is more. History decreed that the biblical southern kingdom was to become the continuation of the covenant community, even though its two tribes were a numerical minority compared to the ten, whose identity and whereabouts evaporated.

The Benjaminite component of the southern kingdom presents a problem. Even a cursory reading of the Book of Judges will show that the tribe of Benjamin was nearly exterminated by the rest of the tribes as a punishment for their cruel rape of the Levite's concubine. And though the tribes are recorded as eventually relenting from their earlier intention to deny wives to the small male remnant of the otherwise extirpated tribe, future references to the tribe of Benjamin are relatively sparse when compared to Judah. Examples include the Benjaminite in 1 Samuel 4, who brings the aged high priest Eli the dreadful news that the Philistines have defeated the Israelites, captured the Holy Ark, and killed his two sons, Hophni and Phineas. The most important mention by far is in the narrative that deals with King Saul, the most noteworthy Benjaminite, with the possible exception of the prophet Jeremiah, who hails from Anathoth in Benjamin. This designation may, however, not make him a Benjaminite, since his father, who was a priest, may have only happened to have been stationed in Anathoth. Though the crowning of the son of Kish, the Benjaminite, indicates a recovery of the standing of the tribe, it is clear that the Benjaminite king is a disaster, both for himself and for the nation, and one is left to wonder whether his Benjaminite origin contributed to this fate or the recording of it. Most significantly, the Benjaminite king is replaced by David, the Bethlehemite—a Judahite!

Ezekiel, at God's command, envisions allotting land to Benjamin in the reconstituted post-exilic community. Nehemiah, after his return from Babylon, counts 928 Benjaminites living in Jerusalem (curiously, almost double the 468 Judahites), as well as other Benjaminites living in sixteen locations outside Jerusalem. He also refers to an official named Benjamin who marched in the procession dedicating the completed wall of Jerusalem. These roughly two hundred references in biblical literature clearly indicate that, while there was a continuous Benjaminite presence, at times even prominently so, the relatively smaller number of these references (and their concentration mostly in a few books) indicates the minor role of Benjamin compared with Judah, which is mentioned more than seven hundred times and in virtually every book of the Tanakh.

There are two more references to Benjaminite origins that deserve special attention. One is in the Book of Esther, where Mordecai is identified as *'îš yĕhûdî, 'îš yĕmînî*, "a Jew, a Benjaminite" (Esther 2:5). This very designation helps to date the book. *Yĕhûdî* had, apparently, already become a name no longer directly associated with the tribe Judah. A Benjaminite could be called a *yĕhûdî*. *Yĕhûdî*, apparently, had become a collective term for all "Jews," regardless of their tribal identifications. Mordechai's alleged Benjaminite roots are authenticated by the citation of his ancestry as the "son of Yair, son of Shimi, son of Kish." Taken literally, Mordechai was the great-grandson of Kish, a deportee of Nebuchadnessar's. The name Kish is, of course, the same as King Saul's father. Regardless of whether Mordechai is a real proper name or designates a follower and devotee of the Babylonian God Marduk, the very fact that the Scroll of Esther traces him back to a Benjaminite root is astounding, especially due to the fact that it calls him *'îš yĕhûdî*, a Judahite. Surely the writer of the Scroll of Esther cannot be accused of confusion. But why not call him simply a Benjaminite? Why insist on *yĕhûdî*? Who was it or what readership was envisaged that could not identify a Benjaminite as a "Jew"? It is puzzling, to say the least.

One other mention in Scriptures of Benjaminite origin deserves

special attention. In Romans 1, Saul identifies himself: "I also am an Israelite, of the seed of Abraham, of the tribe of Benjamin." Similarly in
Philippians 3: "circumcised the eighth day, of the stock of Israel, of the
tribe of Benjamin." Aside from a reference in Revelation 7:8, these are
the only citations of *Benjamin* in the New Testament.

Why all this attention to Benjamin and Judah? The reason, obviously, is that the designation *Benjamin* or *Benjaminite* has not survived,
while *Judah* did. This may not be mere happenstance.

Rachel versus Leah

Let us remember who Benjamin and Judah were originally. The
former was the son of Jacob and Rachel, the latter of Jacob and Leah. Let
us further recall that Torah never hides Jacob's preference for Rachel;
Leah's enforced marriage to Jacob caused him hurt and profound embarrassment. Rachel, Jacob loved. Leah, he never did. Pathetically, Leah is
recorded as saying, "'This time my husband will become attached to me,
for I have borne him three sons.' Therefore he was named Levi. She
conceived again and bore a son and declared, 'This time I will praise the
Lord,' therefore she named him Judah" (Genesis 29:34-35).

And it was not only Jacob who so openly preferred Rachel over
Leah. The sisters were drawn into fateful tension and became involved in
conflict: "And Rachel said, 'A fateful contest I waged with my sister; yes,
and I have prevailed.' So she named him Naphtali" (Genesis 30:8). He
was the son of her maid, Bilha.

"Yes, and I have prevailed"—portentous words, not borne out by
history. It is Leah's son Judah who to this day stamps the identity of "Jew."
Joseph, Rachel's older son, fathered Ephraim and Manasseh. The former
became the very heart of the secessionist northern kingdom, Israel, which
survived as a traceable entity for only some 250 years. Its ten tribes are
lost. Continuity comes from the southern kingdom, named Judah. Or, to
put it differently, though in both the southern and northern kingdoms
Rachel's and Leah's descendants are mingled, the northern is led by
Ephraim/Rachel, the southern by Judah/Leah.

Not only did Rachel not prevail in the contest with Leah originally, but her descendants likewise did not prevail against Leah's. And
while the Esther reference to Mordecai as *yĕhûdî*-and-a-Benjaminite raises
the possiblity of the term *yĕhûdî* losing its root connection to *yĕhûdâ* there
is no gainsaying the fact that it is Leah's son Judah who is perpetuated in
Jew, Judaism, and the like.

Such considerations can throw a specific light on the well-known
Jeremiah 31 passage: Thus said the Lord:

A cry is heard in Ramah—
Wailing, bitter weeping
Rachel weeping for her children.
She refuses to be comforted
For her children, who are gone.
Thus said the Lord: Refrain your voice from weeping,
Your eyes from shedding tears;
For there is a reward for your labor—declares the Lord:
They shall return from the enemy's land.
And there is hope for your future—declares the Lord:
Your children shall return to their country . . .
Truly, Ephraim is a dear son to Me . . . I will receive him
    back in love—declares the Lord.
Thus said the Lord of Hosts, the God of Israel. They shall
    again say this in the Land of Judah . . .
(Jeremiah 31:15-17, 20, 23, Tanakh).

There is no mention here of Leah and her possible grief. Did she not lose her children similarly? Or is Jeremiah's singling out of Rachel's lament not merely the continuance of that preference for her which started out with Jacob, but also an acknowledgment that her children, led by her grandson Ephraim, are truly lost?

But what then of Jeremiah's promise, "There is hope for your future—declares the Lord"? What future? True, according to Nehemiah there was a considerable Benjaminite presence in the second commonwealth, but is it not Judah, the Leahite, who persists and fashions and denominates the "name"?

Interesting and possibly very significant is the blessing upon Ruth as reported in the Scroll of Ruth: "All the people at the gate and the elders said, 'We are [witnesses to Boaz's marriage to Ruth]. May the Lord make the woman who is coming into your house like Rachel and Leah, both of whom built up the house of Israel' "(Ruth 4:11). "Both of whom"? And Rachel, the younger, preceding Leah? Is this wording of the blessing a painful reminder of what is no longer true but remains a fervent hope? Is it evidence of the more loving feelings toward Rachel which are surely a feature of Jewish tradition?

A midrash seems to confirm this impression. It tells that when Rachel learned that Leah and not she was to be given in marrige to Jacob, she feared for her sister's embarrassment and humiliation should Jacob discover the deception. Therefore, she instructed Leah in some of the special love words and gestures that had developed during their courtship, and encouraged her to use them so as to perfect the deception. To my knowledge, there is nothing that indicates that Leah resisted her father's ugly plan or failed to use Rachel's sensitive, caring instructions. Rachel is thus not only more beautiful than Leah, who had "weak eyes," she is also depicted as more gracious and sensitive. Clearly, biblically as well as in the rest of tradition, Rachel comes off better than Leah: "The Lord saw that Leah was unloved," states Genesis 29:31. We who are called Jews to this day are thus linked to the unloved one.

A Final Reconciliation

This brings us back to Saul/Paul the Benjaminite, the Rachelite who becomes the initial major instrument in creating a religious system whose relation to Jews and Judiasm for nearly all of the past 1,800 to1,900 years was, to say the least, deeply stained by antagonism and worse. This is again the conflict between Leah and Rachel, prolonged for generations!

But now, in the second half of the bloody twentieth century, the most significant and, hopefully, lasting reconciliation between Rachelites and Leahites has begun and will spread and last. As Amram Gaon of the Sura Adademy said in the ninth century, "May he who makes peace in his heights make peace among us and among all Israel"; yea, Leahites and Rachelites alike.

When God Speaks:
God and Nature in the Divine
Speeches of Job

BRADLEY J. BERGFALK

The book of Job reaches a dramatic climax when God appears as the "voice of a whirlwind" at the conclusion of the book. Job and the Creator of heaven and earth engage in verbal combat over issues of divine justice. Job challenges the heavenly judge to speak or exonerate him from his sentence of misery. Job does not approach God with his head bowed and hat in hand, but as someone who intends to exact a reversal in fortune before it's too late. After thirty-seven chapters of deafening silence, the voice of God addresses Job's plea. In an extended monologue, God does not consider Job's accusations directly, but rather asks a series of questions, leaving Job tongue-tied in silence. Job thought he understood his place in the moral order in which he lived, and he was "simply intent on presenting himself as the model of a good man falsely accused."[1]

The divine speeches of Job 38-41 have traditionally been the focus of those trying to address the problem of innocent suffering. While this is clearly the theological intent of Job, the divine speeches also provide the modern interpreter with an abundance of material for reexamining the role of nature in wisdom theology. This essay intends to review the content of these divine speeches while paying particular attention to the nature imagery. It is the thesis of this essay that the divine speeches in Job, when viewed in relation to larger themes of creation theology, provide a framework for understanding the role of God and humans in the context of our current ecological crisis.

With regard to wisdom and creation theology, James Crenshaw states that "the function of creation theology within the thought of the sages remains something of a mystery to this day." Crenshaw further observes that any attempt to provide an analysis of creation theology in the wisdom tradition must "clarify the role of creation in the total thought of Israel before going on to demonstrate the distinctiveness of the function of creation theology in wisdom literature."[2] Recent studies have attempted to address the silence of creation theology in the wisdom tradition.[3] Furthermore, there have been a number of significant efforts to understand nature in the life and religion of ancient Israel.[4]

The so-called environmental crisis has provided an additional incentive to come to a more definitive understanding of the role of nature in biblical theology. Many point to the cultural mandate in the creation narratives as the primary contributor to our current ecological predicament. Wesley Granberg-Michaelson has suggested that "Genesis 1:28 has become the proof-text for the industrial age's attitude toward the resources of creation."[5] It is argued elsewhere that an anthropocentric view of creation contributes to an imbalance in the relationship between humans and nature. Lyn White attributes the current crisis to the "Christian dogma of man's transcendence of, and rightful mastery over, nature."[6] This growing ecological concern has prompted biblical scholars to reassess our understanding of nature in light of some of the traditional sources.[7]

Preliminary Observations

The Book of Job is among the most compelling stories in the Jewish and Christian canon. The influence of Job in the history of theology, philosophy, literature, and art is derived in part from the sage's attempt to address perennial questions concerning the human predicament. The value of the Book of Job for the contemporary reader does not arise from its ability to answer such questions unequivocally. On the contrary, Job does not hesitate to leave the reader with painful, unanswered questions about suffering. Furthermore, the Book of Job challenges simplistic appeals to moral order that attempt to ground the human predicament in fate or destiny. At the same time, "the sage does not absolve humans from sharing some of the responsibility."[8] In essence, Job provides a theological challenge to the prevailing view of God, suffering, and personal responsibility. It is at this level of responsibility that the Book of Job has something to say about our understanding of God, nature, and human interaction with both. Before we turn to the wider implications of this study, we first must consider the classification of Job.

On the Classification of Job

As a result of Job's refusal to offer easy answers to the difficult questions that are raised, the history of the interpretation of Job has evoked a variety of readings. This is no less true with regard to the divine speeches. Some have sought to understand Job in the context of its literary environment. Locating the Book of Job in this context does not provide us with many clues to Job's origin or function, because of wisdom literature's tendency to lack identifying characteristics that would otherwise give us a hint concerning these matters.

Recent attempts to determine the genre of the divine speeches have generally concluded that they exhibit a "nature description" genre or a "challenge-to-rival" genre.[9] Gerhard von Rad was one of the first to observe the similarities between the divine speeches in Job 38 and ancient Egyptian wisdom literature.[10] Acknowledging that direct dependence cannot be shown between Job and ancient Egyptian wisdom, von Rad argues that Job represents a genre common among a variety of ancient Near Eastern cultures. This nature description genre appears to enumerate specific categories of nature, including heavenly, cosmological, and meteorological phenomena.[11] Such descriptive lists can also be found elsewhere in the Old Testament and Apocrypha.[12] Whether Job 38 exhibits a so-called nature description genre from Egyptian wisdom or not, the use of the nature list has remote parallels to both the Yahwist and Priestly primeval histories found in Genesis.[13]

Other attempts to determine the genre of the divine speeches have focused on the structural and syntactical form of the speeches.[14] Henry Rowold sees the basic genre of the divine speeches as a disputation in which Yahweh replies to the challenge of Job. This pattern is clearly evident when God responds to Job's accusations with rhetorical questions similar to those a defense lawyer might use when cross-examining a witness. After the challenge has been stated (Job 38:2-3), a "challenge-to-rival" claim is made. God exerts creative lordship and reveals Job's folly as Job stands before God as the rival.[15]

Our review of the form and function of the divine speeches in Job demonstrates the lack of agreement among the various literary approaches. In order to bring further clarity to the function of these speeches, it will be instructive to consider the divine speeches within the context of the cosmology of the wisdom tradition.

The Divine Speeches and the Cosmology of the Wisdom Tradition

The first speech of God (38:1-40:5) begins with a question: "Who is this who darkens counsel with words lacking in knowledge?" This question is important not only because it inaugurates God's response to Job's accusations, but also because it calls into question the one who dares to challenge God's authority over creation. Leo Perdue has suggested that the metaphors of "word" and "struggle" provide the controlling images for the remainder of this disputation with Job.[16] This is evident throughout the divine speeches.

The use of the term *counsel* reflects an understanding of God's mysterious and sometimes paradoxical design in creation. Job's challenge effectively "darkens" God's plan and returns the world to "primordial chaos."[17] Job's plea for divine justice calls into question God's dealing with humanity and subverts God's divine plan.[18] By merely asking the question, Job is setting himself up as an equal to God. In so doing, Job is defrauding God of God's rightful place in creation.

What follows Job's challenge is a series of rhetorical questions that build upon one another until it is clear to Job that he does not possess the ability to understand God's power over creation. Job 38 continues to present God as architect of creation (38:4-7). The language is reminiscent of one who goes out to build a house. This requires both skillful design and construction. One without the other leaves the final structure wanting. In the case of God's creation, it is clear that this is not so. "Where were you when I laid the foundation?" God asks Job rhetorically. The plans were established and the foundation set, and God did not consult Job. And why should God? When God was done, even the cosmos rejoiced. The response of the stars and the heavens is startling in direct contrast to the absence of a human response to God's creative act.

The next section of this poetic diatribe begins at verse 8, where the metaphor changes from architectural to seafaring. God is portrayed as Creator in a more organic sense here. Instead of being concerned with the construction of foundations and measurements, God is occupied by the base elements of creation. God sets the boundaries that keep back chaos (38:11-12). God controls the extent to which this primordial chaos encroaches on the providential order. And, as in the primeval history, the wind from God sweeps over the face of the waters, separating them and thus making the earth habitable for human beings (see Genesis 1:2; 6-8).

A third section begins by looking to the heavens (38:12-15). God is now prepared to indict Job on the basis of his absence. As part of the divine stewardship, God is the one responsible for the cycle of mornings (and by implication evenings). Furthermore, God casts a shadow of darkness upon those who are unrighteous. From the heavens we move to the deep. From the cosmos we must now confront chaos. And while humans cower in fear of the unknown power of the sea, God not only has "walked in the recesses of the deep," but also understands its "broad expanses."

The second speech of God begins at 38:19-21. In a similar fashion to the previous section, the language and metaphor used in this description further reveal God's authority over the elements. Beginning with light and darkness, the theme moves to the meteorological realm.

God's power to bring rain even to those places where people do not dwell underscores the supreme character of this authority. Moreover, God's ability to manipulate the elements challenges Job's anthropocentric worldview. God is portrayed as the sustainer of human and nonhuman life (38:39-39:30). Robert Alter suggests that there is a heightening in the narrative development, leading to the climactic images of Behemoth and Leviathan.[19] It is worth noticing that there is no apparent distinction between human and animal species here.

With each of these metaphors, "it is divine wisdom that is identified with the conceptual design, skill, and power in the origination of creation."[20] For the sage, God creates by containing the powers of chaos with spoken word and skillful act. Thus, the world in which the sage lived embodied both the natural forces of the universe pressing against the boundaries of creation and the moral purposes of the Creator sustaining creation by divine authority.[21]

The next major section of this speech establishes God's relationship to the animal kingdom. Scene one (38:39-41) begins with God's concern for the ultimate predator (the lion) and the ruthless scavenger (the raven). It is God who gives these animals their instinctive skills to hunt their prey and feed their offspring. Scene two and scene three (39: 1-4 and 39:5-12) continue with elaborate descriptions of the world of the untamed animal. There is no apparent ordering to these descriptions, only that each animal here is wild and untamed and thus places humans at risk. Yet to God these dangerous animals pose no risk, for it is God who created them.

At scene four (39:13-25), God's speech turns to the world of the domesticated animal. The foolishness of the ostrich and the horse is revealed every time the ostrich flaps her wings at danger, and the horse rides into the sword in battle without questioning the decision of the rider. Yet God created even these.

In scene four, God wonders out loud whether Job can explain how the hawk can soar effortlessly, while the vulture can see the blood of a slain animal hundreds of feet below. It is God who provides these winged creatures with the instinctual capacity to survive. One can further note that these wild animals dwell in regions that are uninhabited by humans, and are uncontrolled by human constraints.[22] These creatures, unlike those in the Priestly writer's creation narrative and flood story, do not fear humans. Surprisingly, humans do not even figure into God's description of creation here.[23]

The second speech (40:6-41:34) follows the same line of argument as the first. God builds a case carefully, while Job listens in silence. This time, however, God introduces his interrogatory remarks by asking Job whether he embodies the very nature of God in anthropocentric terms. Furthermore, if Job is interested in challenging God's authority by questioning God's justice, then Job must first be prepared to take on two great "incarnations of chaos" that have opposed God in the forms of Behemoth and Leviathan.[24] The description of these primordial creatures draws comparison to many of the earthly creatures with which Job is already familiar. In each instance, however, Behemoth and Leviathan exceed in strength and terror those creatures of the natural world.

Job responds to this fierce inquiry with a doxology. After all of this, Job finally understands his place in the scheme of God's created order. Job ends his inquiry and turns instead toward praise when he says, "I know you are capable of all things, and that no plan you propose will be impossible for you" (42:1).

God, Nature, and the Ecological Crisis

The Book of Job is concerned with one of the oldest problems known to humankind: the suffering of the righteous and the prosperity of the wicked. It would seem unlikely that Job would also address the contemporary issue of the environmental crisis.[25] Yet the climactic position of God's speeches from out of the whirlwind attests to the importance of this section for understanding the theology of the Book of Job. Indeed, these speeches of God cannot be overlooked if one intends to understand the central argument of Job. Robert Gordis has observed how the basic theme of innocent suffering in the Book of Job is abandoned in favor of God's own defense and without any reference to Job's initial questions.[26] What consolation is there for Job, who has sought God's response to his innocent suffering, only to receive a lengthy speech on the transcendent character of God in relation to creation? How can God so soon forget the nature of the inquiry of his sincere inquisitor? Why must God go off on some wild goose chase, extolling the virtues of creation while ignoring Job's plea?

Perhaps the reason for this incongruent response lies in the fact that the sage had another agenda beyond simply dealing with the problem of innocent suffering. From Gordis again: "The speeches out of the whirlwind do not describe the beauties of nature for their own sake; they are concerned with God's nature. . . . [They] underscore the insight that nature is not merely a mystery, but a miracle as well."[27] By analogy, then, since God is in absolute control over every manner of creation, there is also order and beauty in the human sphere, albeit sometimes imperfectly understood by humans.[28] And God's order of creation is not compromised just because humans experience unexplainable suffering from time to time.

What is significant about the imagery of these divine speeches within the context of the cosmology of the wisdom tradition is the diminutive role of human beings throughout the narrative. God has orchestrated the formation of creation from the beginning without human intervention. God contains the primordial forces of chaos. And God continues to sustain creation in all its wonder and terror, in the apparent absence of any human assistance. This naturally places humans in a subservient relationship to God and on equal ground with the rest of animate and inanimate creation. The idea that humans may not be central to God's purpose and joy in creation is hinted at when the stars and heavens rejoice and humans are nowhere to be seen or heard (38:7).[29]

God's authority over the elements of the universe, exhibited in both God's restraint over the primordial waters and the channeling of the torrents of rain, suggests that God continues to have an active role in the confinement of natural forces. The potential for the unleashing of chaos and natural disaster appears to be much greater than we recognize—until a hurricane threatens the inhabitants along the coast of Florida or one of America's great rivers overflows its bank with floodwaters. The direct parallel between God's mastery of the waters in primordial history and in his defense before Job provides a tangible link between creation and wisdom.

The implications of this for our contemporary ecological crisis reaffirm the notion that "the earth is the Lord's and all that dwells therein" (Psalm 24:1). While this is not a perspective unique to the wisdom tradition, it bears repeating in an age when humans behave as if the earth were *theirs* and all that dwells therein. We need not confront God with the complaint of Job to be culpable of challenging God's authority over creation. We need only disregard the subservient role we play in God's creative design, and thus become guilty of the same sin as Job. In the divine speeches, there is no room for anthropocentric arrogance in the presence of the transcendent Creator.

In view of our contemporary ecological crisis, the wisdom tradition can offer some valuable insight for the Christian community by inviting us to behold the creative genius of God's handiwork in the natural world.[30] Before the Creator, Job is made to feel small.[31] And so should we. What begins for Job as a pursuit of divine justice ends with Job receiving an elementary lesson on his place within God's created order. This is an exercise that we would do well to learn. The voice of God in the whirlwind is not done speaking yet. Every now and then, the fury of creation unleashed reminds us of our rightful place and calls us to responsible stewardship in God's divine order. Even now the vast blue-green waters of the Pacific Ocean, the expansive painted landscape of the Grand Canyon, and the delicate beauty of the Florida Everglades all proclaim God's glory, and "heavenly beings shout for joy." Like Job, we too should be speechless with wonder when we consider that we have contributed nothing to this elegant grandeur. When God speaks, nature rejoices—and we must be quiet.

Endnotes

1. Carol Newsom, "The Moral Sense of Nature: Ethics in the Light of God's Speech to Job," *The Princeton Seminary Review* (15:1): 9.

2. James Crenshaw, "Prolegomenon," *Studies in Ancient Israelite Wisdom*, James Crenshaw, ed. (New York: KTAV, 1976). Crenshaw further argues that any such study requires that creation not be divorced from the concept of chaos, and the prevailing view that creation theology has a subservient role to redemptive history must be challenged.

3. Hans-Jurgen Hermisson, "Observations on the Creation Theology in Wisdom," *Israelite Wisdom: Theological and Literary Essays in Honor of Samuel Terrien*, John Gammie et al., eds. (Missoula: Scholar's Press, 1978), 43-57. See also Leo Perdue, "Cosmology and the Social Order in the Wisdom Tradition," in *The Sage in Ancient Israel*, John Gammie and Leo Perdue, eds. (Winona Lake: Eisenbrauns, 1990), 457-78. On a more popular level, see Bill McKibben, *The Comforting Whirlwind* (Grand Rapids: Eerdmans, 1994). For the most extensive discussion of wisdom and creation theology, see Leo Perdue, *Wisdom and Creation—The Theology of the Wisdom Literature* (Nashville: Abingdon, 1994).

4. See George Hendry, *Theology of Nature* (Philadelphia: Westminster, 1980); Ronald A. Simpkins, *Creator and Creation—Nature in the Worldview of Ancient Israel* (Peabody, Mass.: Hendrickson, 1994); and Theodore Hiebert, *The Yahwist's Landscape: Nature and Religion in Early Israel* (New York: Oxford, 1995).

5. As cited by Robert K. Johnston in "Wisdom Literature and Its Contribution to a Biblical Environmental Ethic," in *Tending the Garden—Essays on the Gospel and the Earth* (Grand Rapids: Eerdmans, 1987), 66.

6. This whole debate was prompted in part by an article by Lyn White, titled "Historical Roots of our Ecological Crisis," *Science Magazine* 155:3767 (March 10, 1967): 1203-1207.

7. Theodore Hiebert has observed that in the accounts of primeval history in Genesis, "the Priestly writer's perspective on nature has dominated ancient and modern treatments of biblical thought." For this reason, he has attempted to "rescue from relative obscurity the foundational and distinctive perspectives on nature reflected in the Yahwist's epic." See Hiebert's *The Yahwist's Landscape: Nature and Religion in Early Israel*, 3.

8. Leo Perdue and W. Clark Gilpin, "Introduction," in *The Voice from the Whirlwind*, Leo Perdue and W. Clark Gilpin, eds. (Nashville: Abingdon, 1992), 11.

9. Henry Rowold, "Yahweh's Challenge to Rival: The Form and Function of Yahweh Speeches in Job 38-39," *CBQ* 47 (1985): 203.

10. Gerhard von Rad, "Job XXXVIII and Ancient Egyptian Wisdom," in *Studies in Ancient Israelite Wisdom* (New York: KTAV, 1976), 267-77.

11. Von Rad's list from the Onomasticon finds direct parallels in Job 38, including the following: "dawn," "primeval ocean," "sea," "rain." See his comparative table on pages 268-69 for a more complete listing.

12. See Psalm 148, Sirach 43, The Song of the Three Children, Genesis 1, Psalm 104, and Psalm 147. Rowold has argued that as remarkable as these similarities are, significant differences remain: 1) Job's list appears to explore the outer limits of the human world and is more selective than the Onomasticon; 2) Job's list appears to attach each listing to a purpose result clause that turns one's attention from the phenomena to Yahweh; and 3) the initial pericopes (Job 38:4-7 and 8-11) show considerable influence from the Mesopotamian and Palestinian worlds as well.

13. See the primal history in Genesis 1-2.

14. Henry Rowold, "The Yahweh Speech in Job 38-39," *CBQ* 47 (1985): 205 ff.

15. Ibid., 211.

16. Perdue, *Wisdom and Creation*, 168.

17. Ibid., 169.

18. Leo Perdue, "Wisdom and the Book of Job," in *In Search of Wisdom: Essays in Memory of John Gammie* (Atlanta: Westminster Press, 1993), 92.

19. Robert Alter, *The Art of Biblical Poetry* (New York: Basic Books, 1985), 110 ff.

20. Perdue, "Cosmology and the Social Order in the Wisdom Tradition," 92.

21. Ibid., 464.

22. Perdue, *Wisdom and Creation*, 174.

23. This is in stark contrast to Psalm 8 and Genesis 1-9, where humans are central figures in the creation drama.

24. Perdue, *Wisdom and Creation*, 179.

25. Robert Gordis, "Job and Ecology," *The Hebrew Annual Review* 9 (1985): 189.

26. Ibid., 191.

27. Ibid., 194.

28. Ibid.

29. This can also be seen later, when the wild beast has freedom in the wilderness and "scorns the noise of the city." See Gordis, "Job and Ecology," 195-96, for a discussion of this.

30. I have sought to address this very issue in a four-part Bible study on this topic. See Bradley J. Bergfalk, "When God Speaks—God, Nature, and the Environment in the Book of Job," *The Covenant Companion* 84:11; 84:12; 85:1; 85:2 (November 1995-February 1996).

31. Timothy Weiskel, "In Dust and Ashes—The Environmental Crisis in Religious Perspective," *Harvard Divinity Bulletin* 21:3 (1992).

Reading Scripture with Kenneth Burke: Genesis 38

PAUL E. KOPTAK

For over a decade the work of Robert Alter, Adele Berlin, and Meir Sternberg[1] has offered biblical interpreters and preachers new paths into the narratives of the Hebrew Bible. They have taught us to look closely at characterization, plot, and setting, and, when there is nothing left to see, to look for significance in what is not there in the gaps. Their names have made their way into the preaching textbooks.[2]

Two of the three call their work the study of poetics, defined by Berlin as looking "not only for what the text says, but also how it says it."[3] Yet it is generally agreed that preachers are not only interested in what texts say, or even how, but also in their function—what is a given text supposed to do?

To speak of the function of a text is to speak of its rhetoric. Three recent works on rhetorical criticism of the Hebrew Bible discuss function in terms of effect on a reading or listening audience. Alan Hauser speaks of rhetorical criticism as one color in the spectrum of literary approaches to Old Testament interpretation. He explains that "a rhetorical critic will basically do two things in studying a unit of text: analyze the literary features of the text, to the maximum extent possible, from the perspective of literary style discernible in the works of ancient Israelite writers; and articulate the impact of the literary unit on its audience."[4]

Phyllis Trible takes her definition of rhetorical criticism from James Muilenburg's famous address to the Society of Biblical Literature,[5] which she summarizes as "A proper articulation of form yields a proper articulation of meaning." Her study of the book of Jonah concludes with a catalog of persuasive moves YHWH takes toward Jonah and the reading/listening audience: "In teaching rhetoric as the art of composition, the book of Jonah unfolds rhetoric as the art of persuasion."[6]

Dale Patrick, another of Muilenburg's students, and Allen Scult, a rhetorician, believe that the rhetorical study must not be limited to matters of structure and style, but must consider the intention of writers to influence audiences. They broaden the definition of rhetoric to include "the means by which a text establishes and manages its relationship to its audience in order to achieve a particular effect."[7] The inspiration for this view of rhetoric comes not only from Muilenburg, but also from the late Kenneth Burke. Burke's earliest writings were concerned with the effects writers meant to create in their reading audiences. Over time his focus turned from literary effects to what he began to call rhetorical effects, that is, what literary works are supposed to do for their creators and readers.[8] His work sought to give attention to both poetics and rhetoric without imposing hard and fast boundaries on either.

This essay will show how Burke's recommendations for literary and rhetorical analysis can direct the reading of a biblical text in preparation for preaching. Preaching here is understood to be the communication of a text's message for the purpose of achieving the same rhetorical effect that was intended for the original audience,[9] or, in the case of a radically different contemporary audience/situation, one that corresponds closely to it. If a Scripture text was designed to encourage, convict, or move to action, the sermon based on that text should do the same.

Reading with Kenneth Burke

Throughout his career, Kenneth Burke sought to establish a balance between extrinsic and intrinsic types of criticism through his focus on literature as a "strategy for encompassing a situation."[10] Burke's comments on method were based on his theory that every literary work, as a work of language, has its own network of symbolic action that links the work to the environment within which it was created.[11] He described the internal analysis of the work in terms of poetics, but added that questions about symbolic action "do involve the relation of the work to the author and his[12] environment, insofar as such information is available."[13]

Burke's idea of the symbol as a link that is forged between writer and reader appeared in his first book of criticism, *Counter-Statement* (1931). "The symbol is the verbal parallel to a pattern of experience," and the appeal of the symbol is strongest when the artist's and the reader's patterns of experience closely coincide.[14] Burke's list of symbolic appeals stressed what the symbol, as the basis of a larger work of art, "does" for the writer and the reader. A symbol can interpret a situation, favor the acceptance of a situation, correct a situation, or liberate from a situation. "In sum, the symbol appeals either as the orienting of a situation, or as the adjustment to a situation, or as both."[15]

In order to determine the rhetorical function of a narrative, then, questions concerning the intention and design of the work as a form of symbolic action must be addressed. Burke stressed this function of communication when he defined rhetoric as "the use of language as a symbolic means of inducing cooperation in beings that by nature respond to symbols."[16] Here is an answer to the question, what is the interpreter to look for? The next question is how to look for it, and Burke cautioned that one should not ask one question without the other.

Burke made one of his first attempts to articulate his method in *The Philosophy of Literary Form* (1941), and suggested the following guidelines: First, the critic is to watch for dramatic alignments, or "what is versus what." Then one lists the equation, "what equals what." Attention is given to the beginnings and ends of works as well as the location of the peripety, noting the development "from what through what to what."[17]

Elsewhere, Burke has called this statistical analysis the "principle of the concordance."[18] The critic notices key terms for acts, attitudes, ideas, images and relationships, beginnings and endings of sections, the significance of names, and details of the scene that may stand "astrologically" for motivations affecting character. By focusing attention on the words of a text and their use in their contexts, the interpreter discovers the symbolic function of those terms in relation to the work.[19]

The charting of "what equals what," "what versus what," and "what leads to what" reveals the structure of the work, which in turn reveals the function of the work. Burke's method begins with an internal analysis in order to discover the effect the work is meant to have on its author and audience. Acknowledging that much of the poet's work does things for the poet that it does not do for the reader, he believed that, in general, by discovering what the poem does for the poet, one may discover "a set of generalizations as to what poems do for everybody" (Burke often referred to writers as poets).[20]

> The main point is to note *what the poem's equational structure is*. This is a statement about its *form*. But to guide our observations about the form itself, we seek to discover the *functions* which the structure serves. This takes us into a discussion of purpose, strategy, the symbolic act.[21]

In sum, the basic strategy underlying Burke's method is a charting of the work's structure in order to uncover its "medicine," that is, what it is supposed to do for the writer and the reader. Underlying the method is his primary assumption that an intrinsic analysis of the work will reveal its structure, which in turn will reveal its function or "medicine." Burke's methods of analysis have been summarized as a series of four interpretive steps: 1) cluster analysis: what goes with what? 2) agon analysis: what is opposed to what? 3) analysis of progressive form: from what, through what, to what? and 4) analysis of transformations: what is changed into something or someone else?[22] The four steps and their questions can help us discover the rhetorical strategy and purpose at work in the story of

Judah and Tamar and their dealings with one another.

Genesis 38

While most modern interpreters of Genesis have viewed the story of Judah and Tamar as an unrelated intrusion into the Joseph story,[23] a growing number are following the suggestion of Alter that this chapter is central to the story of Joseph and his family.[24] If one reads the story as part of the larger narrative concerning the family story (*tōlĕdôt*) of Jacob (Genesis 37:2), then the verbal links with Judah's suggestion to sell Joseph in chapter 37 and his later pledge and appeal for Benjamin in chapter 44 come to the foreground.[25] The figure of Tamar can recede in such a reading; it can be forgotten that the story can function on its own, centered on a woman's clever solution to a serious problem. When it is read as an independent short story, Tamar, not Judah, becomes the main character and hero.[26]

CLUSTER ANALYSIS: WHAT GOES WITH WHAT? Cluster analysis identifies key terms, noting either the frequency or the intensity of their use. Symbols and terms that are associated with key words indicate the meanings of those key words and their functions. One can then chart and look for patterns in associational clusters.[27]

The descriptions and associations narrated in verses 1 and 2 of chapter 38 are predominantly masculine. Judah separates from his brothers and settles (Hebrew *nth*, "he turned") near an Adullamite named Hirah. He then sees and takes as a wife the daughter of a Canaanite man whose name, Shua, is given; the woman's is not. The narration of verses 3, 4, and 5 uses descriptions that are predominantly feminine. The wife of Judah builds up a family; she conceives, bears, and names the sons at least two, if not three, times (some scholars emend the Hebrew masculine "he called" in verse 3 to agree with "she called" in verses 4 and 5).[28] The sequence of feminine active verbs, coming after a string of masculine verbs, sets up a distinction between the worlds of men and women that bears watching. Does it continue throughout the story?

In verses 6-11, the verbs are almost all masculine again. Judah "takes" for his firstborn son a wife named Tamar, just as he "takes" a wife for himself in verse 2. When Er's evil moves YHWH to put him to death, Judah directs his second son, Onan, to fulfill the duty of the brother-in-law to father offspring to perpetuate the name and memory of his dead brother (see Deuteronomy 25:25). Onan only pretends to comply and is also put to death for the same reason as his brother: his deeds were "evil in the eyes of YHWH." This time Judah speaks to Tamar. He tells her to go to her father's house until his third son, Shelah, grows up, but the storyteller reveals that Judah blames Tamar for the deaths. Tamar is silent in all of this. No verbs describe her action until she goes to her father's house and stays there.[29]

The separate verbal worlds of men and women continue throughout the story, with the exception of the interaction between Judah and
the disguised Tamar in verses 16-18. Judah is not said to be present for
the births of his twins in verses 27-30. We might speculate that the separation of the worlds of males and females was thought to be normal, but
we cannot be certain. However, we also see that the actions of Er, Onan,
and Judah have left Tamar childless and isolated. She is a woman without a place.[30]

The separation breaks down in the scene that begins in verse 12.
When Tamar hears that the widowed Judah is going up to shear the sheep
at Timnah, she begins to act and speak. First, she disguises herself and sits
by the road. The Hebrew word for "sit" (*ysb*) is the same one used for
"remain" or "live" at the father's house in verse 11; Judah sent her to live
at her father's house, but no one directed her to sit by the road. Second,
Tamar speaks to Judah and bargains with him.[31] He does not "take" her,
as he took wives for himself and his son; he must tell her what he will
"give" (*ntn*), three times (vv. 16-18). Judah later sends a goat to "take"
the pledge back, but when she is not found, he decides to let her keep
(again *lqh*, "take") it. In her disguise, Tamar has entered the man's world.
She belongs to no one, and she directs her own actions, even negotiating
for herself.[32] It may be significant that the masculine and feminine verbs
describing the sex act occur together for the first time in verse 18: "He
went into her and she conceived by him."

So far the study of significant terms and their clusters has supported
the reader's notice that the actions of Tamar crossed the boundaries of
propriety, not just in taking the role of a prostitute, but in taking the
active role that had previously been unavailable to her. Tamar's actions
become even more significant when another cluster of key terms is charted.
Words about seeing and recognition are clustered in verses 14-26. Tamar
disguised herself because she "saw" (*r 'h*) that Shelah had grown and she
had not been given to him (v. 14). Judah "saw" her and took her for a
prostitute (v. 15), for he did not "know" (*yd'*) that she was his daughter-
in-law (v. 16). Judah heard that Tamar was pregnant and ordered her
execution, but she sent out his personal effects and said, "By the man
who owns these I have conceived. Identify [or recognize, *nkr*] them; whose
are they?" (v. 25). Judah identified them and revealed a new insight:
"She is more in the right than I am, because I did not give her to Shelah
my son" (v. 26).

Tamar acted because she "saw." As a result, Judah finally saw and
acknowledged that he had acted unfairly toward his daughter-in-law. The
idea is echoed in the name of the place where Tamar set herself; *petah
'ênayim* can mean "opening of the eyes."[33] Yet Tamar and Judah are not

the only ones who see; YHWH also sees that the acts of Er and Onan are evil (literally, "evil in the eyes of YHWH," vv. 7-10), and that moves YHWH to swift judgment. Judah is also judged for withholding offspring from Tamar, but much more gently. His death is the inner death of self-mortification that recognizes his injustice, and it ultimately leads to life. Are we encouraged to compare these different instances of seeing?

AGON ANALYSIS: WHAT IS VERSUS WHAT? The cluster of words related to seeing also has within it a pattern of opposition, much like the contrast between the worlds of men and women observed earlier. The agon analysis looks for words, themes, images, and principles that stand against one another. Agon analysis completes the work of cluster analysis by discovering the conflicts that may have motivated the work under study.[34]

Certainly there is opposition between the actions of Er, Onan, and Judah that would deny life and the steps Tamar took to give life. There is also opposition between the life-taking judgment of YHWH in verses 7 and 10 and the life-saving intervention or "judgment" of Tamar. Not only did Tamar's actions bring new life to the family (two sons for the two that were lost), but her exposure of Judah gave him the opportunity to mortify or "slay" himself and thereby avert the possibility of a deadly judgment from YHWH.

Why was YHWH merciful to Judah and not to Judah's sons? Perhaps part of the answer is to be found in Tamar's initiative on behalf of the family. The contrast may also be suggested by the use of the idiom "evil in the eyes of YHWH" (vv. 7 and 10), which, as mentioned above, becomes another term in the cluster of seeing. Nothing is said about YHWH seeing or judging Judah's actions, yet Tamar could see what Judah was doing. Judah was spared the judgment that had fallen on his sons when Tamar "saw" his wrong, acted to win her right, and caused Judah to see the injustice for himself. The tragedy that begins the story is turned around so that it ends in comedy.

ANALYSIS OF PROGRESSIVE FORM: FROM WHAT, THROUGH WHAT, TO WHAT? Is the story over? Not until the second set of sons is born; and so we may look at the third step in Burke's method, that of progressive form.[35] Burke also spoke of the "entelechial" test: "Look for *moments* at which, in your opinion, the work comes to *fruition*." The critic is here to attend to the terminology of these moments and then "spin from them."[36]

The story ends not with Tamar's exoneration, but with her delivery of twins. Two birth narratives form a frame around the story that begins with characters described as evil and ends with one who is called righteous, or at least "in the right" (*ṣdkh*). We can observe that verses 1-11 constitute a story of birth and succession that turns for the worse, while verses 12-30 tell another that ends in joy and uplift. One is filled with death and judgment, while redemptive mercy is at work in the other.

Tamar's bearing of twins completes the cycle of two birth narratives, so comparison between the two sets of brothers seems to be in order. Strife between brothers runs throughout the stories of Abraham and Sarah's descendants and appears in Onan's mistreatment of his deceased older brother's wife and memory. Yet we have seen that the sin and judgment of the first narrative (vv. 1-11) are answered with grace and redemption in the beginning of the second (vv. 12-26). Does this comic frame extend into the second birth narrative (vv. 27-30)? Perhaps so, for there is novelty, surprise, and perhaps even delight in the strange birth of the twins.

It is generally assumed that Perez "breaks out" (*prs*) violently and pulls his brother back in order to crawl over him.[37] Yet the brother's hand is withdrawn, not pulled back, and there are no other indications of strife or violence. Could it be that the one marked as firstborn yields his position?[38] Perhaps this is to say too much about a sketchy narrative, but we should notice that there is no clear indication of brotherly strife or of twins fighting in the womb as Jacob and Esau did. The younger rises over the older, just as Joseph sees his youngest blessed first by Jacob (Genesis 48:8-20) and accepts the father's favoritism, just as Judah learned to accept Jacob's love for Joseph and Benjamin. Is there a foreshadow of that resolution here?

ANALYSIS OF TRANSFORMATION: WHAT IS CHANGED INTO SOMETHING ELSE? A number of changes have been noted throughout this analysis, especially in the persons of Judah and Tamar, but perhaps the most significant transformation is the transformation of the story itself. The second narrative parallels the first in structure, word choice, and theme, but it does so to rewrite the story. Tragedy becomes comedy, a widow gains her right, and a wrongdoer begins to see.

Tamar's actions foreshadow those of Joseph, who also hides behind a disguise, uses personal effects to incriminate, and moves Judah to acknowledge guilt and act sacrificially.[39] By framing his brothers with the silver cup and claiming Benjamin as a slave (Genesis 42:6-44:17), Joseph recasts the scene of his own sale, hoping for a better outcome the second time around. In the same way, the second narrative of Genesis 38 begins in verses 12-16 with a second mention of Shua's daughter, the man Hirah, and a journey in which Judah "saw" and "turned" (echoing the vocabulary of vv. 1-2), to indicate that this scene is a replay of the scene in verses 1-11.

There is no lightness in the first narrative, but in the second, the picture of a man leading a goat, looking for a prostitute that no one admits to having seen,[40] is quite comical. Judah realizes this and decides to cut his losses before he and Hirah become a laughingstock, yet the reader is already laughing at the thought that Judah has been beaten at his own game of deception.[41] The laugh signals a brighter ending for this story, and for the larger story of Joseph and his family. Judah has been transformed, not killed; this transformation points to a greater one. Joseph will see God at work, not only in the life of Judah, who offers himself for Benjamin (Genesis 44:33), but in the entire constellation of events: "You meant to do evil to me, but God meant it for good" (Genesis 50:20). The story of Judah and Tamar recommends to the reader the work of God, sometimes hidden, but sometimes revealed to those with eyes to see.

Conclusion

Kenneth Burke's body of work left many approaches to reading that readers and rhetorical critics have used with great profit.[42] Yet more significant than the methods is the perspective that generated them. Richard B. Gregg writes, "Without taking anything away from Burke's concrete methodological advice, his most valuable contribution to the rhetorical critic is his insight into the nature of human symbolic behavior and the potential effect of symbolic inducements.[43]

The above analysis was written to show that Burke's close reading of texts is different from, yet complementary to, the poetics of Alter, Berlin, and Sternberg. His focus on the rhetoric of symbolic action can help the preacher see the effects the writers of Scripture hoped to evoke in their audiences, thus unlocking their persuasive appeal. Preachers may want to highlight the associations and agons in a story-based sermon on Genesis 38, or they may choose to teach the biblical storyteller's point that the injustice done to Tamar is corrected when the scene is replayed with a more active heroine. There ought to be plenty of freedom for invention in sermon writing. Preaching may or may not mirror the form of the biblical text, but it must recapture its function.

In sum, the analysis of clusters, agons, progressions, and transformations has helped us to chart not only the structure of Genesis 38, but its function, the effect it was intended to create. The chapter was written the way it was, the second story rewriting the first, to make us laugh and to make us glad that our own stories are also being written and rewritten by the same divine hand.[44]

Endnotes

1. Robert Alter, *The Art of Biblical Narrative* (New York: Basic Books, 1981); Adele Berlin, *Poetics and Interpretation of Biblical Narrative* (Sheffield: Almond, 1983); Meir Sternberg, *The Poetics of Biblical Narrative* (Bloomington: Indiana University Press, 1985).

2. Sidney Greidanus, *The Modern Preacher and the Ancient Text: Interpreting and Preaching Biblical Literature* (Grand Rapids: Eerdmans, 1988), 188-227; John C. Holbert, *Preaching Old Testament: Proclamation and Narrative in the Hebrew Bible* (Nashville: Abingdon, 1991); Thomas G. Long, *Preaching and the Literary Forms of the Bible* (Louisville: Westminster John Knox, 1989), 66-86.

3. Berlin, *Poetics*, 20.

4. Alan J. Hauser, "Rhetorical Criticism of the Old Testament," in *Rhetorical Criticism of the Bible: A Comprehensive Bibliography with Notes on History and Method*, ed. Duane F. Watson and Alan J. Hauser (Leiden: E. J. Brill, 1994), 1, 14.

5. James Muilenburg, "Form Criticism and Beyond," *JBL* 88 (1969): 1-18.

6. Phyllis Trible, *Rhetorical Criticism: Context, Method and the Book of Jonah* (Minneapolis: Augsburg Fortress, 1994), 224-25.

7. Dale Patrick and Allen Scult, *Rhetoric and Biblical Interpretation*, JSOT Supplement 82 (Sheffield: Sheffield Academic Press, 1990): 12. A similar idea comes from Jerry Camery-Hoggatt, *Speaking of God: Reading and Preaching the Word of God* (Peabody, Mass.: Hendrickson, 1995), 56: "By managing the reader's responses, the evangelist (gospel writer) makes the text a vehicle of transformation."

8. His taxonomy of the "kinds of criticism" distinguished extrinsic criticism (concerned with causes and effects of the work) and intrinsic criticism (analysis of the work itself). Kenneth Burke, "Kinds of Criticism," *Poetry* 68 (Aug. 1946): 274-79. However, Burke meant to appreciate both modes of criticism while seeking to deduce from such analysis the principles of the work, the way a writer crafts a work to produce certain effects. "The Principle of Composition," *Poetry* 99 (Oct. 1961): 52.

9. Camery-Hoggatt, *Speaking of God*, 16, 162.

10. Kenneth Burke, *The Philosophy of Literary Form: Studies in Symbolic Action*, 3d ed. (Berkeley: University of California Press, 1973), 109.

11. Greig Henderson sees symbolic action as a mediatory term: "Because of the ambiguity built into the transaction between text and context, there arises a need for mediation. Symbolic action is the principle of mediation." *Literature and Language as Symbolic Action* (Athens: University of Georgia Press, 1988), 18.

12. Burke's earlier writings do not exhibit the inclusive language he used in his last years of writing and speaking.

13. Kenneth Burke, "Poetics in Particular, Language in General," in *Language as Symbolic Action* (Berkeley: University of California Press, 1966), 42. Burke also labeled the intrinsic approach as formalistic, while he called the extrinsic approach sociological. "Formalist Criticism: Its Principles and Limits," in *Language as Symbolic Action*, 495-99.

14. Kenneth Burke, "Lexicon Rhetoricae," in *Counter-Statement* (Berkeley: University of California Press, 1968), 152-53.

15. Ibid., 156.

16. Kenneth Burke, *A Rhetoric of Motives* (Berkeley: University of California Press, 1969), 43.

17. Burke, *Philosophy*, 69-71.

18. Kenneth Burke, "Fact Inference and Proof in the Analysis of Literary

Symbolism," in *Symbols and Values: An Initial Study*, Thirteenth Symposium of the Conference on Science, Philosophy and Religion (New York: Harper, 1954), 283-306. Reprinted in *Terms for Order*, ed. S. E. Hyman with B. Karmiller (Bloomington: Indiana University Press, 1964), 145-72.

19. Ibid., 148.

20. Burke, *Philosophy*, 73-74.

21. Ibid., 101.

22. William H. Rueckert, "A Field Guide to Kenneth Burke—1990," in *Extensions of the Burkeian System*, ed. James W. Chesebro (Tuscaloosa and London: University of Alabama Press, 1993), 16-17.

23. J. Alberto Soggin, "Judah and Tamar (Genesis 38)," in *Of Prophets' Visions and the Wisdom of Sages: Essays in Honor of R. Norman Whybray on His Seventieth Birthday*, ed. H. A. McKay and David J. A. Clines (Sheffield: JSOT Press, 1993), 281, citing the commentary of Claus Westermann, *Genesis 37-50* (Minneapolis: Augsburg, 1986), 49-57. Westermann's most recent book does not include any discussion of Genesis 38. *Joseph: Eleven Bible Studies on Genesis* (Minneapolis: Fortress, 1996).

24. Alter, *Biblical Narrative*, 1-22. Judah Goldin, "The Youngest Son or Where Does Genesis 38 Belong," *JBL* 96 (1977): 27-44, notes that the problem was seen as early as *Genesis Rabbah*, par. 85.2, stating that the rabbi's "approach of looking for idiomatic or thematic connection or association is sound," 31.

25. Robert Alter, *Genesis: Translation and Commentary* (New York: Norton, 1996), 217-23, 265. Significant repetitions include the directive to "recognize" or "identify" personal effects (Genesis 37:32 and 38:25-26), and the pledge, or offer of security (Genesis 38:17-18 and 44:32). See also Terence Fretheim, "Genesis," in *The New Interpreter's Bible*, vol. 1 (Nashville: Abingdon, 1994), 604-5.

26. So also Harold Bloom, *The Book of J* (New York: Vintage Books), 220-23. The actions of Tamar also relate to the larger theme of the promise of nationhood in Genesis 12:1. Lawrence A. Turner, *Announcements of Plot in Genesis* (Sheffield: JSOT Press, 1990), 170; Gordon J. Wenham, *Word Biblical Commentary, Vol. 2: Genesis 16-50* (Dallas: Word Books, 1994), 365.

27. Sonja K. Foss, *Rhetorical Criticism: Exploration and Practice* (Prospect Heights, Ill.: Waveland Press, 1989), 368-70, 374, citing Burke, *Philosophy*, 20.

28. Westermann, *Genesis 37-50*, 47; Victor P. Hamilton, *The Book of Genesis: Chapters 18-50* (Grand Rapids: Eerdmans, 1995), 430.

29. For a description of these events from Tamar's point of view, see Sharon Pace Jeansonne, *The Women of Genesis: From Sarah to Potiphar's Wife* (Minneapolis: Augsburg Fortress, 1990), 98-106.

30. Susan Niditch, "The Wronged Woman Righted: An Analysis of Genesis 38," *Harvard Theological Review* 72 (1979): 143-48.

31. The change of costume and role may explain the repetition of the word *nth* in verses 1 and 16. It can be translated "turned aside" or even "spread the tent," in the sense of staying with someone. Soggin, "Judah and Tamar," 281, suggests that it be translated "to join in business" in verse 1, but says nothing about verse 16.

32. See Phyllis Bird, "The Harlot as Heroine: Narrative Art and Social Presupposition in Three Old Testament Texts," *Semeia* 46 (1989): 119-39.

33. Ira Robinson, "*běpetaḥ 'ênayim* in Genesis 38:14," *JBL* 96/4 (1977): 509; Johanna W. H. Bos, "An Eyeopener at the Gate: George Coats and Genesis 38," *Lexington Theological Quarterly* 27 (Oct 1992): 119-23; Hamilton, *Genesis*, 40.

34. William H. Rueckert, *Kenneth Burke and the Drama of Human Relations*,

2nd ed. (Berkeley: Univiversity of California Press, 1982), 86, 90. See also Carol A. Berthold, "Kenneth Burke's Cluster-Agon Method: Its Development and an Application," *Central States Speech Journal* 27 (Winter 1976): 302-9.

35. Burke, *Counter-Statement*, 124-25.

36. Burke, "Fact, Inference, and Proof," 167.

37. Westermann, *Genesis 37-50*, 55; Hamilton, *Genesis 18-50*, 453.

38. Perez is listed before Zerah in Genesis 46:12 and 1 Chronicles 2:4-6.

39. Peter F. Lockwood, "Tamar's Place in the Joseph Cycle," *Lutheran Theological Journal* 26 (May 1992): 35-43. Lockwood observes that the transformation of Judah in Genesis 38 "provides a pointer to what will occur in the Joseph cycle at large."

40. Rosemarie Anderson, "A Tent Full of Bedouin Women," *Daughters of Sarah* 19 (Winter, 1993): 34-35. Anderson, citing anthropological research on the nomadic and tribal Bedouin, suggests that Tamar did not act alone, but received help from her village in carrying out the deception.

41. Bernhard Luther saw here an expression of the narrator's friendly attitude toward Judah: "But mixed in with the laughter of the spectator is the joy that the catastrophe has been averted, and, in novelistic terms, that he now has three sons again. Blessing has finally come to him. So affection for Judah is linked with the laughter." "The Novella of Judah and Tamar and Other Israelite Novellas," in *Narrative and Novella in Samuel: Studies by Hugo Gressmann and Other Scholars, 1906-1923*, trans. D. E. Orton, ed. David M. Gunn (Sheffield: Almond Press, 1991), 114.

42. In addition to Foss, see Bernard L. Block, Robert L. Scott, James W. Chesebro, eds., *Methods of Rhetorical Criticism: A Twentieth Century Perspective*, 3d ed. rev. (Detroit: Wayne State University Press, 1990); and Roderick P. Hart, *Modern Rhetorical Criticism* (Glenview, Ill.: Scott Foresman, 1990).

43. Richard B. Gregg, "Kenneth Burke's Concept of Rhetorical Negativity," in *Extensions of the Burkeian System*, 190.

44. An earlier version of this essay was presented at the Annual Meeting of the Academy of Homiletics, December 1996.

CHRISTIAN CANON

On the One Hand . . . On the Other Hand: The Twofold Meaning of the Law against Covetousness

JAMES K. BRUCKNER

A s he was setting out on a journey, a man ran up and knelt before him, and asked him, "Good Teacher, what must I do to inherit eternal life?" Jesus said to him, "Why do you call me good? No one is good but God alone. You know the commandments: 'You shall not murder; You shall not commit adultery; You shall not steal; You shall not bear false witness; You shall not defraud; Honor your father and mother.'" He said to him, "Teacher, I have kept all these since my youth." Jesus, looking at him, loved him and said, "You lack one thing; go, sell what you own, and give the money to the poor, and you will have treasure in heaven; then come, follow me." When he heard this, he was shocked and went away grieving, for he had many possessions. (Mark 10:17-22)

We, too, know the commandments that Jesus quoted in this passage. They are from the "second table" of the ten given at Sinai and found in both Exodus and Deuteronomy. We also have heard them from an early age.

Honor your father and your mother, that your days may be long in the land which the LORD your God gives you. You shall not kill. You shall not commit adultery. You shall not steal. You shall not bear false witness against your neighbor. You shall not covet your neighbor's house; you shall not covet your neighbor's wife, or his manservant, or his maidservant, or his ox,

or his ass, or anything that is your neighbor's. (Exodus
20:12-17)

What Jesus says in Mark 10 contrasts with the familiar order in Exodus. He makes a substitution that would seem to have an intentional
point. Why does Jesus quote the commandments in this way? What sense
is to be made of his inclusion of the commandment "You shall not defraud" (*apostereō*)? Is it possible to explain why this appears where one
might expect to read "You shall not covet" (*epithumeō*)? There is an explanation that has its beginning in the Old Testament and its full prece-
dence in the intertestamental literature, which will shed light on these
questions and add depth to the understanding and interpretation of this
text.

A variety of explanations, most without serious warrants, have been
offered by commentators for the phrase "You shall not defraud." Mann
suggests that "Do not defraud" may be a form of the eighth commandment, "Do not steal."[1] Lane concludes that the prohibition of fraud "appears to be an application of the eighth and ninth commandments." *Defraud* would then be a summary application of the commands just quoted.[2]
This position is also given by Klostermann, that is, that fraud is actually
stealing, by means of bearing false witness.[3]

The burden of proof, therefore, lies in whether or not fraud is a
proper example of stealing. While this seems correlative in English, it is
a much farther reach in Hebrew or Greek. The specific meaning of *gnb*
(steal) has no clear reference to fraud. When it is specifically applied, it
refers to the stealing of persons, that is, kidnapping. Alt's study of this
subject has demonstrated this correspondence especially in Exodus 21:16
and Deuteronomy 24:7, both of which refer to stealing (kidnapping or
enslaving) a citizen of the community.[4] Childs does note that the present
textual form of the command is given a broader scope (as in Deuteronomy
25:16) and may be used generally for any form of dishonesty.[5] While this
general usage is evidenced, it is nonetheless true that when *gnb* is used
with an object in mind, its reference is not specifically to acts of fraud,
but to stealing people.[6]

Other unsupported explanations of the use of *defraud* in Mark 10
include suggestions that it originates from some "Galilean" form of the
decalogue, or that "we must not assume that he is referring only to the
Ten Commandments."[7] Especially interesting is the opinion of E.
Schweizer: "In contrast to the rabbis, Jesus simply reminds him of the
commandments. . . . He quotes from memory the more practical ones
from the second half of the Ten Commandments in a carefree manner
and in random order."[8]

Yet the commands are not random. In contrast to Luke 18:20, the
second table of commands is complete and is quoted in order with the

exception of "Honor your father and mother," which concludes the list.[9] Only Mark includes any reference to fraud.[10] More to the point, Schweizer takes this quotation by Jesus as a cavalier recitation, in part because of the absence of the words "You shall not covet." But there is no indication of this attitude in the text. Jesus gives a straight answer to the man's serious question about eternal life.

One of these various explanations of the absence of the prohibition against covetousness and the presence of *defraud* might suffice were it not for considerable evidence in the intertestamental period that fraud was one of the interpretive proposals made in an effort to answer a larger question. That question had to do with the nature of covetousness. In fact, many commentators do see the phrase "Do not defraud" as a reference to the tenth commandment.[11] It is my intention to uncover the discussion concerning covetousness and fraud that lies historically behind the text.

Jesus' conversation with the rich young ruler in Mark 10 demonstrates a central concern with the theme of covetousness. The evidence will demonstrate that 1) Mark 10 reflects a "conversation" that takes place in the literature of the intertestamental period. Its interest is in whether covetousness is primarily external and observable or is better understood and addressed as an internal problem of the heart. 2) In his quotation of the commandments, Jesus reflects a rabbinic decision that covetousness is externally measurable (as in the practice of fraud), and that the law against it can be kept. 3) In his comment "One thing you lack," Jesus also reflects the pseudepigraphic understanding that covetousness is internal, an engulfing sin that threatens to control the person who does not turn away from it. 4) Finally, Mark 10 echoes the positive use of desire found in the Old Testament. By replacing these positive objects of desire (temple, Torah, God) with himself, Jesus makes a claim that is unprecedented in the previous literature.

The rabbinic material and pseudepigrapha provide fine resources for this conversation. First, however, it is necessary to observe where the discussion concerning covetousness finds its sources in the Old Testament. These texts will not immediately further the argument, but will provide a necessary and familiar starting point for the trajectories of the intertestamental and rabbinic writings.

Old Testament Uses of the Theme of Coveting

"You shall not covet (*ḥmd*) your neighbor's wife and you shall not desire (*'wh*) your neighbor's house, his field nor his manservant, his ox nor his donkey nor anything that belongs to your neighbor" (Deuteronomy 5:12). In this most familiar context, the command against coveting is given as a prohibition, an apodictic command regarding one's relationship to the neighbor. Although the shortened form "You shall not covet" is often used, a survey of the Old Testament usage of the theme of coveting demonstrates that coveting or "desiring" itself is not forbidden.[12]

God covets Zion for his temple (Psalms 68:1; 132:13), and what God desires, he does (Job 23:13). The themes of coveting and desire are used positively for goods (1 Samuel 9:20), land (Isaiah 32:12; Psalm 106:24), homes (Amos 5:11), a lover (Song of Solomon 1:5; 2:3; 5:16), and the temple treasure (Joel 4:5). A more intensified desire is evident in that the temple itself may be coveted (Ezekiel 24:16, 21), the "judgments of the Lord" are to be more desired than gold (Psalm 19:10), and God's name and memory are desired by Judah (Isaiah 26:8, 9). The command forbids desiring what belongs to another. In the pentateuchal usage, this includes the notable examples of the fruit of the tree of knowledge of good and evil and the meat of Egypt.[13]

In the Prophets there are many negative uses of coveting and desire: for example, Aachen's silver (Joshua 7:21), another's fields (Micah 2:2), and young men of Assyria (Ezekiel 23:6). The beauty of an adulteress (Proverbs 6:25) and the delicacies of a selfish man (Proverbs 23:3, 6; 24:1) are but two examples from Proverbs. Both greed (desire for things) and sexual desire are represented in the corpus. In all of these examples, coveting has an object that is forbidden.

Proverbs alone speaks of intense desire (lit. "desiring a desire") without a direct object. Proverbs evidences a concern for coveting as a potential problem for an individual, especially since it may result in slothfulness.[14] Here the interest in coveting and desire is for the sake of a resultant and observable quality of life. Wisdom understands the internal grip of coveting, but makes its arguments by means of what is observable by all.

TWO DYNAMICS OF DESIRE: THE LAW AND THE PROPHETS. The theme of covetousness in the Old Testament may be typified first by Deuteronomy 14:26 and its context: "And you may spend the money for whatever your heart desires, for oxen or sheep or wine or strong drink or whatever your heart asks of you; and there you shall eat before the LORD your God and rejoice, you and your household." This open permission is given at the end of three chapters of laws concerning what is within and what is outside the clean/unclean boundary (Deuteronomy 12-14). "Whatever you desire" in this context means "whatever you desire that I have given for the purpose of desiring." This typifies Old Testament usage in that the positive uses of covetousness presume the restrictions.

The second dynamic evident in Old Testament usage is the theological tension created by the use of 'wh and ḥmd in texts concerning the exile:[15]

2 Chronicles 36:10, 19	to Babylon with desired articles of the house of the LORD
Amos 5:11	pleasant homes destroyed
Isaiah 64:1	precious things are ruined
Jeremiah 25:34	you will fall like a desired vessel
Hosea 9:6	weeds will overtake their coveted silver
Hosea 9:16	I will slay the precious ones of their womb
Hosea 13:15	it will plunder his treasury of every precious article
Lamantations 1:7, 10	precious things lost
Joel 3:5	temple treasure lost
Ezekiel 24:16, 21	the desire of your eyes (wife/temple) is taken away
Ezekiel 26:12	they will destroy your pleasant houses
Zechariah 7:14	they made the desired land desolate

These texts demonstrate the theological tension between what may be desired legally and properly by Israel (the temple splendor) and the harsh reality of the historical outcome. This tension is furthered by the words of Amos 5:18: "Woe to you who long for ('*wh*) the Day of Yahweh."[16] The juxtaposition of even proper desire and sure destruction casts into question the former understanding that one may desire what is given within the boundaries of the law, or even within the boundaries of one's own possession. This may unsettle the reader, or at least raise suspicion about the future of "desire."

SUMMARY AND CONCLUSIONS. 1) There is some textual evidence for an observable distinction in Israel between what may be desired and what may not. This distinction is demonstrated by the presence of both positive and negative uses of *ḥmd* and *'wh* in the canon, as well as by the boundary of the law and the freedom within it, as demonstrated by Deuteronomy 14:26. 2) There is also preliminary evidence for asking about the radicalization of the concept of desire, that is, that desire in itself can be problematic even for the one who desires what is within the boundary (home and family) or at its center (the temple). This is suggested by the use of the word *desire* in the biblical context of God's action to radically remove the object of desire. 3) There is little evidence in the Old Testament for *defraud* as a clear reading of coveting.[17] When "fraud" of the poor is indicated, *apostereō* is used.[18] If the gap between the Old and New Testaments is to be bridged, other written sources are necessary.

Apocrypha

A more radical understanding of the theme of covetousness is evidenced in the Apocrypha. While there are four positive uses of desire, the negative and problematic experiences of coveting predominate.[19] Wisdom of Solomon 4:12 gives us the first translation of *epithumeō* as "concupiscence."[20] Wisdom 16:2, 21 and 19:11 decry the problem of "appetite" (*epithumeō*). Sirach warns the reader against "lust," "concupiscence," or "desires" of the heart.[21] Fourth Maccabees has similar concerns about lust and desire, offering reason and temperance as the means by which one may "root it out" or "rein it in." There is a danger of becoming "enslaved" to it or controlled by it.[22] In these uses, concern for the internal intensification of desire is manifest. While coveting is sometimes externally measurable in its effects, a serious polemic is mounted against its origination in the heart, its grip on the person, and its hiddenness. "Lord, Father and God of my life, give me not a proud look. Turn away concupiscence from me. Let not the greediness of the belly nor lust of the flesh take hold of me and give me not over to an impudent mind" (Ecclesiasticus 23:4-6).

Uses of Coveting in the Pseudepigrapha

In the present line of questioning, we are considering the variety of uses of the theme of covetousness evidenced in the intertestamental era. The pseudepigrapha provide three distinct uses of the theme (besides simply decrying sexual lust or greed). Beyond a simple condemnation of greed and lust, we should ask how the use of the theme implies a theological interpretation or legal application. A few of the texts are concerned with actual deeds, such as fraud. As in the Apocrypha, the theme of covetousness is found in discussions concerning personal, internal control. This second use is predominant in this corpus, while two texts radicalize the power of covetousness even further. They suggest that it is the source of every sin.[23] Each of the following cases is included because of its use of the Greek root *epithum-*. It is variously translated as "covetousness," "desire," "lust," "greed," or "evil desire."

DEEDS. Here we see *desire* used in the context of fraudulent action:

> He did not stop until he succeeded in scattering (them)
> as orphans. He devastated a house because of his *crimi-*

nal desire (*epithumias paranomou*). . . . He is satiated with lawless actions at one place, and then his eyes are on another house to destroy it with agitating word. With all this his soul, like Hades, is not satisfied . . . for they disgracefully empty many people's houses and greedily (*epithumia*) scatter them.[24] (*Psalms of Solomon* 4:10-13, 20; 1st B.C.E.)

Desire (coveting) is applied to criminal practice. *Defraud* is used synonymously with *covet* in 4:22. A similar use is evident in Issachar 4:2 (2nd B.C.E.), where the actions of a proverbial "genuine man" are described.[25]

So also in the *Letter of Aristeas* 211:4 (3rd B.C.E.-1st C.E.), a king is instructed how to rule. When Ptolemy II asks about the qualities of a good king, the advice is given, "A king ought not to desire too much." The advice is repeated in 223:5: "What therefore God gives you, take and keep; do not covet the unattainable." The advice is then rendered to the reader: In everyone, moderation is a good thing.[26]

Pseudo-Philo 9:11-13 (1st C.E.) offers a "go along to get along" sociological argument against covetousness. "You shall not covet your neighbor's house or what he has, lest others should covet your land."[27] In each of these cases the use assumes the observable sociological reality of coveting, as well as a certainty that it can be avoided by the one who wills it. "If someone thinks they render God propitious by means of sacrifice he has deluded himself; he must be honorable, not seduce, commit adultery, steal or slay for gain, or covet. Covet not even a needle's thread for God is nearby and watching you"[28] (*Menander Fragment*; 3rd-2nd B.C.E.).

In another place, the comic poet, repeating a warning of God's "watching," explains the Scripture: "Offer a sacrifice of righteousness and hope in the Lord. Not even a needle, dear friend, should you covet, when it is another's. For God is pleased with just deeds."[29]

ISSUES OF CONTROL. In these texts (primarily from the *Testament of the Twelve Patriarchs*, 2nd B.C.E.), a more internalized reflection on coveting is in evidence. The struggle here is reflected not in the action itself, but in deliberation of the soul. Even more pertinent for our argument is the escalation of the rhetoric to include evil spirits, the blocking of understanding and piety, as well as enslavement and conscience issues.[30]

You heard how Joseph protected himself from promiscuity . . . but his *soul's deliberation rejected evil desire*.[31] (Reuben 4:9; 2nd B.C.E.)

In sexual promiscuity there is *no place for understanding
nor piety* and every passion dwells in *its desire*.[32] (Reuben
6:4)

Take care to be temperate with wine, my children; for
there are in it *four evil spirits: desire*, heated passion, de-
bauchery, and sordid greed.[33] (Judah 16:1)

For those who are two-faced are not of God, but *they
are enslaved by their evil desires*, so they might be pleasing to Belair and persons like themselves.[34] (Asher 3:2)

Here we see that enslavement by desire leads to the clouding of the
mental faculty. "For if anyone is subjected to *the passion of desire and is
enslaved by it,* as she [Potifer's wife] was, even when he hears something
good bearing on that passion he receives it as aiding his wicked desire"[35]
(Joseph 7:8).

One's control of covetousness has implications even for one's direct relation to God. This comes from advice concerning controlling
one's covetous desire: "If you hear some thunder do not flee as long as you
have nothing on your conscience, master. For God is nearby and watching you"[36] (*Menander Fragment;* 2nd-3rd B.C.E.).

In Testament of Dan 4:5 a fearsome threat to the soul from a sinis-
ter source is opened by one's coveting (*epithumeō*). The argument is that,
when one is perturbed by desire for what is transitory, the Lord withdraws
and Belair rules the soul.[37] While this understanding rivals the degree of
Paul's radicalization of covetousness in Romans 7, it still assumes that
one may successfully fight against it. The third category, however, is an
interesting parallel to Paul's radicalized usage.

THE SOURCE OF SIN AND EVIL. This is the most radicalized and
internalized conception of covetousness in the pseudepigraphic literature. "He . . . sprinkled his evil poison on the fruit which he gave me to
eat which is his covetousness. For covetousness is the origin of every
sin"[38] (*Life of Adam and Eve* 19:3; 1st C.E.).

The origin of evil spirits in the world is also explained by means of
covetousness. *First Enoch* 15:8 (2nd B.C.E.-1st C.E.; considerably earlier
than the *Life of Adam and Eve*) posits that they originated in covetousness of the Watchers for the daughters of men. Enoch is called to inter-
cede and to scold the Watchers for this desire and its outcome.[39]

SUMMARY AND CONCLUSIONS. We have observed that at least
two readings of the theme of covetousness developed in the literature of
the intertestamental period. The first regarded coveting as an observable
offense, related to the deeds of criminals, which genuine men, good kings,
and good neighbors will not do and against which God, who is pleased
with just deeds, always watches. The keeping of this reading of the law

against covetousness is possible. The second reading radicalized and internalized the law, claiming that coveting had its roots in the very origins of sin and that this impulse to covet might lead to the bondage or possession of even the faithful. Before we return to Mark 10, we will test this hypothetical twofold interpretation of the law with the rabbis.

Covetousness in the Rabbinic Texts

What uses of the theme of coveting are made in the mishnaic and midrashic texts? This is the operative question in seeking to understand how the command against coveting is understood by the rabbis. The six primary texts that follow demonstrate an important historical shift and rabbinic decision in interpreting the problem of covetousness.

The Mishnah does not usually quote the Ten Commandments directly.[40] Rabbis include the first texts below, however, as part of the discussion of the tenth commandment, the prohibition against covetousness. Coveting is interpreted in relation to the following commandments:[41]

> Leviticus 25:36-7: Do not take usurious interest from him, but revere your God, that your brother may live with you. You shall not give him your silver at interest, nor your food for gain.

> Exodus 22:25-26: If you lend money to my people, to the poor with you, you are not to be a creditor to him; you shall not lay interest upon him. If you ever take your neighbor's cloak as a pledge you are to return it to him before the sun sets.

> Leviticus 19:13-14: You shall not oppress your neighbor, nor rob him. The wages of a hired man are not to remain with you all night until morning. You shall not curse a deaf man, nor place a stumbling block before the blind, but you shall revere your God; I am the LORD.

The focus in the Mishnah text itself is on subtle forms of usury, especially on the prohibition of "apple/orange" type deals in which the more naive may be disadvantaged. The text describes practices that may result in a net loss for the disadvantaged, litigating against the possibility of gain by means of trickery or even by a lender's advantage. It is used in the rabbinic tradition as a practical application of the law against coveting.

MISHNAH, NEZIKIN, BABA MESIA ("DAMAGES, MIDDLE GATE"). Consider the following passage:

> 9. A man may not say to his fellow, "Lend me a *kor* of wheat and I will repay thee at threshing-time," but he

may say, "Lend it to me until my son comes," or "until I find the key." But Hillel used to forbid [even] this. Moreover Hillel used to say: A woman may not lend a loaf of bread to her neighbor unless she determines its value in money, lest wheat should rise in price and they be found partakers in usury.[42]

In the next paragraph one sees further how a fence is set against the possibility of fraudulent dealings in common interactions.

> 10. A man may say to his fellow, "Help me to weed and I will help thee to weed," or "Help me to hoe and I will help thee to hoe." But he may not say, "help me to weed and I will help thee to hoe" or "Help me to hoe and I will help thee to weed." All days of the dry season are accounted alike and all days of the rainy season are accounted alike. A man may not say to another, "Help me to plough in the dry season and I will help thee to plough in the rainy season." Rabban Gamaliel says: There is usury that is paid in advance and usury that is paid afterward.[43]

Establishing the principle that labor in the rainy season may not be counted equal to labor in the dry season assumes an audience in which some kind of deceit was being practiced to the disadvantage of the un-witting neighbor, or that some advantage was being exercised over those who had no choice. This kind of "hidden" usury within the community is forbidden as an observable form of coveting one's neighbor's fiscal re-sources. This applied interpretation of coveting can be, and is, legislated against.[44]

MEKHILTA R. ISHMAEL, BESHALLAH ("WHEN HE LET GO," EXO-DUS 13:17). The Mekhilta is commenting here on the Tosefta Sot. 4:7. There Moses floats the metal coffin of Joseph from its interment in the Nile.[45] Then the coffin of Joseph ascends to the presence of God along-side the ark, which contains the Ten Commandments. The explanation is an account, from proof texts, that Joseph kept the commandments. Thus Joseph's "ark" goes with the ark that contains the commands—the commands and a premier command-keeper, together.[46]

> A. And not only so, but with Jacob went up the retinue of Pharaoh and the elders of his palace, and with Jo-seph went up the ark and the presence of God, the priests, the Levites and all Israel, and the seven clouds of glory.
>
> B. And not only so, but the coffin of Joseph went along-

side the ark of the One Who Lives Forever.

C. And the nations of the world said to the Israelites, "What is the character of these two arks?"

D. And they replied to them, "This is the ark of the One Who Lives Forever and that is the ark of a corpse."

E. And the nations of the world said to them, "What is interred in the ark of the corpse, that it goes along with the ark of the One Who Lives Forever?"

F. And they replied to them, "The one who is interred in this ark carried out what is written concerning the one who is interred in that ark.

G. "Concerning the one that is interred in this ark it is written, 'I am the Lord your God' (Exodus 20:2), and of Joseph: 'For am I in the place of God?' (Genesis 50:19).

H. "Concerning the one that is interred in this ark it is written, 'You shall have no other gods before me' (Exodus 20:3), and of Joseph: 'For I fear God' (Genesis 42:18).

The text continues in this way, demonstrating how Joseph kept each of the Ten Commandments, but omitting the especially relevant and expected "You shall not commit adultery." This tension is resolved with the tenth commandment:

22.Q. "You shall not covet" (Exodus 20:14), and he did not covet the wife of Potifer.

This Mekhilta shows that the commandments can be kept. This includes covetousness, which here has been specifically applied as adultery. The law against covetousness is used here as a central means to Joseph's honor alongside the ark of God, before the nations. The implication is that, by association with Joseph in keeping these commands, the community of faith (offering here no other warrant) will also share in that honor. Let us note especially that obedience to the command is rendered both visible and possible.[47]

MISHNAH, NASHIM, NEDARIM (WOMEN, VOWS). Covetousness is legislated against here, in a variety of conceivable ways, by the multiplication of conditions and words. The effect is that covetousness has been translated from an apodictic command into a casuistic literary context. This oral expansion of the law closes the loopholes through which one might, in this case, help a neighbor avoid paying a variety of offerings.

1.4 If a man said, "May what I eat of thine be a Whole-offering," or "a Meal-offering," or "a Sin-offering," or "a Thank-offering," or "a Peace-offering," it is forbidden to him. But R. Judah permits it. If a man said, "may what I eat of thine be the *Korban*," or "as a *Korban*," or "a *Korban*," it is forbidden to him. . . . If a man said to his fellow, "May my mouth that speaks with thee" or "my hand that works with thee" or "my foot that walks with thee," "be *Konam*," [such an act] is forbidden to him.[48]

While again the word *covetousness* is not used here, it is the theme against which these laws are given.[49] A specific application is made here against the attempted fraud of God. The rabbis, taking the law against covetousness (together with the positive laws of required offering) with complete pragmatism, legislate against those who creatively release their neighbor from an obligation to make an offering to God.[50] In this way their neighbor is fiscally indebted to them, at God's expense.[51] The focus here is on an observable form of covetousness (fraud of God). The operative assumption is that, although people may be very creative in their attempts to avoid this kind of coveting, it can successfully be legislated against.

MEKHILTA BAHODESH.

A. On the one [tablet] was written, "Honor your father and your mother,"

B. And opposite it, "You shall not covet your neighbor's wife."

C. "Scripture thus indicates that whoever covets in the end will produce a son who curses his father and honors one who is not his father."

D. "Thus the Ten Commandments were given, five on this tablet, and five on that," the words of R. Hananiah b. Gamaliel.[52]

Coveting is used here specifically for adultery. The text implies that coveting a neighbor's wife might as well be equated with adultery. There is no room here for identifying coveting as an internal lusting that takes no action. The coveting referred to here is the kind that is necessarily acted upon. "Whoever covets" in this way "will" produce a son.

MIDRASH RABBA, VAYYIKRA ("AND THE LORD CALLED"; LEVITICUS 1:1 FF.) This text tells how the patriarchs, all in their own ways, fulfilled the Torah. The Ten Commandments are included here with a pronouncement of Joseph's fulfillment.[53]

2.10 Joseph fulfilled what is written in the Torah, in which it is said, "Honor thy father. Thou shalt not murder. Thou shalt not commit adultery. Thou shalt not steal. Thou shalt not bear false witness. . . . Thou shalt not covet," etc. (Exodus 20:12 ff.). Even though unto them the Torah had not yet been given, they fulfilled it of their own accord. For this reason the Holy One, blessed be He, loved them with a complete love, and made their name like unto His own great name. Of them He said: "Happy are they who are perfect in the way (Psalm 119:1). "

The argument is that "because they fulfilled commands . . . therefore God loved them with a complete love." The commands function here as a path to God's complete love. For this reason, 1) he loved them with a complete love; 2) he made their name like unto his own; and 3) he said, "Happy are they." These three incentives are given for keeping the commandments. For our purposes, we must finally ask (as the rabbis do in the following final text) how this is possible.

MEKHILTA BAHODESH (54.4.2). The following text has two interests: 1) to state what specifically is included in the prohibition against covetousness, and 2) to prove that only actual deeds are violations of the command. The pertinent problem is raised at G. below. General covetousness could include a desire for almost anything. Therefore, the rabbis ask, "How general is this command?" Here four key decisions are made regarding the limitations of the scope of the prohibition against coveting: 1) The rule of specification, not of generalization, pertains to this command (H). 2) Whatever can be bought or sold is included (J). 3) Whatever can come into one's domain only with the owner's consent is covered by the prohibition (N). (Here one's wife is also covered.) 4) Actual deeds, not words (much less emotions or thoughts), are the only liability covered by this command (R).

Here is the text (54.4.2):

A. "You shall not covet your neighbor's house":

B. This is a generalization.

C. ". . . you shall not covet your neighbor's wife or his manservant or his maidservant or his ox or his ass":

D. These are particularizations.

E. When there is a generalization followed by a specific spelling out of matters, covered by the generalization is only what is made explicit in the specific spelling out of matters.

F. But when Scripture says, "or anything that is your neighbor's," it reverts and presents a generalization once again.

G. But perhaps the generalization at the end is the same as at the beginning?

H. You must say no. Rather what we have is a case in which there is a generalization, a specification of individual items, followed by a generalization.

I. In which case you compose a classification that accords with the details that are spelled out.

J. Just as the details are made explicit that we deal with something which one acquires and one can sell off, so whatever can be bought or sold (is covered by the prohibition against covetousness) . . .

N. And just as the details are characterized by the indicative trait that they come into one's domain only with the owner's consent, so whatever can come into one's domain only with the owner's consent (is covered by the prohibition against covetousness).

O. What is excluded is your coveting his daughter for your son or his son for your daughter.

P. Perhaps covered by the commandment is even expressing covetousness in words?

Q. Scripture states, "You shall not covet the silver or gold that is on them so that you take it for yourself" (Deuteronomy 7:25).

R. Just as in that passage one incurs liability only when one actually does a deed, so here too *one is liable only if one does an actual deed.*[54]

This text describes and proves what is included by the commandment so that it may be kept, so that all know that one incurs liability only when one actually does a deed (R) because the details are made explicit (J).

A scriptural warrant for these rulings is given in Q.: "Scripture states, 'You shall not covet the silver or gold that is on them so that you take it for yourself' (Deuteronomy 7:25)." This represents a typical method of rabbinic interpretation. Any verse of Scripture may be interpreted by another.[55] Here the proof is given that the word "covet" (ḥmḏ) is *limited to* "taking" (lqḥ).

CONCLUSION. The importance of this rabbinic decision is that covetousness is rendered both observable by the community and personally manageable. This law can be kept because it is limited to actual action and to what can be observed.

As we turn back to the Mark 10 text we must note that it is only because the rabbis are aware of the problem of the radical internalization of the law (that is, the problem of desire controlling one's heart) that they define it as they do, in order to make keeping the law possible and observable.[56] It is my argument that Jesus' comments to the rich young ruler reflect positively this defined understanding of coveting. It is precisely from this understanding that he says, "Do not defraud" rather than "You shall not covet."

Two Kinds of Coveting in Mark 10:17-22

It has long been recognized that a central theme of this text is a concern for the allegiance or desire of the heart.[57] This concern is perhaps most easily recognized in verse 22: "But at these words his face fell, and he went away grieved, for he was one who owned much property." More specifically, this text is concerned with the problem of covetousness and two distinct solutions. The key to the distinction is signaled by the word *defraud*.

The two understandings of law, which we have observed in the intertestamental and rabbinic literature, are necessarily linked by the use of the word *defraud* in place of *covet*. The theme of the text has everything to do with what the man desires most. The juxtaposition, therefore, of the so-called misquote of the commandment against covetousness is significant. If the content of the encounter with Jesus did not have as its subject the desire for riches and its binding effect (even to the loss of his eternal life), the use of *defraud* might be dismissed. But because it is the theme, the reader is invited to notice the tension. The tension sets the necessity of both the internal goal (freedom from desire's captivity) and the external form (do not defraud) of law in mutual relief.

ALL THESE I HAVE KEPT: THE EXTERNAL FORM (MORPHĒ) OF THE LAW. "'You know the commandments, Do not murder, Do not commit adultery, Do not steal, Do not bear false witness, Do not defraud, Honor your father and mother.' And he said to him, 'Teacher, I have kept all these things from my youth up.' And looking at him, Jesus felt a love for him" (Mark 10:19-21a).

By saying, "You know the commandments," Jesus shows how highly he esteems the Law as containing the norm of conduct.[58] Jesus accepts without question the ruler's claim that he has kept the external form (*morphē*) of the commandments. He assumes that such keeping is possible (Mark 10:20). While Jesus critiques the tradition of the elders, he does not attack the commandments. The response of the pious man, "All these I have observed from my youth," does not earn a rebuke. Jesus does not question the man's integrity. The commandments can be kept.[59] The law is measurable and its keeping observable. This is especially evident in the formulation "You shall not defraud."[60] This law can be kept. Jesus immediately accepts it.[61] The assumption, moreover, is that it must be kept to inherit eternal life.

GO, SELL, GIVE, AND YOU WILL HAVE TREASURE IN HEAVEN: THE RADICALIZATION OF THE LAW. "'You lack one thing; go, sell what you own, and give the money to the poor, and you will have treasure in heaven; then come, follow me.' When he heard this, his face fell and he went away grieving, for he had many possessions" (Mark 10:21b-22).

Jesus says, "One thing you lack." For this lack he commands two actions: sell, and follow me. In the first command, "Go, sell all you possess and give it to the poor, and you shall have treasure in heaven," he reflects the radicalized understanding of the command "You shall not covet." It is radicalized in that the object of his desire is his own property.[62] Under the measurable law, this is no crime. Jesus then adds that, as a part of his wholeness, his treasure (the object of his desire) will be located in heaven.[63]

The ruler's response echoes the intensified theme of captivity to desire found in the pseudepigrapha.[64] The expression "He went away, grieved" indicates that he was in emotional conflict, either unwilling or unable to meet the criteria given. Both by his question (What shall I do?) and by his response (grief), his interior conflict is indicated. The locus of that conflict is his own wealth ("For he was one who owned much property."). Jesus' admonition is to sell it, not only for the sake of the poor, but in order to escape its grip. His sadness in walking away confirms that grip for the reader.

Jesus says, "How hard it will be for those who are wealthy to enter the kingdom of God" (10:23). This amazes the disciples, who have been brought up on the rabbinic teaching that worldly wealth, though it involves great responsibility, is on the whole a sign of God's favor and an advantage for those who desire to keep the law.[65]

The same double radicalization of the law (that is, captivation by interior covetousness and captivation by legitimately owned wealth) is evident in the other Synoptics. The observable form of the law "You shall not defraud" is not present in Matthew or Luke. They simply omit any reference to coveting at all. It may be that this omission rhetorically sets up Jesus' response. What the ruler lacks is that he covets, in the radical sense of the word, so he cannot follow Jesus. He is captivated by his desire for his own wealth. This stands as the insurmountable obstacle to his discipleship.[66]

SUMMARY. The law against coveting has a radical dimension, which is enjoined by Jesus in addition to observable command keeping. The fulfillment is only possible, this text argues, by the transfer of the ruler's desire away from his own possessions (that which has the possibility of possessing the heart of the owner). The internal goal of the law is freedom from covetousness, that is, freedom from desire's captivity. The text argues that this is possible only by the ruler's obedience to the command to go, sell, and give. The implied argument is that to escape this kind of covetousness, or to fulfill the law against it, you will need to be with Jesus. In this sense, Jesus claims to be the *telos* of the law.

THEN COME, FOLLOW ME: THE INTERNAL GOAL (*TELOS*) OF THE LAW. "'Good Teacher, what shall I do to inherit eternal life?' And Jesus said to him, 'Why do you call me good? No one is good except God alone. . . .' And looking at him, Jesus felt a love for him, and said to him . . . 'Come, follow me'" (Mark 10:17, 21).

The second command Jesus gave for the sake of the ruler's eternal life was "Follow me." This is an unprecedented move in the literature. In these words, Jesus has made himself the only legitimate object or goal (*telos*) of radicalized desire. He says, "I am the way to inheritance of eternal life." This may be construed as blasphemy if he is not God. The precedents for positive uses of a radicalized covetousness in the Old Testament include the Torah, the temple, and the name and the memory of God.[67]

There is another fruitful comparison to a text we have noted previously. Here we are reminded that God loved Joseph because he kept the commandments. "For this reason the Holy One, blessed be He, loved them with a complete love, and made their name like unto His own great name. Of them He said: 'Happy are they who are perfect in the way'" (Psalm 119:1).[68]

Why does Mark say that Jesus looked at the ruler and loved (*ēgapēsen*) him? Certainly because he kept the commands. Although there is no causal link between these texts, Mark certainly echoes the understanding of the previous literature, in which the complete Torah keeper, Joseph, is "loved completely" by God. This claim by Mark about Jesus may even be consonant with the claim that he is the Son of God (Mark 1:1). A midrashic exegetical warrant might suffice for this linking of texts, but it need not stand alone. Both of these texts are set in the context of a discussion on the nature of radicalized covetousness. Both make ultimate claims about the way to eternal life. Moreover, the echo of the Shema in Jesus' response, "No one is good but God alone," ironically signals his claim to be the *telos* of the law-keeping.[69]

SUMMARY. This text makes the claim that in Jesus a positive radical covetousness finds its true goal. There is precedent in the Old Testament for this kind of positive reversal in the theme of covetousness (Ezekiel

24:16, 21; Psalm 19:10; Isaiah 26:8, 9). The claim that Jesus is the locus of desire for the one seeking eternal life may be seen as an offense, inasmuch as the former scriptural objects commended were the temple, the Torah, and God's own name and memory. Moreover, the references to "God alone" and to Jesus' unconditional love for the man who had kept the commandments echo scriptural and rabbinic claims made only about God.

Conclusion

It has been the thesis of this paper that Jesus' conversation with the rich young ruler in Mark 10 demonstrates a central concern for the theme of covetousness. The task was to demonstrate that: 1) Mark 10 reflects a "conversation" that takes place in the literature of the intertestamental period. Its interest was whether covetousness is primarily external and observable or is better understood and addressed as an internal problem of the heart. 2) In his quotation of the commandments, Jesus reflects a rabbinic decision that covetousness is externally measurable (as in the practice of fraud), and that the law against it can be kept. 3) In his comment "One thing you lack," Jesus also reflects the intertestamental understanding that covetousness is internal, an engulfing sin that threatens control of the person who does not turn away from it. 4) Finally, Mark 10 echoes the positive use of desire found in the Old Testament. By replacing these positive objects of desire (temple, Torah, God) with himself, Jesus makes a claim upon humanity that is unprecedented in the previous literature.

Finally, we may generally conclude from our inquiry into the uses of the law against covetousness that, in the first century C.E., three responses to the experience of the radical internalization of sin are discernible. The rabbinic response was to radically externalize the law, so that it could be observed and measured by the community of faith. Their primary means of externalizing were to extensively define and describe the law, as is done in the Mishnah. The second response was the belief that, in addition to external holiness, interior holiness was possible. This was the response of the Qumran community and may be called the radical internalization of the law.[70] It may also be seen in the Sermon on the Mount. Third, the Mark 10 response reflects both concepts. The external validity of law is recognized as a useful but not primary means for the God-human relationship. On the other hand, the law is radically internalized, but unto hopelessness, not unto hope. It functions to demonstrate the impossibility of inner human righteousness, finding hope for righteousness through faith in the righteousness of God, Jesus Christ.

When preaching and teaching God's commandments in the church, it is helpful to remember both uses of the law found in Mark 10. We may strongly teach that the laws of God ought to be kept and can be kept in their outward form. This is necessary for the sake of order in the life of the community and the well-being of the individual. In biblical tradition, this is especially necessary for the sake of the weaker members of society, particularly children. Simultaneously, it is our calling also to declare that God's commands cannot be wholly kept. When we plumb our hearts and motivations, we are fugitives from the law. We are driven from the holy God, or else to Jesus and the cross for forgiveness and freedom from the bondage of the law offered in the one who calls us by name.

Endnotes

1. C. S. Mann, *Mark* (Garden City, N.Y.: Doubleday & Co., 1986), 400.

2. W. Lane, *The Gospel According to Mark* (Grand Rapids: Eerdmans Publishing Co., 1974), 366.

3. Erich Klostermann in F. C. Grant, *The Interpreter's Bible*, Vol. 7, G. Buttrick, ed. (New York: Abingdon, 1951), 802.

4. A. Alt, "Das Verbot des Diebstahls im Dekalog," *Kleine Schriften* I (1953), 333-40. Also M. Noth, *Exodus*, trans. J. S. Bowden (Philadelphia: Westminster, 1962), 165-66.

5. B. Childs, *The Book of Exodus* (Philadelphia: Westminster, 1974), 423-24; cf. also T. Fretheim, *Exodus* (Louisville: John Knox, 1991), 235-36.

6. In the Masoretic Text fraud is designated by *'šq* and in the LXX by *apostereō*. See specific uses of *apostereō* below. The Greek for "steal" is *kleptō*. Its usage is very general, although it too can be used specifically for stealing people (cf. Matthew 24:43; Luke 12:39; 1Thessalonians 5:2). W. Bauer, *A Greek-English Lexicon of the New Testament and Other Early Christian Literature*, 2d ed., trans. W. F. Arndt and R. W. Gingrich (Chicago: University of Chicago Press, 1957), 434.

7. Ernst Lohmeyer in Grant, *The Interpreter's Bible*, 802.

8. E. Schweizer, *The Good News According to Mark*, trans. D. Madvig (Atlanta: John Knox Press, 1970), 211.

9. Taylor, et al., raise the question of the accretion of the parental command. V. Taylor, *The Gospel According to St. Mark* (Grand Rapids: Baker Book House, 1981), 428.

10. Cf. Matthew 19:20 and Luke 18:20

11. "Most commentators," Taylor, *St. Mark*, 428. "Some commentators," Mann, *Mark*, 400.

12. *'wh* occurs forty-five times and *ḥmd* occurs fifty-eight times in the MT. They are generally translated as "desire" and "covet" respectively. Sometimes, however, the reverse occurs. *'wh* is usually thought to be the more inward desire, but the distinction does not always hold. The LXX translates both as *epithumēo*, even in Deuteronony 5, where the Hebrew verbs occur together. As always, context determines the English translation, which results in rendering both the Hebrew and the Greek as covetousness, desire, precious, pleasant, fitting, trea-

sure, longed for, lust, appetite, concupiscence, and craving.

13. Genesis 2:9; 3:6; Numbers 11:4-5,18, 34-35; 33:16-17; Deuteronomy 9:22. Both *'wh* and *ḥmd* are used in the Genesis 3:6 text. Cf. also Deuteronomy 7:25.

14. Proverbs 13:12; 18:1; 21:26; 1:22.

15. For the variety of English renderings of *'wh* and *ḥmd*, cf. footnote 12. These texts represent about 15 percent of the Old Testament usage of these verbs.

16. Jeremiah 17:16 expresses a similar tension between desire and woe: "I have not longed for the woeful day."

17. There is a clear and consistent LXX usage of the infrequent word *defraud* or *rob* (*apostereō*). The LXX and Apocrypha use it eight times in six texts. Every occurrence except one has a poor laborer as its object, with the command or admonition not to defraud him. The biblical usage of *defraud*, therefore, is limited to a very specific and observable transgression. This specific meaning also persists in the only other New Testament occurrences, 1 Corinthians 6:7-8 and 7:5.

18. Exodus 21:10; Deuteronomy 24:14; Malachi 3:5; Ecclesiasticus 4:1; 29:1,7; 31:21-22.

19.The positive uses are found in Ecclesiasticus 6:37; 14:14; 3:29 and Wisdom of Solomon 6:17, 20. *Desire* in these texts is for wisdom, goodness, the ability to listen, and discipline.

20. C. L. Brenton, *The Septuagint with Apocrypha* (Peabody, Mass: Hendrickson Publishers, 1986). Webster's notes the source of the English: Covet > convoiter (F) > cupiditare (L); *covet* is therefore from the same root as *cupiscence*. *Webster's New International Dictionary*, Second Edition, Unabridged. W. A. Neilson, ed. (Springfield: G. & C. Merriam Co., 1944).

21. Ecclesiasticus 5:1; 16:1; 18:30-31; 20:4; 23:5.

22. 4 Maccabees 1:3, 22, 31, 32; 2:1, 4, 6; 3:2, 11, 12, 16; 5:23.

23. 1 Enoch 15:4, 8; Life of Adam and Eve 19:3; cf. discussion below.

24. J. H. Charlesworth, *The Old Testament Pseudepigrapha*, 2 vols. (Garden City, New York: Doubleday and Co., 1983/1985), 656; cf. also *Psalms of Solomon* 14:7.

25. Issachar 4:2

26. Charlesworth, *Pseudepigrapha*, vol. 2, 27.

27. Ibid., 319.

28. Ibid., 830.

29. Ibid.

30. Cf. also Reuben 5:6-7; 6:4; Issachar 4:2-4.

31. Charlesworth, *Pseudepigrapha*, vol. 1, 784.

32. Ibid., 784.

33. Ibid., 799; cf. also Judah 13:2 f.; 14:1, 3.

34. Ibid., 817; cf. Asher 6:4-5.

35. Ibid., 821; cf. Joseph 3:10; 4:8; 7:6, 7; 9:1.

36. Charlesworth, *Pseudepigrapha*, vol. 2, 830.

37. Charlesworth, *Pseudepigrapha*, vol. 1, 809.

38. R. H. Charles, *Apocrypha and Pseudepigrapha of the Old Testament*, vol. 2 (Oxford: Clarendon Press, 1966), 279; *Life of Adam and Eve* 19:3 (Apocalypse of Moses).

39. Cf. also 1 Enoch 6:2; 15:4-8.

40. Only three times is the sabbath law quoted, and once the command against false witness.

41. R. A. Hyman, *Torah ha-kethubah Vehamessurah*, vol. 1 (Tel-Aviv: Dvir Publishing Co., 1979), 131, 283. Solomon Goldman, *The Ten Commandments* (Chicago: University of Chicago Press, 1956), 186-87. This traditional reading is also given in Schachter's edition of *The Babylonian Talmud*, vol. 5 (London: Soncino Press, 1935), 240, and in vol. 6, 740. See the general index under the word *covet*.

42. *The Mishnah*, trans. H. Danby (Oxford: Oxford University Press, 1933), 355-57; Mishnah 4.2.5, paragraphs 1-11.

43. Ibid., 357.

44. The Tosefta text that follows Mishnah 4.2.5 expands the mishnaic comments on usury by false assessment of property and usury by means of a second party. Its import is that usury may be practiced with Gentiles, but not between Jews. If a Gentile converts to Judaism, previous interest may not be collected. The idea of covetousness is used here as a control for equity within the community of faith. This kind of observable coveting is bad for corporate life. J. Neusner, *Tosefta*, vol. 4 (New York: KTAV Publishing House, 1981), 100-104.

45. The Tosefta commentary is on Exodus 13:19 ("And Moses took the bones of Joseph with him").

46. *Mekhilta According to Rabbi Ishmael*, vol. 1, trans. J. Neusner (Atlanta: Scholars Press, 1988), 129; Mekhilta 4.1.22 (Beshallah 22).

47. When "the nations" (rather, someone in the community) ask about Joseph's coffin (ark) and the ark of Moses, an accounting of Joseph's command-keeping will provide the answer. The argument is given in relation to the nations, but this must be a pedagogical device for the community of faith. This setting belies the setting of the community over against the nations. Eschatological arguments for command-keeping are made typically by communities in crisis or by marginalized communities. "Glory" and "an eternal place" were given to Joseph because of his command-keeping.

48. *The Mishnah* 3.3.1, trans. Danby, 264-65.

49. Cf. note 41.

50. Cf. a similar problem regarding *Korban* in Josephus, *Wars*, 2.9.4, and in Mark 7:11.

51. Cf. Nedarim 1.2 in *The Mishnah*, trans. Danby, 264. "If a man said to his fellow, '*Konam*' or '*Konah*' or '*Konas*' . . . " These words are substitutes for *Korban*, by which one could also slip through a loophole by communicating the exchange with a neighbor without formally breaking the law. This tractate seeks to close those loopholes by describing eventualities by which an act of fraud against God might be perpetrated. The operative assumption is that this kind of measurable covetousness may be stopped by means of this kind of legislation.

52. Circa 80-120 C.E. *Mekhilta*, vol. 2, trans. J. Neusner, 87; Mekhilta Bahodesh 54.3.5.

53. *The Midrash*, vol. 4., H. Freedman, ed. (London: Soncino Press, 1939), 30; Vayyikra 2:10.

54. *Mekhilta*, vol. 2, trans. J. Neusner, 87; Mekhilta Bahodesh 54.4.2.

55. For R. Ishmael's eleven principles of interpretation, cf. the introduction to the Sifra. Also on the exegetical rules, cf. E. Schurer, *The History of the Jewish People in the Age of Jesus Christ*, vol. 2, ed. G. Vermes, F. Millar, and M. Black (Edinburgh: T. & T. Clark, 1973-1987), 343-44.

56. Even today, where there is a discussion of the law against coveting, the question of whether it is internal desire or external action that constitutes actual coveting is raised. For example, see Fretheim, *Exodus*, 237; B. Childs, *The*

Book of Exodus, 425; G. von Rad, Deuteronomy, 59; M. Noth, Exodus, 166. The discussion is motivated by exactly this question. Can it be kept? Adultery, murder, false witness, etc., lend themselves to observable social measure. Does coveting? Is it to be defined as an outward action or an internal emotion? It is not surprising to discover that both interpretations have voices in the literature.
    57. D. H. Juel, Mark (Minneapolis: Augsburg Fortress, 1990), 142; D. E. Nineham, The Gospel of Saint Mark (Baltimore: Penguin Books, 1963), 272; Lane, Mark, 368; Taylor, St. Mark, 430.
    58. Taylor, St. Mark, 427.
    59. Juel, Mark, 142. Nineham says, "'You know the commandments' is no mere reminder but part of the answer to the man's question about eternal life." Nineham, Saint Mark, 273. Cf. also Mann, Mark, 400.
    60. Taylor reviews the textual variants on page 428. On defraud: apostereō in the LXX is used overwhelmingly to denote protection of the powerless, especially the needy laborer. So also in Sirach. Exodus 21:10; Deuteronomy 24:14; Malachi 3:5; Ecclesiasticus 4:1; 29:1, 7; 31:21-22.
    61. Also in Luke 18:22/Matthew 19:21.
    62. I. Abrahams, Studies in Pharisaism and the Gospels (New York: KTAV Publishing House, 1967), 113 ff. There had been since the time of the psalmists an understanding by some in Israel that the poor equals good and pious, and the rich equals sinners. Taylor says that Jesus' standpoint is nearer to that of the Rechabites and the Essenes. Taylor, St. Mark, 429. Cf. also Nineham, who notes that there is more than one tradition concerning wealth, that even one's own wealth can be a temptation in Judaism. Nineham, Saint Mark, 271.
    63. Epithum- is translated as "treasure," "that which is desired" (a synonym of thēsaur), in Daniel 11:38, 43; 2 Chronicles 20:25; 36:10, 19; et al.; cf. "For where your treasure is there will your heart be also," Matthew 6:20-21.
    64. A similar use is predominant in the pastorals.
    65. Nineham, Saint Mark, 271.
    66. For the problem of desiring one's possessions in Luke-Acts, cf. D. Juel, Luke-Acts, (Atlanta: John Knox, 1983), 91-92.
    67. The temple itself may be coveted (Ezekiel 24:16, 21), the "judgments of the Lord" are to be more desired than gold (Psalm 19:10), and God's name and memory are desired by Judah (Isaiah 26:8, 9).
    68. The Midrash, vol. 4., H. Freedman, ed. (London: Soncino Press, 1939), 30; Vayyikra 2.10.
    69. On the ironic God-talk in Mark, cf. Juel, Mark, 228.
    70. For this idea, which has not been dealt with in this paper, cf. H. Braun, "Römer 7:7-25 und das Selbstverständnis des Qumran-Frommen" Zeitschrift für Theologie und Kirche 56 (1959):1-18; and H. Braun, Qumran und das Neue Testament, 2 vols. (Tübingen: Mohr Seibeck, 1966).

"The Servant of the Lord": Israel (Isaiah 42:1-4) and Jesus (Matthew 12:18-21)

PETER FIEDLER

The Gospel of Matthew is well known for its fulfillment/formula quotations. The longest of these, Matthew 12:18-21, is introduced in verse 17 as a word of God through Isaiah the prophet (Isaiah 42:1-4) and explicitly set in the context of verses 15 ff. At first glance this connection with the context seems to exist only for Matthew 12:19, 20a, b. Jesus does not intend to continue the confrontation with Pharisaic adversaries after dealing with them in defense of his disciples (12:1-8) and in the incident of the man with the withered hand (12:9-14). But why didn't Matthew confine himself to quoting Isaiah 42:2, 3b? Is it because he depends on a source containing biblical proof texts? Is there actually a text in Matthew with which such a source might be connected to Isaiah 42:1-4? There is none. The pre-Matthean source of Matthew 12:12-16 is obviously the Gospel of Mark. The same difficulties arise in the following units where there is a mixture of Markan and Q passages.

If Matthew 12:17-21 is to be considered as redactional material, then what is Matthew's purpose here? Can a relationship with the closer and wider context be ascertained?[1] What christological and ecclesiological consequences can be derived from this passage? Are they in accordance with the biblical text cited? Have they been influenced by Matthew's polemics against the Pharisees? And last, but not least, if the answers to these questions are to be of any help for our faith as Christians, we must consider the question: how can the Matthean "fulfillment quotation" be understood in the light of today's Jewish-Christian dialogue? In view of this question, we must be aware that the relationship between Christianity and Judaism today substantially differs from the relationship between Matthew and his church on the one hand and a synagogue community and its Pharisaic leaders on the other.

Synoptic Comparisons

In 9:17 Matthew quotes the Markan story (2:22), and in 12:1 he returns to it (Mark 2:23). These pericopes, Mark 2:23-28 (par Matthew 12:1-8: plucking corn on the Sabbath) and Mark 3:1-6 (par Matthew 12:9-14: healing of the man with the withered hand on the Sabbath), are followed by a summary of Jesus' preaching and healing activities. These are further connected with the command to the evil spirits (as to healed persons) not to tell who he is (Mark 3:7-12). Matthew 12:15 f. has significantly abbreviated and changed the Markan text he had already used in 4:24 f. In verse 15a Matthew adds that Jesus knew the Pharisaic intentions against him. His departure turns out to be a deliberate "retiring from confrontation"[2] (cf. 12:19).

In 12:15b the evangelist writes, "Jesus healed everybody" (against Mark "many people"). This is usual Matthean enhancement, with regard to verse 20a. Unlike Mark, however, Matthew does not mention evil spirits. Therefore, the command of Jesus to silence in verse 16 refers to the healed people and is thus directly connected with verses 15a and 19. The following pericopes of Matthew 12 unite Markan and Q traditions with the Markan account in chapter 3. (Mark 3:13-19 has been drawn forth in Matthew 10:1-14, and Mark 3:20 f. eliminated.) We will see that the topics of these pericopes are also related to Matthew 12:18-21. By writing *tote* (a Matthean favorite) and "he healed" (v. 22), the evangelist has explicitly announced a link to 12:15. The title "Son of David" (v. 23) refers immediately to the *pais* of verse 18, in view of the fact that the messianic "Son of David" is called "servant" according to King David's title in 2 Samuel 7 *'ebed* (MT) and *doulos* (LXX) in Ezekiel 34:23 f. and 37:24 f.[3]

The Biblical Text

Isaiah 42:1-4 belongs to the Songs of the Lord's Servant. The pericope is usually seen as the first of these songs. But the preceding unit, 41:8-16, should also be considered in this account since in this unit Israel/Jacob has already been addressed as God's servant (41:8 f.) An additional question is whether Isaiah 42:1-4 is the complete Servant Song or only a part of a larger unit.

For our purposes, it is important to interpret these verses with regard to their context. The context consists on the one hand of other Servant Songs, and on the other hand of the whole Book of Isaiah, containing related topics.[4] The Lord's Servant is the people of Israel. This is the meaning of the present biblical text (MT), confirmed by the LXX through the addition of Jacob and Israel in 42:1 (cf. 41:8 as well as 49:3 MT). The election motif, also present in the surrounding chapters, points out God's loyalty. In the Bible, election always means mission too. Therefore it is said, the gift of God's Spirit, as fulfillment of Numbers 11:29 and promise for all generations (Isaiah 44:32 and 59:21), enables the people of Israel to bring out God's *mišpāṭ* to the nations (42:1; this task is repeated in vv. 3 f.).

What does the noun *mišpāṭ* mean here? In correspondence with ṣedeq/ṣĕdāqâ *mišpāṭ* stands for the order intended and guaranteed by God (cf. 33:22), or likewise the procedure that induced this order. Therefore, the translation of "justice" or "judgment" can be correct. But we can more precisely grasp the meaning of *mišpāṭ* here. According to Isaiah 9:6, the new son of David will bring a reign of *šālôm*, inducing and keeping up God's order. Like this and other passages in the Book of Isaiah (cf. especially 11:4), Isaiah 42:1-4 lays stress on social aspects, on liberation from oppression, that contribute to a life worth living. Isaiah 42:3 shows that *mišpāṭ* is concerned with the fact that the poor and weak are supported and saved (cf. 10:2; 42:7; 6:12). It is, therefore, also legitimate to understand *mišpāṭ* here as salvation.[5]

This understanding of *mišpāṭ* indicates, on the one hand, the gentle behavior of the Servant as described in 42:2. In comparison to 9:1-6 and 11:1-9 (cf. also Psalm 72), the description of the Servant's activity to bring the *mišpāṭ* to the nations like a judge or even a warrior is missing. On the other hand, it is God's salvation that the nations expect. Therefore, the Servant's gentleness corresponds with the nations' expectations (42:4). This gentleness characterizes his *tôrâ*, that is, his teaching of YHWH's *mišpāṭ* revealed to Israel (cf. 30:18-26) for the universal establishment of this *mišpāṭ*. Israel becomes God's instrument to bring salvation to all humankind, "the light for the nations" (49:6; in 51:4-8 the same promise of salvation is expressed as God's own activity).

Israel's prophetic/messianic role must be realized through an enduring commitment that does not conform to the usual expectations of respect and honor. Isaiah 42:4a underlines the Servant's endurance that is guaranteed by God's support of the Servant (cf. 41:8 ff.). The other Songs of the Lord's Servant point out the hostility and humiliation that he must face as he carries out his mission, and from which he is finally saved by God. Thus Isaiah 42:1-4, including its referent texts, provides a comprehensive characterization of Israel's prophetic/messianic role within God's saving action in favor of all humankind. This fulfills the promise given to Abraham (Genesis 12:2c, 3c). Now we will consider whether and how the quotation in Matthew 12:18-21 corresponds with this meaning of the biblical text.

Did Matthew Use a Collection of "Testimonia"?

To understand the Servant in the sense of a messianic figure as Matthew does here and elsewhere, alluding to Isaiah's Servant texts, is not problematic. Such an identification is attested by the Targum.[6] We must, therefore, ask if the quotation of Isaiah 42:1-4 is supported by the portrayal of Jesus Christ in Matthew's gospel. But can we do so? Should we not also take into account that the evangelist depended on a source containing such biblical quotations?

If the quotations in Matthew originate from such a collection of biblical proof texts produced by Jewish-Christian scribes, we should expect that there are divergences between Christ's portrait rendered by these proof texts and the one given by the evangelist. But instead of such divergences, we can observe a close connection between the biblical quotations and their Matthean context. We will examine this more closely in our example: Matthew 12:18-21.

The relevance of this pericope concerning the fulfillment quotations in Matthew is clearly expressed by U. Luz. He declares that 12:18-21 contains the weakest links regarding the context, vocabulary, and content. But he concedes the difficulties of maintaining his thesis of a pre-Matthean collection of biblical proof texts already connected with the units now found in Matthew.[7] Indeed, these difficulties are verified when we take into consideration the argument of Verseput and Neyrey.[8] These authors have convincingly shown the close relationship between 12:18-21 and its wider context with regard to both vocabulary and content. Here we will only discuss the impressive ones.

The correspondence between 12:19 and verses 15 f. is commonly accepted. The connection of verse 20a, b with the preceding pericopes (1-8 and 9-14) has already been mentioned. By defending the disciples and healing the sick man, the Matthean Jesus exemplifies what he has announced in 11:18-30. We can add here 8:16 ff., where, in view of Jesus' healing activity, Isaiah 53:4 is cited as a fulfillment quotation as well. Matthew's use of Hosea 6:6 in 12:7 is a supplementary reinforcement because of its accentuation of Jesus' compassion with tired people (in the same sense already 9:13; see below).

The Isaiah quotation is also connected with the following pericopes. Instead of focusing upon the gentleness of God's Servant, they concentrate on the Servant's success granted by God. Matthew continues reporting Jesus' healing activity. It produces new controversies. But these pericopes do not contradict verse 19a. For the controversies are caused by Jesus' adversaries, the Pharisees (v. 24). The broad disputes (vv. 24-37 and 38-45) explain what verse 20 means: "He causes *krisin* to triumph." Both pericopes deal with the judgment theme, explicitly (vv. 27, 33-37, 41d) and inclusively (vv. 30, 31 f., 38-40, 43-45). The final triumph of this Servant of the Lord, Jesus, can be forecast by his victory over the demons (cf. *ekballō* in vv. 24-28); for it is God's Spirit that gives Jesus the power to drive them out. Jesus as God's elected one is imbued with God's

Spirit (12:18a, c). God's adversaries, now rebelling against Jesus, will be forced by the last judgment to acknowledge that they have refused God's Spirit.

This judgment theme that underscores Jesus' authority has already been discussed in Matthew 11:16-24. The preceding units center on the figure of John the Baptist and contain Jesus' self-testimonies (vv. 2-15). The first of these responds to Jesus' role as God's gentle Servant (vv. 2-5; v. 6 alludes to the judgment). Matthew 11:25-37 summarizes his mission in an excellent self-testimony that is testified by God himself, who has spoken through the prophet Isaiah (12:17-21). Jesus' followers have accepted these testimonies by orienting their lives around Jesus' explications of God's will (12:46-50). Thus Matthew 11 and 12 are closely connected with the quotation from Isaiah 42:1-4. Between the discourses in chapters 10 and 13, chapters 11 and 12 form a great unit with a clear christological scope that includes ecclesiological consequences.

Regarding the biblical quotation in Matthew 12:18-21, the evidence above enables us to take a clear position with respect to the alternative question posed by Verseput: Did "the form of quotation determine the context or did the context influence the form of the quotation?"[9] Like W. D. Davies and D. C. Allison Jr.,[10] I am convinced that the evangelist himself has created the text, using the Isaiah quotation according to his own purposes. There is, therefore, no need to assume a source used by Matthew (just as we need not suppose such a collection of biblical proof texts for the Apostle Paul). Hence we have to consider the relationship the evangelist has established between his Isaiah quotation and the kerygmatic purpose of this book.

Matthew's Interpretation of the Biblical Text

The divergences of Matthew 12:18a, c from Isaiah 42:1 in both the MT and LXX result from the evangelist's Son of God Christology.[11] For the noun *pais* is to be understood in the strict Matthean sense of the unique son of God, Jesus Christ. That is underlined by the relative clause "whom I have chosen" (cf. Haggai 2:23 LXX) and by *agapētos*, which "is no doubt explained by the baptismal tradition" (3:17; cf. Isaiah 41:8; 44:2).[12] This "my beloved one" also "anticipates the transfiguration" (17:5). The future tense in Matthew 12:18c, "I will put," which agrees with the Targum against MT and LXX, "points up the predictive character of the passage."[13]

It is important to see that this predictive character is valid specifically for Matthew 12:18d (and 21). For, according to Matthew's own view, this promise has not been fulfilled by Jesus, but only by the post-Easter preaching (*apangelei*) initiated by the risen Lord (28:19 f.). And this fulfillment has only just begun. What will be preached by the church is *krisis*. What does this mean for Matthew? According to the targumic *dînā'* that means both justice and judgment,[14] the evangelist could be alluding both to the "justice" of God's reign (that is, "almost righteousness")[15] and to the "judgment" carried out by Jesus Christ over all nations (25:31-46).[16] Viewed in the context of 12:21, the first meaning has the preponderance of support. This is underlined by 23:23: *krisis* here combined with *eleos* and *pistis*.

In 12:19 Matthew refers to the characterization of the gentle, humble Messiah in 11:29a, b, also in 21:5 (again as a biblical quotation). He hints at the fact that during his earthly ministry Jesus is not publicly acclaimed as Messiah.[17] The clause verse 19b could have been formulated by the evangelist "for a contrast with his distinctive picture of hypocrites who pray standing on street corners (6:5)."[18] The imagery of verse 20a can be connected with both Jesus' healing activities (cf. 8:17, see above) and his kindness towards sinners. For, apart from 12:7, Matthew has already cited Hosea 6:6 in 9:13. We should then include all those "who are tired from carrying heavy loads" (11:28; cf. 9:36). This saving ministry of Jesus is effected through God's Spirit. It may also be noted that this stands in accordance with the meaning of the Isaiah quotation in Luke 4:18 f.

In 12:20c the evangelist changes his perspective. Here he has changed the clauses Isaiah 42:3c and 4b. The assumption "that Matthew's line has been influenced by Habakkuk 1:4 (MT) is a real possibility, especially since 1QH 4:25 seems to bring together Isaiah 42:3 and Habbakuk 1:4."[19] The scope of verse 20c points to the future and final success of the Son of God. This success cannot be hindered, for Jesus is God's elected one, his beloved Son, who is provided with all authority (cf. 11:27a and 28:18). He "establishes God's will and righteousness in the world" (that is, justice) and carries out God's judgment against those who reject him (cf. 12:24-45; 25:31-46).[20] From this perspective, the evangelist could not take over from Isaiah the clause verse 4a. For he now wants to point out the ultimate triumph of the ministry and person of Jesus Christ without reservation. In this respect, we must remember that the passion does not belong to the themes Matthew recognized being announced by Isaiah (including chapter 53).[21]

Regarding the horizon of eschatological success of the Son of God, Matthew 12:21 (=Isaiah 42:4c LXX) views (like v. 18a) the post-Easter opening of the Jewish church to the Gentiles as commanded by the risen Christ (28:19 f.). Because of this opening, Matthew understood the promise of universal salvation given in Isaiah 42 as being fulfilled. It is surely not an accident that the Apostle Paul cites a corresponding biblical text (Isaiah 11:10 LXX in Romans 15:12) by referring to the same experience of the young church. The fact that Matthew prefers with LXX *onomati* instead of MT *tôrâ* may be explained by an allusion to baptism. At any rate, the "name" sums up Christ's saving person and work.

Although Matthew clearly shows that Jesus was "sent only to the lost sheep of the house of Israel" (15:24), he gives several references to the situation of his community, where there are Jewish and heathen Christians together (cf. 4:13-16 and 24 f.). As a part of the complete quotation, verse 21 connects the earthly ministry of Jesus and his post-Easter work carried out through his church. These christological and ecclesiological references point to the eschatological success of Jesus Christ.

The Matthean *Sitz im Leben* of the Bible Quotation

The evangelist's redaction of Isaiah 42:1-4 reflects the circumstances of the faith in Jesus Christ that Matthew and his community face. The context of 12:18-21 embodies several attacks of the Pharisees and scribes. Moreover, chapters 11 and 12 contain negative statements concerning "this generation." Is it therefore justified to say that Matthew speaks about "Israel's culpable rejection of their Messiah"?[22] Is this where the evangelist has Jesus' "separation from Israel" begin?[23]

Such generalized assertions can be refuted by the gospel itself. We confine ourselves to Matthew 12:18-21 and related texts.[24] Immediately before the Isaiah quotation, it is said that "many people followed him" (12:15), that is, they do not agree with the plan of the Pharisees against Jesus told in verse 14. These people, as well as the crowds of verses 46-50, are exclusively Jews. We must also take into account that Matthew and the majority of his church were Jews. Therefore, the evangelist cannot assume that Jesus is rejected by Israel. Instead, what he really does is reproach the Pharisees and scribes because of their opposition against Jesus Christ.

But we must differentiate these accusations.[25] On the one hand, the evangelist says (cf. Mark 3:6) that "the Pharisees made a plan against Jesus to ruin him" (12:14). Their opposition is answered by the Matthean Jesus with extraordinarily harsh condemnations and threats. On the other hand, the same Jesus gives his disciples an order "to obey and follow everything" the Pharisees and scribes tell them to do (23:3a). This order is very well founded. The differences between the Pharisaic *halachic* traditions and the *halachic* rules of the Matthean Jesus are really small and unimportant. The same fundamental agreement appears with regard to the way of life that transcends *halachic* rules. Both the Pharisaic *ṣaddîq* (righteous) and Jesus' disciples are concerned with the "imitation of God," that is, with the imitation of God's mercy and love.[26]

These agreements are usually concealed by the evangelist's polemics against the Pharisees and scribes when the evangelist insinuates that they plan to eliminate Jesus because of a divergence in understanding the

Sabbath command (12:14), or when Matthew describes their way to fulfill God's will as legalistic (5:20 ff.). We must ignore those polemics for
the above mentioned reasons. Then we can see that the real point at
issue is the christological question: is Jesus the Son of God or not? This is
the definitive controversy between the evangelist and his Pharisaic opponents.

In order to sharpen this controversy, Matthew connects it with the
teachings of his Messiah, whose "yoke is easy" (11:30) while the Pharisees and scribes "tie heavy loads on men's backs" (23:4). The Isaiah quotation 12:18-21 in the context of chapters 11 and 12, therefore, is intended to intensify the persuasive power of Matthew's christological
preaching. By rejecting Jesus as God's gentle Servant, his opponents show
their own lack of gentleness. This manner of connecting the christological
controversy with moral attacks on his Pharisaic opponents enabled the
evangelist to warn the members of his church, especially the Jewish members, not to fraternize with these Pharisees and scribes whose teachings
for daily life are requested—despite their refusal to acknowledge Jesus as
Messiah.

Isaiah 42:1-4/Matthew 12:18-21 in the Light of Today's Christian-Jewish Dialogue

Today we must consider that the *Sitz im Leben* of Matthew and his
church does not exist. The gospel shows a full acceptance of the Torah
(5:17-19), including Pharisaic interpretation (23:2, 3a).[27] The affiliation
of heathens has not dissolved the Jewish character of Matthew's church.
We can further conclude from the above cited passages that the heathen
members of his community had to observe the "Apostolic Decree" (Acts
15:20; cf. v. 28 f.). Thus the christological controversy is the decisive
issue. We face in Matthew's work an inner-Jewish conflict portrayed by a
member of one conflicting party, the weaker party. The evangelist's faith
that Jesus is the Messiah is questioned by the Jewish people. The evangelist employs varying manners to refute the Pharisaic opponents. These
include sharp polemics and argumentation with biblical proof texts. Our
fulfillment quotation exemplifies how Matthew translates Isaiah in order
to express his faith in Jesus Christ according to the *Sitz im Leben* of his
community. The methods of biblical interpretation he uses correspond
with those of his opponents. Faith in Jesus Christ, or its refusal, causes
differing results.

These observations distinguish us from Matthew as well as from
other New Testament authors. As Christians of today, we not only have
other methods of biblical interpretation, but our Bible has also changed.
The Jewish Bible is no longer the unique Bible, because Christians have
appropriated the New Testament writings as Holy Scripture as well. But

the formation of the New Testament canon was connected with the growing distance of the heathen church from Judaism. Here we face the most
important difference between us and the evangelist. Christians of today
lack the understanding of the Jewish background that was shared by
Matthew and his Pharisaic opponents. As a consequence, the heathen
church has altered the inner-Jewish christological controversy of Matthew into a conflict between Christianity and Judaism, using Matthew's
arguments and polemics from outside.

In our days the "new encounter between Christians and Jews"[29]
requires returning to the Jewish roots of our Christian faith (cf. Romans
11:18 in connection with v. 29). Here the Gospel of Matthew can become a guide. Thus it must no longer be used to provide an argument
from the separation of the heathen church from Israel, but it can rather
bring us nearer to the Jewish people. I will now try to illustrate this with
several elements of the fulfillment quotations in Matthew 12:18-21.

Isaiah 42:1-4 shows that Israel's election through God refers to the
salvation of all humankind (cf. Genesis 12:1-4). This universal role of
Israel has been the presupposition for Matthew's interpretation of the
Isaiah text in favor of Jesus Christ. "The Isaianic expectations about Israel's
role are understood to be fulfilled by the obedient Jew, Jesus."[30] For the
evangelist, as well as for the Book of Isaiah, there is no mutual exclusion
of the messianic figure and the messianic role of the people.[31] Regarding
Matthew's Jewish presuppositions, we must acknowledge, in the light of
Romans 9:4 f. and 11:28b, 29, that the messianic role of the Jewish people
has not been taken away by the heathen church. Our christological interpretation of Isaiah 42:1-4 (et al.) can be justified only under the presupposition of the remaining election and mission of the Jewish people as
God's Servants for the salvation of all nations. Thus we can define our
own role as heathen church in dependence on, but not in contrast to,
Israel's role.

Isaiah 42:1-4 and its messianic interpretation in the targumic tradition show that the idea of the one Jewish expectation of the Messiah,
that is, the expectation of a king like David who defeats the people's
enemies and establishes a political reign, originates from a Christian bias.
Instead, we have to acknowledge that there is a plurality of Jewish messianic expectations. We must also add that a crucified Messiah was not
included in those expectations. The Jewish disciples of Jesus had to learn
this characteristic on Good Friday and Easter. If they accepted Jesus as
Messiah, they could do so only by faith in those events. Such faith is
God's gift, and therefore our gratitude toward God, who gives us faith
through Jesus Christ, must not be linked with polemics (like Matthew's)
against the Jews, whose faith in God does not require the acceptance of
Jesus as Messiah.

Isaiah 42:1-4 shows that the Servant of the Lord must aim to bring God's righteousness to the nations. The kernel of this righteousness is the vital rights of all who are disadvantaged.[32] "The way of Torah" is therefore Israel's task. "God is the compassionate one who has called the Israelites to be partners in creating a society that will reflect divine (com)-passion for people. God's teachings provide room for everyone to live, expand, and find fulfillment."[33]

Matthew knew that Jesus' teachings followed on the way of Torah. By his polemics he has concealed that Pharisaic teachings are moving in the same direction. Therefore we now have to learn that Jesus' Torah explications are in full agreement with the Torah interpretation of the Bible itself, that is, of prophetic and wisdom traditions. Moreover, we have to acknowledge that when Matthew sums up Jesus' saving activity with Hosea 6:6 (in 9:13 and 12:7), it is "sound Rabbinic doctrine . . . at its best."[34] The challenge for the church gathered from the nations is that "Christians should take seriously the claims of Sinai in shaping their Christianity."[35]

Isaiah 42:1-4 (and therefore Matthew 12:18-21) shows that the messianic task of Israel and of Jesus carried out by his church is still open for fulfillment. Both Jews and Christians can live and work in the hope that the biblical promises will be realized by God "who created us and taught us how to be truly human."[36]

Endnotes

1. U. Luz, *Das Evangelium nach Matthäus*, EKK I/2 (Zürich/Braunschweig & Neukirchen-Vluyn: Neukirchener Verlag, 1990), 246, admits only a slight link between the Isaiah quotation and its context; see below.

2. D. Verseput, *The Rejection of the Humble Messianic King: A Study of the Composition of Matthew 11-12* (Frankfort: P. Lang, 1986), 190.

3. Cf. E. Schweizer, *Das Evangelium nach Matthäus*, NTD 2 (Göttingen: Vandenhoeck and Ruprecht, 1973), 185 f. Psalms 78 (77), 70 (-72), and 89 (88), 21 f. must be added.

4. The following considerations in accordance with I. Fischer, *Tora für Israel—Tora für die Völker. Das Konzept des Jesajabuches*, SBS 164 (Stuttgart: Verlag Katholisches Bibelwerk, 1995): 79-89.

5. "Rettung": G. Liedke, THAT II, 1976, s.v. "richten," col. 1006.

6. Cf. also the cited passages from Ezekiel and Psalms (above note 3).

7. Luz, *Das Evangelium nach Matthäus*, 244.

8. J. Neyrey, "The Thematic Use of Isaiah 42:1-4 in Matthew 12," *Bib* 63 (1982): 457-73.

9. Verseput, *The Rejection of the Humble Messianic King*, 194 f.

10. W. D. Davies and D. C. Allison, *The Gospel According to Saint Matthew*, ICC vol. II (Edinburgh: T. and T. Clark, 1991), 323 f.; cf. vol. I (1988), 31 f.

11. D. R. A. Hare, *Matthew*, Interpretation (Louisville: Westminster/John Knox Press, 1993): 136.

12. W. D. Davies and D. C. Allison, *Matthew*, vol. II, 324 f.

13. R. H. Gundry, *Matthew: A Commentary on His Handbook for a Mixed Church under Persecution*, second edition (Grand Rapids: Eerdmans, 1994), 229.

14. Cf. K. Elliger, *Deuterojesaja*, BK X1/1 (Neukirchen-Vluyn: Neukirchener Verlag, 1978): 198.

15. R. H. Gundry, *Matthew*, 229.

16. W. D. Davies and D. C. Allison, *Matthew*, vol. II, 325.

17. Cf. D. A. Hagner, *Matthew 1-13*, WBC 33A (Dallas: Word, 1993), 338.

18. R. H. Gundry, *Matthew*, 229.

19. W. D. Davies and D. C. Allison, *Matthew*, vol. II, 326.

20. Ibid., 327.

21. Cf. J. Gnilka, *Das Matthäusevangelium*, Herder's ThKNT, vol. I (Freiburg: Herder, 1986): 453.

22. D. Verseput, *The Rejection of the Humble Messianic King*, 205.

23. U. Luz, *Das Evangelium nach Mattäus*, 244. In the same sense G. N. Stanton, *A Gospel for a New People, Studies in Matthew* (Louisville; Westminster/John Knox Press, 1993), Part II, "The Parting of the Ways."

24. For a comprehensive examination, see A. J. Saldarini, *Matthew's Christian-Jewish Community* (Chicago and London: University of Chicago Press, 1994).

25. Cf. M. Davies, *Matthew* (Sheffield: Sheffield Academic Press, 1993), 95.

26. Cf. my essay "Das Matthäusevangelium und 'die Pharisäer,'" in *Nach den Anfängen fragen: Festschrift G. Dautzenberg* (Giessen, 1994), 199-218.

27. I have pointed out (ibid., 208-211) this common basis against J. Neusner. *A Rabbi Talks with Jesus: An Intermillennial Interfaith Exchange* (Garden City: Doubleday, 1993).

28. Cf. C. Tassin, *L'Evangile de Matthieu* (Paris: Centurion, 1991), 131.

29. J. M. Osterreicher, *The New Encounter between Christians and Jews* (New York: Philosophical Library, 1986).

30. M. Davies, *Matthew*, 95.

31. It is surprising that W. L. Kynes, *A Christology of Solidarity: Jesus as the Represenative of His People in Matthew* (Lanham: University Press of America, 1991), gives attention to Matthew 12:18-21 only in a footnote (193, n. 2). The contended separation of Jesus and his "new community" from Israel (193 f.) ignores that Matthew's church retains its Jewish character.

32. Cf. I. Fisher, *Tora für Israel*, 86: The Servant's Torah is "das Lebens-Recht der Schwachen."

33. F. C. Holmgren, "The Way of the Torah: Escape from Egypt," in *Preaching Biblical Texts*, ed. F. C. Holmgren and H. E. Schaalman (Grand Rapids: Eerdmans, 1995), 117-128, cf. 118 f.

34. C. G. Montefiore, *Rabbinic Literature and Gospel Teachings* (London: MacMillan, 1930; reprint New York, 1970), 242.

35. J. Neusner, *A Rabbi Talks with Jesus*, 153.

36. F. C. Holmgren, "The Way of the Torah," 128.

"When You See These Things Take Place" (Mark 13:29): An Apocalyptic Timetable in Mark 13?

DAVID M. FREEDHOLM

Beginning with the work of T. Colani in the nineteenth century, it became commonplace to refer to Mark 13 as the "little apocalypse" or the "synoptic apocalypse."[1] Today, however, scholars hesitate to call Mark 13 an apocalypse. In fact, in the past twenty-five years they have debated over the question of the relationship of Mark 13 to Jewish apocalyptic literature and thought. In the course of the debate, scholars have answered this question in varying and sometimes contradictory ways. For some, Mark 13 has little in common with apocalyptic literature. For example, K. Grayston examined Mark 13 according to the eight motifs characteristic of apocalyptic literature as identified by Koch, and concluded that in Mark 13 "the marks of apocalyptic are scarce."[2] Similarly, G. Beasley-Murray has argued that Mark 13 has two features that distinguish it from Jewish apocalyptic literature: 1) its lack of "specifically apocalyptic traits," and 2) its paraenetic content.[3] Likewise, in his commentary W. Lane points to the paraenetical material in Mark 13, as well as to the constant form of address in the second person plural, and concludes that these features "serve to distinguish Mark 13 from Jewish apocalyptic documents contemporary with it."[4] T. Geddert, in the most recent full-length study on Mark 13, says, "We join the chorus of those who insist that Mark 13 as a whole shares little in common with typical Jewish apocalyptic as a literary genre."[5]

Others have recognized an apocalyptic element in Mark 13, usually identifying this element as an apocalyptic source (for example, a "Flugblatt") that Mark has incorporated into his gospel for the purpose of correcting or "toning down" its apocalyptic character. These scholars, of whom R. Pesch is the primary example, believe that Mark is really "anti-apocalyptic."[6]

In contrast to both of these understandings of the relationship between Mark 13 and Jewish apocalyptic literature and thought is the understanding of E. Brandenburger. In his book *Markus 13 und die Apokalyptik*, Brandenburger argues that there is abundant evidence of apocalyptic motifs, form elements, and thought patterns in Mark 13, in both pre-Marcan and redactional material.[7]

Which of these evaluations is correct? What relation, if any, does Mark 13 have to Jewish apocalyptic literature and thought? In this paper I shall attempt to bring into clearer focus the relationship between Mark 13 and Jewish apocalyptic literature and thought. It seems to me that many have been quick to deny that Mark 13 is related to Jewish apocalyptic literature and thought, but have not compared the two in any detail. As I proceed, it will become clear that I believe that Mark 13 is closely related to apocalyptic literature and thought. I ask only that the reader reserve judgment until I have made my case. I shall first consider the question of whether Mark 13 belongs to the genre of apocalypse. I will then point to a number of features that Mark 13 shares with Jewish apocalyptic literature and thought. Next I will show that Mark 13 has within it a certain "apocalyptic timetable," a feature that is rather common within apocalyptic literature. I will suggest that the identification of this apocalyptic timetable is important for understanding how the various parts of Mark 13 relate to one another. I think here particularly of the rather vexing question of the relation of Mark 13:29 to Mark 13:32. Finally, I will draw together the conclusions of this paper and assess their implications for the study of Mark 13. I would only note at the outset that I am leaving aside the question of whether Mark used a Jewish apocalyptic document in writing Mark 13 (cf. Pesch, Brandenburger, et al.), though my investigation may have implications for that question.

The Genre of "Apocalypse"

In recent decades there have been attempts to define better what is meant by terms such as "apocalypse," "apocalyptic," "apocalypticism," and "apocalyptic eschatology." There has been a general acceptance of Koch's distinction between "apocalypse" as a literary genre and "apocalyptic" (or "apocalypticism") as a sociological movement. The term "apocalyptic eschatology" has been generally accepted to refer to the eschatology found in apocalypses or recognized by analogy with them.[8]

In 1979 the Apocalypse Group of the Society of Biblical Literature Genres Project, led by J. J. Collins, surveyed all the texts that might be or have been classified as apocalypses and that might be plausibly dated between 250 B.C.E. and 250 C.E., in order to see how far they can be regarded as members of one genre.[9] They drew up a paradigm of elements commonly found in these texts and then identified those few elements that are constant in every work they called an apocalypse. This common core of constant elements enabled them to draw up a comprehensive definition of a genre. Their definition is: "'Apocalypse' is a genre of revelatory literature with a narrative framework, in which a revelation is mediated by an otherworldly being to a human recipient, disclosing a transcendent reality which is both temporal, insofar as it envisages eschatological salvation, and spatial insofar as it involves another, supernatural world."[10] Within that genre they identified two types: apocalypses that do not have an otherworldly journey (Type I) and those that do (Type II). Within each of these types they make further distinctions in view of the eschatological content of the texts: a) the "historical" type, which includes a review of history, eschatological crisis, and cosmic and/ or political eschatology; b) apocalypses that have no historical review but envisage cosmic and/or political eschatology (this type lacks the review of history that distinguishes type a, but retains some public character in its eschatology, as opposed to the purely individual interest in type c; and c) apocalypses that have neither historical review nor cosmic transformation but only "personal eschatology."[11]

This definition of the genre of apocalypse by Collins et al. represents a move toward a more comprehensive definition and away from the making of "checklists" of traits to define the genre (which were often used in the past, for example, by Koch).[12] As some have correctly pointed out, there was often little correspondence between items in these checklists and works commonly considered to be apocalypses.[13] While the definition of the genre of apocalypse by Collins has been acknowledged as a move in the right direction, others have offered even more "essentialistic" definitions. E. P. Sanders has argued that "what is peculiar to the works which have traditionally been considered Palestinian Jewish apocalypses is the combination of revelation with the promise of restoration and reversal."[14] J. Carmignac has given this definition of the genre of apocalypse: "a literary genre which presents, through typical symbols, revelations either about God, or about angels or demons, or about their supporters, or about the instruments of their action"[15] (my translation). These two definitions are not necessarily in conflict with that of Collins et al., and they do cover texts commonly considered to be apocalypses, but they run the danger of being too broad in that they might cover a whole range of revelatory works not commonly considered to be apocalypses. In my opinion, Collins's definition seems best. It is the product of extensive analysis, and it fits works considered to be apocalypses while not being so broad as to fit other kinds of literature as well.

Does Mark 13 fit this definition? It is revelatory in that it is a prediction of events that are to come (Mark 13:23b—*proeirēka humin panta*). These events in Mark 13 serve as signs of the coming of the Son of Man (Mark 13:29: "When you see these things taking place, you know that he is near, at the very gates"). It is set in a narrative framework. The revelation is disclosed to human recipients. Mark 13 does disclose a transcendent reality that is temporal, insofar as it envisages eschatological salvation (Mark 13:26-27—the coming of the Son of Man and the gathering of the elect), and spatial, insofar as it involves another, supernatural world (Mark 13:26-27—the mention of the Son of Man, angels, and heaven). The one element of the description that Mark 13 may lack is that the revelation is supposed to be "mediated by an otherworldly being." As A. Yarbro Collins says of Mark 13, "Whether this text and its parallels fit our definition of an apocalypse depends on whether Jesus is to be understood as an otherworldly mediator."[16] Yarbro Collins concludes that in the Gospels the pre-resurrection Jesus is not an otherworldly figure in the same sense as the post-resurrection Jesus and the angels who appear as mediators in other apocalypses. She describes the role of Jesus in Mark 13 as a kind of oracle-giver or prophet. Thus Yarbro Collins does not categorize Mark 13 as an apocalypse, though she admits it is very close in terms of form and content.

While Yarbro Collins may be right in refusing to call the pre-resurrection Jesus an otherworldly mediator, the evidence might not be all that clear. As she notes, this decision depends on one's understanding of the Christology of the synoptic Gospels, in this case, the Christology of Mark. While I cannot discuss in detail here the Christology of Mark, it seems to me that Jesus is portrayed by Mark as an otherworldly figure. From the beginning to the end of the Gospel, Jesus is identified as God's Son (Mark 1:1, 1:11, 15:39, etc.). He is recognized as such by demonic powers, and he has authority over them (Mark 3:11, 5:7). In an important text, Jesus is transfigured before Peter, James, John, and Andrew (three of whom appear in Mark 13); and Elijah and Moses appear and speak with him (Mark 9:1-8). In this transfiguration scene, Jesus is also declared to be God's Son by a voice from heaven (Mark 9:8). Certainly in this scene Jesus is shown to be an otherworldly figure. This is not to say that in Mark Jesus is only or even primarily represented as an otherworldly figure. It is to say that there is some reason to argue that in Mark Jesus is presented in such a way that would justify an understanding of him as, among other things, an otherworldly mediator. Thus I would claim that Mark 13 does fit the definition of an apocalypse made by Collins et al.[17] If so, it would be, according to their typology, a type Ib apocalypse—that is, an apocalypse that has cosmic and/or political eschatology but no historical review or otherworldly journey.

I believe that Mark 13 is an apocalypse; but, even if it is only very close, as Yarbro Collins argues, what is important to note is that, in terms of basic form and content, it displays a close relation to apocalyptic literature. It should also be noted that the presence of paraenesis does not, as some have argued, distinguish Mark 13 from apocalyptic literature, either Jewish or Christian. As P. Vielhauer says, "All apocalypses include paraenesis."[18] C. Münchow, in an extensive study, has demonstrated the connection between ethics and eschatology in Jewish apocalyptic literature.[19] In Christian apocalypses this connection is even stronger. As E. S. Fiorenza says, "Early Christian writings frequently combine the apocalyptic pattern of eschatological events with paraenesis. Either the apocalyptic pattern is introduced and framed by paraenesis or it is interlaced with hortatory statements."[20]

Having shown that Mark 13, in terms of its form, is very close to other apocalypses, it is appropriate to show how the individual elements of the chapter are related to elements in apocalyptic literature.

Apocalyptic Elements in Mark

As a way of beginning, let me show some of the elements that Mark 13 shares with apocalyptic literature. The setting of Mark 13 on the Mount of Olives is significant. Note that in Zechariah 14:4 the Lord is to stand upon the Mount of Olives on the "day of the Lord" (cf. Ezekiel 11:23). Apparently the Mount of Olives was a place of significance for those expecting the end of time. Josephus (AJ 20.169 f. and BJ 2.261f.) tells of an Egyptian prophet who gathered a large group of supporters and led them to the Mount of Olives, promising that at his command the walls of Jerusalem would fall and he would then defeat the Roman garrison.[21] It seems that the followers of this Egyptian expected some sort of divine intervention or miracle. Though Josephus does not say so specifically, it may be that the Egyptian claimed to be the Messiah. Also, the Mount of Olives provides the setting for a number of early Christian apocalypses (cf. the *Apocalypse of Peter*, the *Apocalypse of the Holy Mother of God*, the *Mysteries of St. John the Apostle and Holy Virgin*, etc.). Evidently the Mount of Olives was a place that had eschatological significance and hence was an appropriate place for the discourse in Mark 13.

The question asked by the disciples in Mark 13:4 provides the springboard for the discourse. This is a common technique in apocalyptic literature (cf. 4 Ezra 4:33; 6:33; 8:63; *2 Apocalypse of Baruch* 26:1; 41:1; etc.). The question in Mark 13:4 has two parts: 1) *pote tauta estai* 2) *kai ti to sēmeion hotan mellē tauta sunteleisthai panta*. The first part of the question probably refers back to the prediction of the destruction of the temple, in verse 2. The plural *tauta*, which is referring to the singular event of this destruction, points to the fact that the destruction of the temple was understood as part of a complex of events surrounding the end of time.[22]

The second part of the question is tied to the first and is an expansion of it. The *pote* of the first part is further defined as *ti to sēmeion* in the second part. *Tauta* is made more explicit by the addition of *panta*. *Estai* becomes in the second part *mellē sunteleisthai*.[23] Thus the two parts of the question in verse 4 are not separate questions, one referring to the destruction of the temple and the other to eschatological events in general. They are, rather, parallel questions and represent an attempt by Mark to link the destruction of the temple with these eschatological events (*tauta panta*).

Many have noted that the second part of the question is reminiscent of Daniel 12:7 LXX—*suntelesthēsetai panta tauta*. Lambrecht has correctly noted that the phrase *panta tauta* has become a *terminus technicus* for the occurrence of the end time, which Mark has taken over.[24] See, for instance, the phrase (Heb. *kol 'ēlleh*, Syr. *hlyn clhyn*) in Daniel 12:7 and 4 Ezra 6:33 (cf. Daniel 12:8; 1 Enoch 93:2; 4 Ezra 4:33; 6:30; 2 Apocalypse of Baruch 14:2; etc.). Thus there is no doubt that *tauta panta* in Mark 13:4 refers to the events at or near the end of time. This is made explicit by Matthew, who changes the second part of the question to read *ti to sēmeion tēs sēs parousias kai sunteleias tou aiōnos*. This question, then, is the springboard for the following discourse, which describes the events that are to take place at or near the end of time.

The various signs discussed in Mark 13:5b-8 (wars, rumors of wars, earthquakes, famines) are common stock in apocalyptic literature, (for example, 4 Ezra 9:1-4; 16:18-34; 2 Apocalypse of Baruch 70; Sibylline Oracles 2:154 f.). Relatively unique to Mark 13 is the inclusion of false Christs (Mark 13:6, 21-22) among these other signs. Note, however, Sibylline Oracles 3:63 f., in which Belial arises and raises the dead and performs many signs. In this text it is predicted that Belial will "also lead men astray, and he will lead astray many faithful, chosen Hebrews, and other lawless men who have not yet listened to the word of God" (Sibylline Oracles 3.67-68). In any case, the false Christs in Mark 13 apparently were of great concern for Mark and his community.

The relationship between Mark 13 and Daniel has long been noted (cf. Hartman). There is a similarity, for instance, between the phrase *all' oupō to telos* in Mark 13:7 and Daniel 11:35 (*kî 'ôd lammô'ēd*). It seems that "end" in these texts refers to the time of God's intervention in history and the beginning of the new age. Note 4 Ezra 7:112-113, which says, "This present world is not the end. . . . But the day of judgment will be the end of this age and the beginning of the immortal age to come."[25] The point that is being made in Mark 13:7 and in Daniel 11:35 is that the events described in the verses preceding are not to be construed as a sign that "the end" has arrived; there is more yet to come. This point is made even more clear in Mark 13:8, which calls the sign the *archē ōdinōn*.

The imagery of the "birthpangs" or, perhaps more appropriately, "labor pangs" is fairly common in apocalyptic literature. In *1 Enoch* 62:5 the imagery is used to describe the condition of the ruling class when they recognize the Son of Man. The text says, "Then pain shall come upon them as on a woman in travail with birth pangs." In 1QH 3.6 f. the imagery of birthpangs is used in connection with the birth of a messianic figure (1QH 3.10 *pl' yw'ṣ* "a wonderful counselor"). In 4 Ezra 4:33 f. this imagery is used in connection with the coming of the new age. In this text, when asked about the delay of the "end," Uriel responds by saying, "Go and ask a woman who is with child if, when her nine months have been completed, her womb can keep the child within her any longer" (4 Ezra 4:40). When Ezra admits that a woman cannot, Uriel says, "In Hades the chambers of the souls are like the womb. For just as a woman who is in travail makes haste to escape the pangs of birth, so also do these places hasten to give back those things that were committed to them from the beginning. Then the things that you desire to see will be disclosed to you." More striking is the use of this imagery in 4 Ezra 16:35 f.: "Behold, the calamities draw near, and are not delayed. Just as a woman with child, in her ninth month, when the time of delivery draws near, has great pangs about her womb for two or three hours beforehand, and when the child comes forth from the womb, there will not be a moment's delay, so the calamities will not delay in coming forth upon the earth, and the world will groan, and pains will seize it on every side."[26] Thus in Mark 13:8 the phrase *archē ōdinōn* would seem to indicate that the events in Mark 13:5b-8 are to be seen as the beginning of the eschatological woes at the end of time.

Mark 13:9-13, which contains a description of the persecution of Christians, is without direct parallel in apocalyptic literature in early Judaism, but the persecution of the church is a common theme in Christian apocalypses.[27] Note, though, that Mark 13:9-13 is at least indirectly paralleled by Daniel 11:33-35, which tells of the persecution of the *maśkîlîm*. The other parallels between Mark 13:14-20 and Daniel 11-12 are more obvious and do not need to be dwelled on here.[28] They include the mention of the "desolating sacrilege" (Mark 13:14; Daniel 11:31) and the time of the unsurpassed tribulation (Mark 13:19; Daniel 12:1). The coming of a messianic figure at the end of time to save God's people, as seen in the coming of the Son of Man in Mark 13:24-27, occurs frequently in apocalyptic literature (for example, 4 Ezra 7:26 f.; 12:32 f.; 13:21f.; *2 Apocalyse of Baruch* 70:9, 72-72; etc.). The notion of gathering together the elect at the end of time (Mark 13:27) is paralleled in 4 Ezra 13:39 f.

From this brief treatment, it is clear that there are numerous and significant points of contact between Mark 13 and Jewish apocalyptic literature. These are concentrated in Mark 13:3-7. But Mark 13 displays another feature that is commonly found in apocalyptic literature: it has a peculiar understanding of the timing of the end, which might be called an apocalyptic timetable.

An Apocalyptic Timetable

It has long been recognized that one of the distinctive characteristics of some of the most important Jewish apocalypses (for example, Daniel 7-12, the Apocalypse of Weeks, 4 Ezra, *2 Apocalyse of Baruch*) is the periodization of history—that is, the dividing of history into time periods.[29] Often this periodization of history is highly schematized and replete with symbolic language (for example, *2 Apocalyse of Baruch* 55-74). Of course, the periodizations of history found in these apocalypses do not merely involve past events, but include the present situation of the author as well as the future. Specifically, these apocalypses wish to plot the end of this present evil age and the dawning of the reign of God (or the Messiah) in the new age to come within their overall historical schema. As Lars Hartman says, they are "texts which periodize history until the end in such a way that an informed reader should be able to spot his place in the developing drama."[30] Not only do some of the authors of these texts give the readers information (sometimes explicit and sometimes vague) in the form of *ex eventu* prophecy that enables them to spot their place in the apocalyptic drama, but they also provide readers with a description of the future events that will mark the culmination of this drama.

I will briefly examine the timing of the end (that is, the end of the present age and the dawning of the new age) as it is presented in Jewish apocalypses and other apocalyptic literature.[31] These presentations of the timing of the end might be called (for the lack of a better term) apocalyptic timetables.[32] After doing this, I will examine the timing of the end, or the apocalyptic timetable, which I believe is in Mark 13.

Before examining these apocalyptic timetables, I will make three observations. The first is rather basic. Invariably, it seems, the authors of apocalyptic literature believe that they and their readers live very near the time of the end. This time, for them, is a time of evil; and in some documents one finds the idea that the evil in the world has been increasing throughout history and has reached its highest level in their present time. In this time period there are various woes and calamities that come upon the world and sometimes upon the elect. This time period is often referred to as the "last days" or "the time of the end."[33] Second, however, there is the often overlooked notion in much apocalyptic literature that before the dawning of the new age there will be a short period of greatly intensified evil, sometimes called a tribulation.[34] Some documents describe this period as the time when the forces of good and the forces of evil will have their final battle. This period might be called the final "stage" of the end. What differentiates this stage from the one described in my first observation is that, in most cases, this stage had yet to occur in the minds of the authors.[35] I believe that it is proper to link many descriptions of the so-called messianic woes with this period. Third, in most apocalyptic literature we find a description of the intervention of God in history on behalf of his elect. This stage is usually marked by the destruction of all evil in the world and the establishment of the kingdom of God upon the earth. Sometimes this intervention involves a messianic figure, and sometimes not.

What I am positing here is that Jewish apocalyptic literature conceived of the end as something that would occur in a number of stages.[36] As we shall see, the documents differ considerably in the number of the stages they enumerate and in their descriptions of the stages. Also, some documents integrate the stages of the end within a broader periodization of history (for example, Daniel, 2 Apocalyse of Baruch). I do think, however, that a remarkable unanimity exists in these documents in the description of a future time of tribulation (my second observation above), which is the final stage of the end before the inaugurating of the new age. Let us look, then, at how the timing of the end is portrayed in several documents: Daniel 10-12, 1QM, 4 Ezra, and 2 Apocalypse of Baruch. Special attention will be paid to the final stage of intense evil (tribulation) as it appears in these documents.

DANIEL 10-12. In Daniel 10:2-14 an angelic figure (Gabriel?) appears to Daniel and gives him a vision of that which is to come upon Daniel's people in the last days (Daniel 10:14: ăšer yiqrāh lĕ'ammĕkā). In Daniel 11 we find, in the form of prophecy, a description of history from Alexander the Great to Antiochus IV Epiphanes. Daniel 11:31 tells of the profaning of the temple by Antiochus IV and the setting up of the haššiqqûṣ mĕšômēm (LXX—bdelugma ēphanismenon). Daniel 11:33-35 describes the suffering of the maśkîlîm, a suffering that is intended to purify them "until the time of the end, for it is not yet the appointed time" ('ēt qēṣ kî 'ôd lammô'ēd). Several things should be noted thus far: 1) The events described in these chapters are the events of the last days. These events encompass both the past and the present of the author and his community (the suffering of the "wise"). 2) Although the events described thus far are those of the last days and thus are part of the apocalyptic timetable, there is the sense that the end has not yet arrived (Daniel 11:35).

If up until 11:39 the author of Daniel has engaged in ex eventu prophecy, in 11:40-12:4 he foretells the future. In 11:40-45 we find predictions that "in the time of the end" Ptolemy would attack Antiochus and that Antiochus would conquer Libya and Ethiopia. The angel predicts that upon returning "with great fury to bring ruin and to utterly destroy many," Antiochus would meet his end. However, these predictions in 11:40-45 never came true. Still, following the author's timetable, the angel predicts in 12:1 that the angel-prince Michael would rise up as the protector of Daniel's people. It seems likely that the author believed that Michael would intervene in history and perhaps do battle with the forces of evil. Then the text says, "And there shall be a time of tribulation such as has never been from when the nations came to be until this time" (Daniel 12:1). Here, then, is the tribulation, the "time of anguish" (*'ēt ṣārâ*—LXX *hēhēmera thlipseōs*. No description of this time of anguish is given beyond that it will be unsurpassed in terms of suffering. What follows the tribulation in 12:1-3 is a description of the deliverance of the elect. What is crucial to note is that the tribulation in 12:1 is, in the mind of the author, a future event.[37] Its prediction comes in the context of 11:40-12:4, where the author is genuinely foretelling the future.

Thus in Daniel 10-12 we find an apocalyptic timetable that describes the events leading up to the end of time. The culmination and final stage of these events is the great tribulation, a time of unparalleled anguish.

THE QUMRAN LITERATURE: 1QM. One may find in the Qumran literature, and particularly in 1QM, evidence that the Qumran community (or certain members of it) may have harbored ideas about the timing of the end similar to those found in Daniel and other Jewish apocalyptic literature. Of course, it is difficult to know whether the Qumran community had one particular and consistent eschatological outlook.[38] But, regardless of the answer to this question, it is possible to show that the literature produced by the community displays eschatological ideas and patterns that resemble those in apocalyptic literature. The Qumran community, of course, did not produce apocalypses, but early apocalypses (for example, Daniel and *1 Enoch*) were evidently valued by the community and apparently influenced their literature.[39] This has led some to cautiously refer to the Qumran community as an apocalyptic community.[40] But let us turn to the issue at hand.

It is clear that the Qumran community considered itself to be living in the last days (*'ḥryt hymym*), a phrase that is repeated frequently in the community's literature and particularly in the *pesharim* (for example, 1QSᵃ 1.1; 1QpHab 2.5-6; 4QpIsᵇ 2.1). These last days were for the community a time of distress and suffering (cf. 1QpHab 5.5-6, etc.). They thought of themselves as the "last generation" (*hdwr h'ḥrwn*—1QpHab 7.2), and they were waiting to be delivered by God on the *ywm hmṣpṭ* (cf. 1QpHab 12.14). They believed themselves to be living in the "last endtime" (*hqṣ h'ḥrwn*—1QpHab 7.12), and expected God's intervention in history at any moment.[41] Yet it is also clear that, before the time of eschatological salvation, the community expected one final conflict between the forces of good and evil.

This conflict is described in 1QM (the War Scroll); 1QM 1.9 f. reads: "On the day that the Kittim fall there shall be a mighty battle and carnage before the God of Israel, for that day is the day appointed by him from ancient times for the battle of destruction of the sons of darkness, on which they shall engage with great carnage the congregation of angels and the assembly of men, the sons of light and the sons of darkness." In this battle, Michael is the leader of the sons of light, while Belial leads the sons of darkness. This battle rages back and forth, but finally, "in the seventh lot," God intervenes, bringing down the forces of evil (1QM 1.14 f.). In 1QM 15.1 the time of this battle is called an 'ēt ṣārâ (a time of anguish). This echoes Daniel 12:1, which also speaks of an 'ēt ṣārâ before the final deliverance of the people. There may be references to this 'ēt ṣārâ in other Qumran documents. For instance, 4QpPs^a frag. 1-10 2.10 and 3.3 refers to a mw'd ht'nyt (a time of affliction), which is marked by sword, famine, and plague.[42] However, it is unclear whether these references in 4QpPs^a are to a future time (such as the 'ēt ṣārâ in 1QM) or to some afflictions in the present time of the author. Also note 4QpIsa^a frag.7-10 column 3, which seems to envision the battle outlined in 1QM.[43]

In any case, two things are clear. 1) The Qumran community believed itself to be living in the last days. In their eyes, these last days were evil and full of trials. Though they believed that they were living in the end-time, they knew that the end-time had not reached its completion (1QpHab 7.7-14). 2) It is clear from 1QM that the Qumran community (or at least part of it) expected a great tribulation, a great apocalyptic battle, before the time of final deliverance. This battle was clearly to take place in the future.

4 EZRA. As M. S. Stone has pointed out, 4 Ezra has present in it the idea that the times and their order and length have been fixed by God.[44] Included in this, I believe, is an understanding that the events of the end are ordered by God as well. By "end" I refer here to the events that are to occur at the end of the present age and the beginning of the coming age, though I realize that this term has varied referents in 4 Ezra.[45] Thus in 4 Ezra there are a number of interesting passages that reveal another apocalyptic timetable.[46] In the first vision (4 Ezra 3:1-5:20), Ezra asks Uriel why Israel has been given over to the Gentiles. Uriel responds that it is "because the age is hastening swiftly to its end" (4:26). Ezra asks in 4:33, "How long and when will these things be?" Uriel responds by giving a number of signs of the end (5:1-13), but not all of them. In fact, as bad as these signs are, Ezra is told to expect "greater things than these" (5:13). In the second vision (5:21-6:34), Ezra requests from Uriel that he be shown "the end of the signs" (6:12) from the previous night. However, instead of Uriel giving the signs, a voice (probably that of God) gives them. The voice says, "Behold, the days are coming, and it shall be that when I draw near to visit the inhabitants of the earth . . . and when the humiliation of Zion is complete, and when the seal is placed upon the age which is about to pass away, then I will show these signs" (6:18-19). At the completion of these signs, the voice says, "It shall be that whoever remains after all that I have foretold to you shall be saved and shall see my salvation and the end of my world" (6:26).

What is important to note here is that the "signs" preceding the end pass through several stages. In the first vision Ezra is given an initial lot of signs to watch for. Then in the second vision he is given the signs that are to immediately precede God's coming. There is good reason to believe that the second group of signs are not *ex eventu* prophecies, but predictions of the future. Note that in 6:19 the humiliation of Zion is said to be complete. It seems reasonable to equate the woes of these signs with the time of tribulation found in other documents.

This understanding is supported by a further discussion of the end and the signs preceding it, which occurs in the fourth vision. In 8:63 Ezra asks, "Behold, O Lord, you have now shown me a multitude of signs which you will do in the last days, but you have not shown me when you will do them." The angel responds in 9:1 f.,

> Measure carefully in your mind when you see that a
> certain portion of the predicted signs have passed, then
> you will know that it is the time when the Most High is
> about to visit the world which he has made. So when
> there shall appear in the world earthquakes, tumult of
> peoples, intrigues of nations, wavering of leaders, con-
> fusion of princes, then you will know that it was of these
> that the Most High spoke from the days of old, from
> the beginning. For just as with everything that has oc-
> curred in the world, the beginning is evident, and the
> end is manifest; so also are the times of the Most High.
> The beginnings are known by portents and by signs and
> mighty works, and the end by punishments and signs.
> And it shall be that everyone who will be saved . . . will
> survive the dangers which I have predicted, and will
> see my salvation in my land.

In this text, Ezra is told to watch carefully the signs, for they are to proceed in a particular order up to the coming of the Most High. The times
when these signs occur are called the "times of the Most High." These
signs have a discernible beginning and end, which are marked by specific

kinds of signs (6:6).[47] Thus, here we see stages in the timing of the end, culminating in a final age of intense evil.[48]

It may be objected that the signs in all the stages of the apocalyptic timetable in 4 Ezra seem to be equally horrible and evil. But there is the notion in 4 Ezra that evil will worsen in the eschatological age until the time of salvation. In 4 Ezra 4:15-16 it says, "For evils worse than those which you have seen happen now, afterwards shall happen. For the weaker the world gets from old age, the greater the evils shall be upon the inhabitants of the earth." This increase in evil is also reflected in the imagery found in 4:28, in which Uriel says, "For the evil has been sown about which you ask me, but the harvest of it has yet to come."

2 APOCALYPSE OF BARUCH. In *2 Apocalypse of Baruch* 26-28 there is a detailed periodization of the eschatological age that is to precede the coming of the messiah. It is divided into twelve parts. The first part is called the "beginning of the disturbances." The next ten parts are made up of various woes (for example, earthquakes, famine, slaughtering, fire). The twelfth part consists of disorder and "a mixture of all that has been before" (27:13). In this twelfth part, all the other parts are mixed together and confused so that no one will comprehend that it is the end-time, except for those who "understand" (27:15-28:1). Thus here we see the eschatological age divided into distinct stages. The last is seen as a time of intense evil (that is, tribulation). This last stage is a prediction of the future. Note the invitation in 28:1 for the reader to discern this last stage.

In another apocalyptic vision, *2 Apocalypse of Baruch* 55-76, there is a highly schematized periodization of history (which is reminiscent of the one in the *Apocalypse of Weeks* in *1 Enoch*). History is divided into twelve "waters." The vision presents history in such a way that the waters alternate between "black waters" and "bright waters." For instance, the first black waters is the transgression of Adam (56:5), and the first bright waters is Abraham (57:1). After these twelve waters, the last of which is the return from the exile and the rebuilding of the temple, there comes a final black waters. This black waters is undoubtedly the eschatological age preceding the coming of the messiah.

In *2 Apocalypse of Baruch* 70 these final black waters are described: "Therefore, hear the exposition of the last black waters. This is the word. Behold, the days are coming and it shall be when the time has ripened and the harvest of the seed of the evil ones and the good ones has come. . . ." Then a series of calamities is described (70:2-6). After this comes an interesting passage, 70:7 f., which says, "Then the Most High will give a sign (*ngl' dyn mrym'*) to those nations whom he prepared before and they will make war with those leaders who are left. And it will be that everyone who saves himself from the war will die in an earthquake." Here again we see the end divided into stages. There are first a number of calamities (70:2-6). Then God gives a sign and there is a final battle and conflagration. This is reminiscent of the tribulation in Daniel 12:1 and 1QM.

MARK 13. I have attempted to show here that one can find in Jewish apocalyptic literature a consistent interest in the timing of the end of this world and the beginning of the new age.[49] I have also attempted to demonstrate that there is a tendency in this literature to divide the end-time into various stages. This division of the end-time varies from document to document, but there seems to be at least one common motif in all of them: that the final stage of the end-time would be a period of intense evil (sometimes called a tribulation). This final stage was always future in the minds of the authors, and was to be followed by the intervention of God into history.

It is my contention that Mark 13 has a similar understanding of the timing of the end. In other words, it also has an apocalyptic timetable. Mark 13:1-5a provides the introduction to the discourse in verses 5b-37. This introduction is divided into two different scenes. The first scene takes place outside the temple (vv. 1-2). The second occurs on the Mount of Olives, where the discourse is given. The discourse in Mark 13:5b-37, I suggest, is divided into two parts. The first part contains the description of the events of the eschatological age (vv. 5b-27), culminating in the coming of the Son of Man. The second part contains two parables, the parable of the Fig Tree (vv. 28-30) and the parable of the Unknown Day and Hour (vv. 32-37). A key question is how these two parables relate to the first part of the discourse and to each other. In particular, does Mark 13:32 represent an attempt to cool the fervent expectations of the end evident in the previous verses? I shall leave this question for later.

The first part of the discourse in Mark 13 can be divided into three time periods or stages.[50] These time periods are sequential, representing the general course of eschatological events leading up to the end of the age. The first period of time (vv. 5-13) consists of those events marking the beginning (v. 8—*archē*) of the eschatological woes that indicate that the present evil age is about to end and the new age is about to begin. The events of verses 5b-13 are to be the sign that the eschatological woes have begun, but, as the author of verse 7 is eager to point out, "the end is not yet." This period is marked by the appearance of false Christs (v. 6), wars, earthquakes, and famines (vv. 7-8). It is also marked by persecution of the church (vv. 9-13). The transition from this time period to the second is marked by the appearance of *to bdelugma tēs erēmōseōs* in verse 14. The second time period, marked by the coming of the "desolating sacrilege," is a short time of *thlipsis* (v. 19) and is described in verses 14-23. This period is a time of unsurpassed suffering. It is also marked by the presence of "false Christs" and "false prophets" (vv. 21-22, cf. v. 6). The third and final time period is the time *meta tēn thlipsin ekeinēn* (v. 24), and is described in verses 24-27. In this time period the Son of Man comes and the "elect" are gathered together from earth and from heaven by angels. This is the period of eschatological salvation.

Thus the core of Mark 13 has within it an apocalyptic timetable much like those found in other apocalypses and in other literature influenced by apocalyptic thought.

Summary

Let me summarize here the results of this study. Using a current, basic definition of the genre of apocalypse, it is evident that Mark 13 does indeed fit that definition. There are numerous and significant contacts in content, language, and imagery between Mark 13 and apocalyptic literature. The basic structure of Mark 13:5b-27 reveals an apocalyptic timetable similar to others found in various apocalyptic works. Thus it is beyond doubt that Mark 13 exhibits in form and content a basic affinity with apocalyptic literature. The attempts by some scholars to deny this affinity are groundless.

How does this help us understand Mark 13? To answer this question fully would require another full-length study. However, some basic answers can be given. First, it seems very probable that Mark shared with the authors of apocalyptic literature the conviction that he and his community were living in the last days (Mark 13:30). Mark believed that the evil events of his time (war, famine, persecution, etc.) were the eschatological woes that marked the nearness of the end. He believed that God would soon intervene in history through the coming of the Son of Man, which he probably interpreted as the parousia of Jesus. For Mark, in parallel and in contrast to the worsening of evil in the last days was the secret growth of the kingdom (Mark 4:26-29). The same kind of parallelism is found in *2 Apocalypse of Baruch* 70:2: "Behold, the days are coming and it shall be when the time of the world has ripened and the harvest of the seed of the evil and the good ones has come."

Second, by recognizing the relation of Mark 13 to apocalyptic literature, we can remove the seeming difficulty between Mark 13:28-31 and 32-37. Mark 13:29 says, "So also, when you see these things taking place, you will know that he is near, at the very gates." Verse 32 says, "But of that day or that hour no one knows, not the angels in heaven, nor the Son, but only the Father." Some have seen in verse 32 a contradiction of vese 29, a contradiction which they believe indicates that Mark is really "anti-apocalyptic" (see above). This contradiction is only apparent, however. Upon identifying the apocalyptic timetable in Mark 13, we can understand that 13:29 is an exhortation to recognize the events narrated in 13:5b-23 for what they are—signs of the stages that the present age must go through before the coming of the Son of Man and the closing of the age. Mark 13:29 has a close and illuminating parallel in a text from 4 Ezra that we have already seen: "Measure carefully in your mind, and when you see that a certain part of the predicted signs are past, then you will know that it is the very time when the Most High is about to visit the world which he has made" (4 Ezra 9:1-2).

In Mark 13:29 and in 4 Ezra 9:1-2 the emphasis is on the ability to recognize that one is living in the last days and that the end is near. This emphasis is common in apocalyptic literature, along with the related conviction that the present generation is the last generation (Mark 13:31, cf. 1QpHab 7.2, etc.). Mark 13:32 f. emphasizes that the exact day or hour of the coming of the Son of Man is not known, and thus there is a need for preparedness. This notion is found in apocalyptic literature as well. In *2 Apocalypse of Baruch* 85:10 f. we find this:

> The youth of the world has passed away, and the power of creation is already exhausted, and the coming of the times is very near and has passed by. And the pitcher is near the well, and the ship to the harbor, and the journey to the city, and life to its end. Further, prepare yourselves so that, when you sail and ascend from the ship, you may have rest and not be condemned when you have gone away. For behold, the Most High will cause all things to come. There will not be an opportunity to repent anymore, nor a limit to the times, nor a duration of the periods, nor a chance to rest, nor an opportunity to prayer.

This text, like Mark 13, holds that, while the signs of the end of the world are observable, there is still the need for preparedness in that the final denouement will be sudden. Thus Mark 13:32 is not an indication that Mark is "anti-apocalyptic."

In conclusion, it seems that Mark, living in a time of apparent evil and persecution, provided his community with an apocalyptic timetable. This timetable was not, I think, intended to be used as a chart for them to calculate their place in history vis-à-vis the end of time. Rather, it has a comforting and exhortative purpose. On the one hand, it tells the readers that history is proceeding according to God's plan (that is, as their Lord predicted). It tells the readers that the suffering and the evil they are experiencing indicate that the new age is about to arrive. On the other hand, the warning of the time of tribulation indicates to the readers that things may get worse before they get better. The promise of the coming of the Son of Man in this text serves to bolster the readers for hard times to come. Hence Mark says, "When you see these things taking place, you know that he is near, at the very gates."

Endnotes

1. T. Colani, *Jésus Christ et les Croyances messianiques de son Temps* (Paris, 1864). I am uncertain as to when the term "little apocalypse" was first applied to Mark 13, though it seems to have come into vogue after Colani's work.

2. K. Grayston, "The Study of Mark 13," *BJRL* 56 (1973-74): 380. The eight motifs of apocalyptic literature identified by Koch are 1) the urgent expectation of the impending overthrow of all earthly conditions in the immediate future; 2) a cosmic catastrophe; 3) the time of this world is divided into predetermined segments; 4) armies of angels and demons contend and intervene; 5) beyond the catastrophe there is a paradisal salvation; 6) God (or the Son of Man) ascends the throne, and the kingdom of God becomes visible on earth; 7) there is an eschatological mediator; 8) in the new age the condition of man and the world is glory. See K. Koch, *The Rediscovery of Apocalyptic* (London: SCM Press, 1972), 28-33. One wonders how Grayston reaches his conclusion that the marks of apocalyptic are scarce in Mark 13. Many of the above motifs, as he himself notes, are present in Mark 13 in some form. The one he denies categorically (No. 3), we shall argue is present in Mark 13. Furthermore, one wonders how well any one recognized piece of apocalyptic literature would fit Koch's paradigm. Does every motif have to be present for a document to qualify as apocalyptic? If not, how many are required?

3. G. Beasley-Murray, *A Commentary on Mark 13* (London: Macmillan & Company, 1957), 17; and idem, *Jesus and the Future* (London: Macmillan & Company, 1954), 223-24.

4. W. Lane, *The Gospel of Mark*, NICNT (Grand Rapids: Eerdmans, 1974), 445. Also cf. C. E. B. Cranfield, "St. Mark 13," *SJT* 7 (1954): 295. These scholars (and especially Beasley-Murray) seem to want to stress the uniqueness of Mark 13:5-37 (that is, Mark 13 is not related to Jewish apocalyptic literature) in order to argue for its authenticity (to the historical Jesus). Differently, J. Lambrecht, *Die Redaktion der Markus-Apokalypse* (Rome: Papal Bible Institute, 1967), has stressed the redactional element in Mark 13 but seems to reach similar conclusions as to the relation between it and Jewish apocalyptic literature. For instance, he concludes that, for Mark the redactor, "die Paränese aktueller und wichtiger war als alle apokalyptische Unterweisung," 287.

5. T. Geddert, *Watchwords: Mark 13 in Markan Eschatology*, JSNTSS 26 (Sheffield: JSOT Press, 1989), 205. Geddert does not give any evidence to back up his position. Also, he exhibits no knowledge of the current state of the discussion surrounding the genre of apocalypse (see below).

6. See R. Pesch, *Naherwartungen* (Düsseldorf: Patmos-Verlag, 1968), 119 and passim. See also F. Neirynck, "Le discours anti-apocalyptique de Mk., XIII," *ETL* 45 (1969): 154-64. Similarly, H. Conzelmann, "Geschichte und Eschaton nach Mk 13," *ZNW* 50 (1959): 215, speaks of Mark as fending off "zeitgeschichtlichen-apokalyptische Spekulation" and giving in turn "positive eschatologische Belehrung." Note also W. Marxen, *Mark the Evangelist*, trans. J. Boyce et al. (Nashville: Abingdon, 1969), 189, who says that "Mark transforms apocalyptic into eschatology." Here Marxen is in essential agreement with Conzelmann; F.

Busch, *Verständnis der synoptischen Eschatologie, Markus 13 neu untersicht* (Gütersloh: Bertelsmann, 1938), 80; and W. Kümmel, *Promise and Fulfillment*, trans. D. Barton (London: SCM Press, 1957), 104. L. Hartman, *Prophecy Interpreted* (Lund: CWK Gleerup, 1966), who believes that Mark 13 is a midrash on Daniel 7-12, is reluctant to speak of all or part of Mark 13 as an apocalypse. He asserts that it is "uncommon in the Jewish apocalypses for the eschatology to be so closely bound up with the paraenesis," 175. He considers Mark 13 to contain "partly apocalyptic and eschatological material and partly paraenesis," 235.

7. E. Brandenburger, *Markus 13 und die Apokalyptik* (Göttingen: Vandenhoeck & Ruprecht, 1984), 12. Geddert, 18, criticizes Brandenburger, saying that "he fails to read the chapter in its Gospel context, choosing rather to read it in the light of contemporary apocalyptic literature, as so many scholars have done in the past." Thus with one sentence Geddert dismisses Brandenburger, and indeed a whole approach. In fact, Geddert spends a little over two pages in dismissing most scholarly attempts to understand Mark 13.

8. See on these terms J. J. Collins, "Apocalyptic Literature," in *Early Judaism and Its Modern Interpreters*, ed. R. A. Kraft and G. W. E. Nickelsburg (Atlanta: Scholars Press, 1986), 345-47; idem, *The Apocalyptic Imagination* (New York: Crossroad, 1984), 1-11; and P. D. Hanson, "Apocalypticism," *IBD* (Supp. vol.), 28-34.

9. The work of the Apocalypse Group can be found in *Semeia* 14 (1979), which is entitled "Apocalypse: The Morphology of a Genre" and is edited by J. J. Collins.

10. Collins, "Morphology of a Genre," 9.

11. Ibid., 13. For examples of these six categories, see ibid., 14-15: for example, (Ia) Daniel 7-12; 2 *Apocalyse of Baruch*; (Ib) Revelation; (Ic) *Apocalypse of Adam*; (IIa) *Apocalypse of Abraham*; (IIb) *1 Enoch* 1-36; and (IIc) 3 *Apocalyse of Baruch*

12. See above, note 2, for Koch's "checklist." Another commonly used list of traits was drawn up by P. Vielhaur, *New Testament Apocrypha*, vol. 2 (Philadelphia: Westminster, 1965), 582-600.

13. See on this E. P. Sanders, "The Genre of Palestinian Jewish Apocalypses," in *Apocalypticism in the Mediterranean World and the Near East*, ed. David Hellholm (Tübingen: J. C. B. Mohr, 1983), 456.

14. Ibid.

15. J. Carmignac, "Qu'est-ce que l'apocalyptique? Son emploi à Qumrân," *RevQ* 10 (1979-81): 20.

16. A. Yarbro Collins, "Early Christian Apocalypses," *Semeia* 14 (1979): 97.

17. Brandenburger, *Markus 13*, 13, says, "ja muß man Markus 13 durchaus eine Apokalypse nennen." Others might be reluctant to call Mark 13 as it stands an apocalypse, but might use the term to describe a source that stands behind the chapter. For instance, Pesch, *Naherwartungen*, 208, calls the source he identifies behind Mark 13 an "apokalyptischen Flugblatt." See also F. Flückinger, "Die Redaktion der Zukunftsrede in Mark 13," *ThZ* 27 (1970): 408.

18. Vielhauer, *New Testament Apocrypha*, 587.

19. C. Münchow, *Ethik und Eschatologie: Ein Beitrag zum Verständnis der frühjüdischen Apokalyptik* (Göttingen: Vandenhoeck & Ruprecht, 1981).

20. E. Schüssler Fiorenza, "The Phenomenon of Early Christian Apocalyptic: Some Reflections on Method," *Apocalypticism in the Mediterranean World and the Near East*, ed. David Hellholm, 300.

21. See on this incident E. Schürer, *The History of the Jewish People in the Age of Jesus Christ*, vol. 1, rev. and ed. Vermes, Millar, and Black (Edinburgh: T. & T.

Clark, 1973), 464.

22. See Beasley-Murray, *A Commentary on Mark* 13, 27; Lambrecht, *Die Redaktion der Markus-Apokalypse*, 86; and Brandenburger, *Markus, 13*, 95. L. Gaston, *No Stone on Another*, SNT 23 (Leiden: Brill, 1970), 12, notes, "It is assumed by the disciples, according to Mark, that the fall of Jerusalem and the end of the world are related, even simultaneous events." Pesch, 103 f., agrees that the destruction of the temple and the end of the world perhaps were thought to be related, but leaves open the question of their exact relationship.

23. This parallelism has been noted by Beasley-Murray, *A Commentary on Mark* 13, 27; Cranfield, "St. Mark 13," 195; and Lambrecht, *Die Redaktion*, 86.

24. Lambrecht, *Die Redaktion*, 87.

25. Translations from the pseudepigrapha are taken from The Old Testament Pseudepigrapha, ed. J. H. Charlesworth (Garden City, N.Y.: Doubleday, 1983). The meaning of the word *end* in apocalyptic literature is difficult to pin down. See, for instance, M. E. Stone, "Coherence and Inconsistency in the Apocalypses: The Case of 'the End' in 4 Ezra," *JBL* 102 (1983): 229-43.

26. Of course, 4 Ezra 15 and 16 were not originally part of 4 Ezra, but are early Jewish-Christian writings.

27. See Schüssler Fiorenza, *The Phenomenon of Early Christian Apocalyptic*, 301. See also the Greek Apocalypse of Ezra 3:11-14.

28. See on these parallels see Hartman, *Prophecy Interpreted*, 151-54.

29. For instance, Koch, *The Rediscovery of Apocalyptic*, makes periodization of history one of the eight motifs he finds characteristic of all apocalyptic literature, 28-33. In contrast, the SBL Apocalypse Group in 1979, led by John J. Collins, recognized that only some apocalypses have this periodization of history, and made them a subgroup within the genre.

30. Lars Hartman, "The Functions of Some So-called Apocalyptic Timetables," *NTS* 22 (1975-76): 1.

31. The reader will note here that I broaden my discussion to include documents that are not "apocalypses" in terms of genre but might be considered "apocalyptic" in that they are influenced by apocalyptic thought. This is because, in my opinion, other Jewish literature reveals a concern for the timing of the end (for example, *Sib. Or.* 3, 1QM, *Jubilees* 23).

32. I borrow here Hartman's term, "The Functions of Some So-called Apocalyptic Timetables," 1.

33. It is important to note here the important (but often neglected) work of Jacob Licht, "Time and Eschatology in Apocalyptic Literature and in Qumran," *JJS* 16 (1965): 177-82. Licht notes that in apocalyptic literature there is often "a veiled condemnation of the real writer's own period, which is regarded as the inevitable time of hardship preceding the expected salvation," 179.

34. It is interesting that many scholars either ignore this period or give it scant attention. For instance, it is not mentioned by Licht or by Hartman, *Prophecy Interpreted*, ConB 1 (Lund: WK Gleerup, 1966), 28 f. Hartman finds a different division of the eschatological age in the literature of early Judaism: a) The description of the background of the divine intervention—evil times, moral evil, catastrophes, etc.; b) a divine intervention (by God or the messiah); c) the passing of judgment; d) the fate of sinners, their punishment, etc; e) the time of salvation, the blessed state of the elect, etc. See also D. S. Russell, *The Method and Message of Jewish Apocalyptic: 200 b.c.—a.d. 100*, OTL (Philadelphia: Westminster Press, 1964), 271-76; and Christopher Rowland, *The Open Heaven: A Study of Apocalyptic in Judaism and Early Christianity* (New York: Crossroad, 1982), 156-60. The most detailed treatment of the time of tribulation is found

in Dale C. Allison, Jr., *The End of the Ages Has Come: An Early Interpretation of the Passion and Resurrection of Jesus* (Philadelphia: Fortress Press, 1985), 5-25. However, Allison's treatment of the literature is very general and fails to see the distinctions I am making in terms of the timing of the end.

35. As John J. Collins, "The Date and Provenance of the Testament of Moses," in *Studies on the Testament of Moses*, ed. George W. E. Nickelsburg (Missoula, Mont.: Scholars Press, 1973), 20, says that an "accurate generalization of apocalyptic patterns might say that the final judgment is preceded by a time of great distress, which may on occasion contain a description of the time of the author, but most often is future prediction, either entirely or in part." Allison, 6-7, notes Collins's viewpoint and contrasts it with that of H. H. Rowley, who speaks of the great tribulation as being a present reality for the authors of apocalyptic literature. Allison believes that both viewpoints are tenable because both can draw on different texts for support. I, however (contra Rowley and Allison), believe that when the concept of the tribulation is present in the literature it is always (or almost always) future. Rowley and Allison err in equating the tribulation with the woes and trials that make up the earlier stages of the end and which do indeed represent the present reality of the authors.

36. This is suggested but not elaborated on by Licht, "Time and Eschatology," 179, when he says, "It is only at the end of the whole process—after several protracted stages of eschatological transition—that a New Heaven and a New Earth will transpire and the process of 'historical development' will cease."

37. This is against Allison, *The End of the Ages*, 7-8, who does not examine Daniel 10-12 in detail but seems to argue that for the author the tribulation is present.

38. See Morton Smith, "What Is Implied by the Variety of Messianic Figures?" *JBL* 78 (1959): 66-72, who argues that the diversity of messianic expectations in the Qumran literature indicates that the community was not organized around a single eschatological argument. Smith argues that eschatology at Qumran may have been a highly individualistic matter. John J. Collins, "Patterns of Eschatology at Qumran" in *Traditions in Transformation*, ed. Baruch Halpern and Jon D. Levenson (Winona Lake, Ind: Eisenbrauns, 1981), 351-75, while recognizing the diversity of eschatological doctrines held at Qumran, has argued that these doctrines presupposed an underlying coherent perception of reality that can be described as apocalyptic in character. See the argument to the contrary by Philip R. Davies, "Eschatology at Qumran," *JBL* 104 (1985): 39-55.

39. As Jean Carmignac, "Qu'est-ce que l'apocalyptique? Son emploi a Qumrân," 325, says in regard to the genre of apocalypse, "Ce genre littéraire était connu et apprécié à Qumrân, non seulement dans ses emplois bibliques, mais aussi grâce à des oeuvres comme Jubilés ou Hénoch, dont les auteurs étaient plus ou moins apparentés à Qumrân." It is debated whether 1QM can be considered to be an apocalypse. See Jean Duhaime, "La régle de la guerre de Qumrân et l'apocalyptique," *ScEs* 36 (1984): 67-88, for a review of the debate. What is not doubted is the influence of apocalyptic thought on the literature of Qumran (particularly in the case of 1QM).

40. This is a hotly debated issue; see, for instance, *JNES* 49 (1990), which devotes a whole issue to the discussion of Qumran and apocalyptic. Those who have called Qumran an apocalyptic community include Frank Moore Cross, Jr., *The Ancient Library of Qumran and Modern Biblical Studies*, rev. ed. (Garden City, N.Y.: Doubleday, 1961), 76-78; Martin Hengel, *Judaism and Hellenism*, vol 1; trans. John Bowden (London: SCM Press, 1974), 218 f.; John J. Collins, *The Apocalyptic Imagination* (New York: Crossroad, 1989), 140; and idem, "Was the

Dead Sea Sect an Apocalyptic Movement?" in *Archaeology and History in the Dead Sea Scrolls*, ed. Lawrence H. Schiffman, JSPSup 8 (Sheffield: JSOT Press, 1990) 25-51. This opinion has been challenged by Hartmut Stegemann, "Die Bedeutung der Qumranfunde für die Erforschung der Apokalyptik," in *Apocalypticism in the Mediterranean World and the Near East*, ed. David Hellholm, 525; and P. R. Davies, "Qumran and Apocalyptic or Obscurum per Obscurius," *JNES* 49 (1990): 127-34.

41. As Lawrence H. Schiffman, *The Eschatological Community of the Dead Sea Scrolls*, SBLMS 38 (Atlanta: Scholars Press, 1989), 7, says, "Equally important is the notion of the immediacy of the eschaton. The old order would soon come to an end. The forces of evil and those opposing the sect would soon be destroyed. . . . The sect lived on the verge of the eschaton, with one foot, as it were, in the present age and one foot in the future age." Schiffman argues that because of this, the community organized itself on the model of what its members expected the eschatological community to look like. This model of the eschatological community is found in 1QSa.

42. For the questions surrounding the translation of *mw'd ht'nyt*, see Maurya P. Horgan, *Pesharim: Qumran Interpretations of Biblical Books*, CBQMS 8 (Washington, D.C.: The Catholic Biblical Association of America, 1979), 206-7.

43. On the restoration of this damaged column, see, ibid. 82-86.

44. M. S. Stone, *Fourth Ezra*, Hermeneia (Minneapolis: Fortress, 1990), 102.

45. See here Stone, "Coherency and Inconsistency," and idem, *Fourth Ezra*, 103-4.

46. Stone also uses the word *timetable* in reference to these matters, cf. *Fourth Ezra*, 103.

47. This understanding may help to explain 4 Ezra 6:1, a text that has given scholars a bit of trouble. It says *qdmy byd br 'ns' swlm' dyn b'ydy dyly* ("the beginning by the hand of man, but the end by my hands"). The "beginning" here, I suggest, is the start of the eschatological age, caused perhaps by the actions of foreign nations (cf. 4:3, 6). The "end" is the end of this age, marked by the signs shown by God (cf. 6:20). See on this verse Michael E. Stone, *Features of the Eschatology of IV Ezra*, HSS 35 (Atlanta: Scholars Press, 1989), 84-85.

48. This understanding is supported by Stone, *Fourth Ezra*, 294.

49. Due to space and time, I have not examined other texts that reveal this same interest. I think here of many other apocalypses (for example, the *Apocalypse of Weeks*, *2 Enoch*) and documents like *Jubilees* 23, *Sibylline Oracles* 3, *Testament of Levi*. See also Revelation and Mark 13 in the New Testament.

50. This threefold division of Mark 13:5b-27 is recognized by Brandenburger, *Markus 13*, 17-18, but he does not compare this periodization with similar patterns in Jewish apocalyptic literature. The same can be said of F. Rousseau, "La structure de Marc 13," *Bib* 56 (1975): 157-72. For a review of other proposals on the structure of Mark 13, see J. Mateos, *Marcos 13* (Madrid: Ediciones Cristiandad, 1987), 171-92.

The Foreigner and Association with Foreigners in the Old and New Testaments

Lothar Ruppert

C ountless masses worldwide are fleeing famine zones and war-torn areas, pleading for asylum. Many of these people seek refuge in Germany. People hope to stop or regulate the flow of refugees with suitable legislation. Of course, this raises not only political issues. Christians must also wrestle with the question of foreigners, refugees, and those seeking sanctuary, especially in light of what the Savior of the world says in Matthew's Gospel: "I was a stranger and you welcomed me" (Matthew 25:35)—the theme of this conference.[1] When this theme was introduced as the topic of the academy's program, the leaders could hardly foresee how acutely relevant it would become in a literal sense.[2] Christians must decide for themselves in this matter; they cannot remain distant observers. Of course, this decision, which is also politically relevant, must not be arrived at without consideration. Rather, one must keep in mind what God expects from Christians here, today. Therefore, it is necessary to begin by listening to God's word as transmitted and delivered in the human words of the Holy Bible, the Old and New Testaments. Yet I implore you, do not look to this lecture on basic principles for any concrete advice that could solve the refugee problem in Germany for good. A Christian solution must take the Bible into account, but also requires socio-political understanding. Here it is good to begin by listening carefully to the many voices of the Holy Bible and then trying to "translate" the biblical message sent forth 2,000 years ago (and even earlier in Israel) from that time and environment. This translation, necessary for responsible Christian practical, political action, can only be outlined here. The Bible is the basis and plumb line of Christian belief, yet it certainly

This essay was translated from German by Beth I. Jenkins.

does not therefore offer an arsenal of political actions to which one can help oneself as one pleases. As an exegete of the Old Testament (also called the "First Testament"), I would like to concentrate my observations on the first part of the two-part Christian Bible, without neglecting the New Testament.

The Foreigner in the Old Testament

Old Testament statements about foreigners and association with foreigners differ widely.[3] Christians can easily become confused because of this. However, the difference in attitudes toward foreigners is easy to understand when one considers that the books of the Old Testament emerged from their sources over a period of almost 1,000 years. Their statements are to be understood in light of the differing times in which the relevant texts emerged and the very different audiences to which their message was originally addressed. It makes quite a difference whether the people of God were living in a sovereign Israelite or Jewish nation (that is, in the Northern Kingdom of Israel or in the longer-extant Southern Kingdom) or in a more or less autonomous temple community centered in Jerusalem under Persian, Egyptian, or Syrian sovereignty, not to mention in a totally foreign environment, the Babylonian Exile (as from 597 or 586 to 538 B.C.E.). One must also take into consideration whether the foreigner is encountered in more judicial biblical texts, such as the so-called Book of the Covenant (Exodus 20:22-23:19), or in more characteristically religious or theological sections. Even though religious vision and theological evaluation permeate the Law of Israel, in the final analysis it is still understood as law given to Israel by YHWH, Israel's God.

I would like to cover the Old Testament portion of my lecture in four steps: I want 1) to acquaint you with the different groups of "foreigners" in ancient Israel by discussing the relevant Hebrew expressions that describe each group's social status. I would then like 2) to demonstrate, with the help of theological texts and legal determinations, the development undergone by Israel's attitude toward strangers. Thereafter I would like 3) to show how Israel's ethos provided a theological and concretely salvation-historical basis for the requisite attitude toward strangers, in order to 4) sum up the relevant message of the Old Testament.

THE DIFFERENT HEBREW TERMS FOR "STRANGERS" AND THE LEGAL STATUS OF THOSE GROUPS OF PERSONS. The Hebrew Bible uses several words to designate "strangers": If the stranger is a *foreigner* who is only temporarily staying in Israel, *nokrî* is used, or sometimes *zār*. A more negative connotation accompanies the latter word, as with the English "strange." This term mostly used with members of foreign peoples with whom Israel has had unpleasant, even painful, experiences, such as the Egyptians and Babylonians. Finally, in later ritual texts *zār* can mean "layperson," or "unauthorized" in a cultic sense.

Two groups are most interesting for our question: the *gēr* and the *tôšāb*. The *gēr* is distinguished from the foreigner (that is, from the *nokrî*, or occasionally *zār*) in that he is a settled stranger, one who has established himself for a certain time in the country and to whom a special status is therefore granted. Perhaps we could equate the *gērîm* in Old Testament times with our foreign laborers, from whom only certain rights are withheld (such as the right to vote). Likewise, the *gēr* "does not have all the rights of an Israelite, for instance, she may not own land. . . . She is generally in the service of an Israelite, who is her lord and protector (Deuteronomy 24:14). Usually the *gēr* is poor (cf., however, Leviticus 25:47) and is therefore counted among the 'economically disadvantaged.' "[4]

In a similar but socially more deprived situation was the so-called sojourner (*tôšāb*), who, mostly descending from the original Canaanite population, "found lasting shelter on foreign (Israelite!) land as a ward of the resident tribe or one of the single *owners*."[5]

Thus one can fundamentally differentiate between two major groups of strangers in Israel: strangers who have become resident in Israel, although without possessing land and with restricted legal rights (*gēr* and *tôšāb*), and those temporarily staying in Israel, that is, foreigners (*nokrî*) or people of a foreign religious cult and way of life (*zār*).

THE HISTORICAL DEVELOPMENT OF ISRAEL'S ATTITUDES CONCERNING STRANGERS. YHWH's *Privilegrecht* (Exodus 34:10-26)[6] forbade Israel to make a covenant with the Canaanite inhabitants of the land (Exodus 34:12) so that Israelite men could not marry Canaanite women (cf. Deuteronomy 7:3). However, ancient Israel by no means spurned contact with the Canaanite population or foreigners until long into the monarchic era. Foreigners were present as David's soldiers (2 Samuel 11:1-27), among his officials (2 Samuel 8:15-18), and among the sailors and merchants of the kings of Israel and Judah (1 Kings 9:26 f.; 10:11; 20:34); and most of the traders in the country were Canaanites ("Canaanites" meant, more or less, "traders," cf. Hosea 12:8; Zephaniah 1:11; Proverbs 31:24). The relationship with the original inhabitants, as with foreigners, was thus for the most part uncomplicated. It was not considered a scandal that even Moses, as is witnessed in the tradition, had a Midianite wife (Exodus 2:15-22), that a charismatic leader like Samson courted a Philistine (Judges 13:14), or that Israelite spies went in to a prostitute in Jericho (Joshua 2). Of course, the ancient Israelites had to learn by experience that too close a contact—for instance, a marriage relationship with the Baal-worshiping Canaanite population—carried with it great danger for the purity of Israel's YHWH worship, and even for the identity of Israel. Increasingly, the Deuteronomic movement late in the monar-

chy recognized this (cf. Deuteronomy 7:3), as did the Deuteronomistic
History in retrospect, and made King Solomon, due to his (politically
justified) marriage to "idol-worshiping" foreign women, responsible for
the desertion from, the breaking of, the covenant of God's people
(1 Kings 11:1-3). From this negative experience came the conviction in
the late pre-exilic era that YHWH wanted, indeed commanded Israel before their entry into the Promised Land, to consign the idol-worshiping
Canaanites to destruction (Deuteronomy 7:2; 20:16-18), a practice that
the Deuteronomic law provided for in the siege of an enemy city in a
later period only under very specific circumstances (Deuteronomy
20:10-15). According to older Deuteronomic thought, YHWH had promised Israel to drive her Canaanite enemies out of the land (cf. Deuteronomy
6:19; Exodus 23:27-31). That God did not completely fulfill this promise
is later explained by Deuteronomistic theology as God's preserving the
rest of the people in the land as punishment for Israel's breaking the
covenant (cf. Joshua 23:12 f.). Nevertheless, the ban,[7] the religious order
to consign the peoples to destruction (an ancient oriental praxis in no
way limited to Israel that, according to Scripture, was used to some extent in the taking of the land [cf. Joshua 6-8]), was essentially only a
simple theological postulate derived from later reflection on bad experiences. Finally, the Canaanites actually remained among the Israelites in
Canaan. The later distancing of Israel from one part of the land's population happened in no way for ethnic or racial reasons. Rather, it sprang
from the sad historical experience that these non-Israelites represented a
great danger for the faith, the religion, indeed the existence of the people
of God. For this reason, even one hundred years after the Babylonian
exile, the scribe Ezra (Ezra 9 f.) and the governor Nehemiah (Nehemiah
13:15-22) took decisive action against mixed marriages: gentile wives
had to be dismissed.

At the same time, there are exilic and post-exilic witnesses who
resist a chauvinism regarding salvation among the people of God that
dared to dispute foreigners' capacity for repentance and the possibility of
their inclusion in the salvation offered by YHWH through Israel. The testimony of those books of edifying history, Jonah and Ruth, should be
mentioned first: the God-fearing, pagan sailors, as well as the inhabitants
of Ninevah who respond to the prophet's call to repentance, shame the
salvation-chauvinist Jonah, who, as a deserting prophet, functions as a
negative example. And that, of all people, Ruth, a Moabitess who gave
up her people and her homeland out of loyalty for and devotion to her
Israelite mother-in-law, should become ancestress of King David (cf. Ruth
4:13-17)! Likewise, the numerous prophetic oracles concerning salvation for pagan peoples give us pause to consider; one thinks of the word
of salvation regarding the nations making pilgrimage to Zion (according

to Isaiah 2:2-5 *par.* and other references). According to the eschatological outlook of Psalm 47, the princes of the pagan peoples are gathered "as the people of the God of Abraham" (NRSV, v. 10). Thus, one finds in the Old Testament no trace of ethnically motivated xenophobia, or indeed of race discrimination.

What information does Israel's law give us about the position and rights of foreigners? Perhaps the oldest provision in the Book of the Covenant reads, "You shall not oppress a resident alien (*gēr*)" (Exodus 23:9 without the later salvation-historical argument). A similarly grounded prohibition in the same place appears to be just as ancient: "You shall not wrong or oppress a resident alien (*gēr*). . . . If you do abuse them, when they cry out to me, I will surely heed their cry" (Exodus 22:21a, 23, original form). Therefore, in order to warn Israel against such actions, YHWH himself guarantees a hearing for oppressed people—though they may not exactly be YHWH worshipers—who cry for help to YHWH, the God of the oppressing Israelites. Thus, already in a relatively early time in Israel the oppression/exploitation of even a single resident alien in the land is strictly forbidden by law, and even by divine law.

The Deuteronomic law expresses itself often regarding the resident alien (*gēr*): In Israel, grain fields, olive trees, and vineyards were not allowed to be harvested completely because the resident aliens (along with other representatives of the socially disempowered, the orphans and the widows) had the right to glean (Deuteronomy 24:19-22). In the area surrounding each town, a tenth of the year's harvest had to be stored so that resident aliens (along with orphans and widows) could eat of it (Deuteronomy 14:28 f.)—a rather high rate of social taxation, to use modern terms! The stranger also (like male and female slaves, orphans, and widows) should participate in harvest festival celebrations (Deuteronomy 16:9-15), and the stranger is included in the sabbath rest (Deuteronomy 5:12-15). Deuteronomy 24:14 f. forbids withholding "the wages of poor and needy laborers, whether other Israelites *or aliens* who reside in your land in one of your towns." They must also be paid on the same day, without exception.

And yet even Deuteronomy certainly does not gloss over the differing status of strangers and foreigners vis-à-vis the Israelites. While it is forbidden for Israelites to eat carcasses (that is, torn or dead animals, which were considered ritually unclean), the carcasses may be left (gratis) for the alien living in Israel and may even be sold to the foreigner (*nokrî*; Deuteronomy 14:21). An Israelite believer may even take coercive legal action against a foreigner (Deuteronomy 15:3) or charge interest to a foreigner (Deuteronomy 23:20), while such is forbidden in dealings with a "brother" (an Israelite). Of all foreigners, the Ammonites and the Moabites were denied entrance into the assembly of YHWH (due to their hostile behavior during the Exodus of Israel from Egypt), while the Edomites (because of their tribal kinship with Israel) and even the Egyptians (because Israel had sojourned as guest in Egypt) were allowed entry (Deuteronomy 23:3-8).

Also, the Priestly law (the law concerning ritual) calls for a portion of the harvest to go to resident aliens (Leviticus 19:9 f.) and forbids oppressing them (Leviticus 19:33). Furthermore, "The alien who resides with you shall be to you as the citizen among you; you shall love the alien as yourself" (Leviticus 19:34a)—surely a peak formulation in the Old Testament. A foreigner residing in Israel (*gēr*) may eat of the Passover lamb if he allows himself to be circumcised (Exodus 12:48). Citizens as well as aliens who live in Israel are ruled by the same law (Exodus 12:49; also Numbers 15:14-16). A common cult with foreigners is therefore possible under certain preconditions.

A prophetically inspired community code from the early post-exilic era takes things even further. It says,

> Do not let the foreigner (*ben-hannēkār*) joined to the LORD say, "The LORD will surely separate me from his people." . . . And the foreigners who join themselves to the LORD, to minister to him, to love the name of the LORD, and to be his servants, all who keep the sabbath, and do not profane it, and hold fast my covenant— these I will bring to my holy mountain, and make them joyful in my house of prayer; their burnt offerings and their sacrifices will be accepted on my altar; for my house shall be called a house of prayer for all peoples. Isaiah 56:3a, 6-7[8]

This last prophetic text from the early post-exilic period concerns itself with foreigners who, through accepting the worship of YHWH, have in a certain way joined the *people* of God. There is also an exilic prophetic text with a background in Priestly theology which allows even foreigners (*gērîm*) to receive their portion of the land at its new division following the Exile (Ezekiel 47:22 f.). Bound by one faith and a common cult, people of different origins and different traditions can grow together as the people of God into a greater Israel.

By analogy, carried over to the political plane which interests us today, this certainly means that foreigners—those seeking asylum, for instance—who take on German citizenship want to be Germans without renouncing their cultural heritage. At any rate, this prophetic text is a clear message against any chauvinism of the elect and expulsion of foreigners.

How Does the Ethos or Law of Israel Theologically Justify This Positive Attitude Toward Foreigners? Several of the legal texts I have cited justify their positive attitude toward foreigners or the "rights" they give foreigners by referring to the fact that the Israelites were once strangers in Egypt. For example, "You shall not wrong or oppress a resident alien, for you were aliens in the land of Egypt" (Exodus 22:21).[9] This salvation-historical motivation in regard to the social attitude vis-à-vis strangers is typical for Deuteronomic/Deuteronomistic theology, whose presence here as well must be presumed. That is to say, the motivation of the law is in keeping with a later, Deuteronomic/Deuteronomistic editor.

The best known of these is the salvation-historical motivation for the sabbath which also includes foreigners (Exodus 20:10 *par.*), in the Deuteronomic version of the Ten Commandments: "Remember that you were a slave in the land of Egypt, and the LORD your God brought you out from there with a mighty hand and an outstretched arm; therefore the LORD your God commanded you to keep the sabbath day" (Deuteronomy 5:15).[10] Likewise, the ritual law of the Priestly Code gives a similar reason for loving even the resident alien: "You shall love the alien as yourself, for you were aliens in the land of Egypt: I am the LORD your God" (Leviticus 19:34).

In several places in the Pentateuch we find references to the fact that the patriarchs of Israel had to live as foreigners in the land promised to themselves and their descendants.[11] Thus, the foreigner reminded the Israelites of the foreignness and vulnerability of their ancestors, not only in Egypt, but also before that even in Canaan: "A wandering [or "homeless," or "close to destruction"] Aramean was my ancestor; he went down into Egypt and lived there as an alien, few in number" (Deuteronomy 26:5 ff.)—so runs the brief historical creed that Israelites were to use in giving thanks to God for the first fruits of their produce. The ancestor here referred to is Jacob (with the honorary name Israel), who had to live as a foreigner (Aramean) among Canaanites in the land of Canaan and, in conjunction with a famine, emigrated to the fertile pastureland of the eastern Nile delta in Egypt to live there also as a stranger. The Genesis tradition already knows that, in the Promised Land, Abraham was dependent upon the goodwill of the indigenous peoples in order to purchase a burial place, the cave of Machpelah at Mamre/Hebron (Genesis 23). The only possession in the Promised Land—a burial place! The Priestly tradition coined the eloquent expression for the promised, not yet possessed, land: "the land in which you sojourn" (Genesis 17:8 and frequently). Without possession of land, the patriarchs of Israel had to live in tents in the country (cf. Genesis 18:1 and other places). Thus the Israelite farmer, now residing on his own land, was required in the old laws to recognize in the lot of the unpropertied stranger—whether Israelite or landless Canaanite sojourner—the hard lot of his own tribal fathers or ancestors. Moreover, foreigners who had found refuge with Israelite property owners were considered guests. Hospitality was highly valued in the Near East at that time, and still is today; to violate hospitality was a serious sacrilege (cf. Genesis 19:4-8; Judges 19:22-26). Thus, the tradition of hospitality and the knowledge of the experience of their own foreignness and homelessness in the early history of their people contributed to a fundamentally positive attitude towards foreigners.

THE TESTIMONY OF THE OLD TESTAMENT IN REGARDS TO BEHAVIOR VIS-À-VIS FOREIGNERS IN ANCIENT ISRAEL. Let us summarize briefly. The Old Testament understood as "foreigners" the foreigner settled in a place (*gēr*), who had become impoverished and placed himself under the protection of and in service to a free Israelite (usually a propertied farmer). Usually it refers to an Israelite from another place, though it can also be a Canaanite, one of the original inhabitants of the country; these are usually called sojourners (*tôšāb*). An Israelite's behavior toward these was to be similar to her treatment of a *gēr*. An exception was in the cultic domain: the foreigner could take part in the Passover meal of the extended Israelite family only if he had allowed himself to be circumcised, thereby joining the community of Israel as the people of YHWH. Such became an explicit entitlement even for foreigners in a strict sense in a post-exilic community code. Edomites and even Egyptians were allowed to participate in more civic assemblies of YHWH.

Israel's (divine) law expected behavior vis-à-vis foreigners ranging from a ban on oppression and suppression, from the punctual payment of daily wages and guaranteed subsistence, through a type of social taxation (the tithe of the harvest profits), through enjoyment of sabbath rest and participation in the great harvest festivals, to the demand to love the foreigner as oneself. This exceedingly positive view of foreigners has, finally, two roots. One root is the common Eastern institution of hospitality, which still today above all else enjoys high esteem in the Bedouin region of the Orient. The other root is of a historical and religious sort. It is the Israelite consciousness that Israel itself was earlier (through its ancestors, even the original patriarchs) a foreigner, the alien in Canaan, and that its God, YHWH, had freed it from its bondage in Egypt, a foreign place. Just as the Israelites experienced YHWH's favor when they were near destruction and oppressed as foreigners, so should they behave correctly towards the alien Canaan, which was once a land of foreign sojourn for Israel's patriarchs; still more, they should offer it protection and provision and, yes, seek its good. Of course, Israel drew the line when the aliens, as worshipers of foreign gods, could be a snare for or temptation to the Israelites themselves to turn to the gods of the aliens, that is, fall away from YHWH, breaking the covenant. This danger appeared to be greatest when a large number of foreigners lived in immediate proximity to Israelites, and when a greater number of mixed marriages threatened to take away Israel's identity as the people of YHWH, its God, such as in the Persian province of Judah in the Second Temple period (cf. Ezra 9 f.; Nehemiah 13:23-30). Mind you, it was an issue of losing not the ethnic identity, but rather the religious identity of Israel!

The Foreigner in the New Testament

I would now like to touch briefly upon foreigners in the New Testament,[12] and to do this in three steps: 1) the Greek word for "foreign/foreigner" in the New Testament, 2) places where the New Testament speaks of foreigners and proper or improper behavior toward foreigners, and 3) the motivation for love of foreigners in the New Testament.

THE GREEK WORD FOR "FOREIGN/FOREIGNER." The Greek word for "foreign" (adjective) and "foreigner" (noun) is *xenos*, which, as an adjective, besides "foreign" can mean "exotic" or "strange" and, as a noun, besides "foreigner" can mean "visitor" or "guest" or again "host." "The variable meaning of 'foreigner' is explained by the system of hospitality, whose goal it is to integrate the foreigner in a certain group. If this does not succeed, the stranger is required to withdraw."[13]

PLACES WHERE THE NEW TESTAMENT SPEAKS OF FOREIGNERS AND PROPER OR IMPROPER BEHAVIOR TOWARD FOREIGNERS. The New Testament speaks of Jesus as a foreigner and about people's behavior towards him as such. Jesus himself speaks twice in the Gospels about behavior towards foreigners. In the non-Gospel writings of the New Testament, right or wrong behavior towards foreigners (mostly nonresident Christians, including missionaries) is addressed. Finally, Christians themselves are understood as foreigners on this earth.

Jesus as foreigner. The prologue of the Gospel of John reflects the foreignness of Jesus. The rejection by his own, who did not comprehend the Incarnate Word (the *Logos*), allows Christ himself to be seen as a foreigner in his own realm (John 1:11; cf. v. 14). Jesus can say of himself: "Foxes have holes, and birds of the air have nests; but the Son of Man has nowhere to lay his head" (Matthew 8:20 // Luke 9:58).

Jesus' words regarding the proper behavior vis-à-vis foreigners. Well known is Jesus' parable of the Good Samaritan who showed mercy to the Jew fallen victim to robbers, that is, to a stranger, even a so-called enemy of the Samaritan (Luke 10:29-37). Jesus makes plain with this parable that the foreigner, in his indigence and need, can be the neighbor whom an Israelite must love as himself according to the instructions of Mosaic law (Leviticus 19:18). The law itself applies to foreigners the identical formula "love as yourself" (Leviticus 19:34).

Equally well known is the great apocalyptic discourse of the Son of Man at the Last Judgment, transmitted only in Matthew (Matthew 25:31-46). According to this text, the Son of Man, or rather the King (in this context Jesus himself), appears in court to judge and reward or punish the people according to their works, not of piety, but rather of love of neighbor. Among these works of love of neighbor, the welcoming of foreigners is mentioned by name: "I was a stranger and you welcomed me" (v. 35), he would say to those on his right, but to those on his left: "I was a stranger and you did not welcome me" (v. 43). That is to say, the judge of the world identifies himself with the least of his brothers (and sisters) (vv. 40-45). Since Christians address each other as "brothers," as witnessed in the New Testament, those strangers mentioned in this passage can be understood as Christians who come to a foreign Christian community.[14] If this is the case, then this judgment discourse, at least in its present form, is also to a great extent first coined by the evangelist Matthew.[15] Of course, the passage breathes the spirit of the historical Jesus through and through. The rabbinical literature likewise bears witness to the idea that God reckons a good deed done to the poor as done to himself (*Midr. Deuteronomy* 15:9). What is new here is that, in the final analysis, the act of love is counted as done to Jesus Christ (Matthew 25:40, 45).

The witness of non-Gospel books of the New Testament. The author of 3 John praises the addressee of Gaius's letter as faithful in everything that he does concerning the brothers (that is, fellow Christians) and even strangers (apparently itinerant Christian preachers; v.5). In this context belongs also the already cited apocalyptic discourse of the Son of Man at the last day; for there also the hospitable reception of foreign brothers, that is, Christians, is obviously valued just as if the good deed were rendered to Jesus Christ himself (Matthew 25:35, 38; cf. v. 43).

The reason for the absence of any admonition to do good deeds to strangers in the sense of pagans is not so much that close contact with outsiders, particularly unknown pagans, was dangerous for the Christian community, which even at this early date was in constant danger of persecution. It is rather that close contact with pagans easily led to unbelief or apostasy, or could at least endanger the solidarity of Christians. Of course, Christian solidarity could not be permitted to lead to a withdrawal into defensive isolation; on the contrary, if summoned and called upon, Christians were obligated to give witness before the pagans: "Always be ready to make your defense to anyone who demands from you an accounting for the hope that is in you; yet do it with gentleness and reverence. Keep your conscience clear" (1 Peter 3:15 f.). In the Christian community of Corinth, even pagans had apparently been admitted to the community gatherings. At least, when interested pagans came, they were not excluded (1 Corinthians 14:23).[16]

But the last reason why Christians kept a certain distance from their pagan fellow-citizens was their own general understanding of themselves as living as foreigners in this world. According to Paul (2 Corinthians 5:6), Christians know that they live far from the Lord (that is, from Christ) in a foreign country "while we are at home in the body." In the same way, the great Old Testament saints, such as the patriarchs, knew that they were "strangers and foreigners on the earth" (Hebrews 11:13). First Peter admonishes Christians to "live in reverent fear during the time of your exile" (1:17). The Christians are "aliens and exiles" (2:11). Indeed, according to Paul, Christians hold their true citizenship "in heaven" (Philippians 3:20) as "members of the household of God" (cf. Ephesians 2:19; 2 Corinthians 5:1-10).

Christians who had come from paganism were, of course, formerly "foreign" in a different sense of the word: they stood before God "once estranged and hostile in mind, doing evil deeds" (Colossians 1:21). As heathens, they were formerly "aliens from the commonwealth of Israel," that is, from the chosen people of God (Ephesians 2:12). Yet, through their belonging to Christ and his commonwealth, their alienation was overcome: "So then you are no longer strangers and aliens, but you are citizens with the saints and also members of the household of God" (Ephesians 2:19). Where people have become new persons in Christ, "there is no longer Greek and Jew, circumcised and uncircumcised, barbarian [that is, foreigner], Scythian [an example of a foreigner], slave and free; but Christ is all and in all" (Colossians 3:11). In Christ—that is, in the Christian community—former barriers pass away: first of all the barrier between the people of the old covenant with God and the pagan peoples; then national barriers (as vis-à-vis foreigners, in Greek "barbarians"), for example, with the Scythians; and finally social barriers (between the free and the slaves). Thus, through communion with Christ and among Christians, all previous estrangement and isolation are overcome.

A SUMMARY OF THE MOTIVATION OF LOVE TOWARD STRANGERS IN THE NEW TESTAMENT. Since through his incarnation in this world, which rejected him, Jesus Christ himself became a stranger, and since Christians also have no fixed abode, but rather are strangers, there is for Christians no natural barrier or demarcation vis-à-vis those who are strangers in a worldly sense. This is especially true when former strangers, that is, foreigners, have become "members of God's household" together with Christians. Thus, hospitality to Christian strangers is quite natural for Christians. According to the witness of the New Testament, such openness and hospitality fits with the will of Jesus, or of God, not only when exercised toward Christian strangers. Much more, as the parable of the good Samaritan (Luke 10:29-37) shows, in certain situations a stranger (translated: non-Christian!) who needs help can actually be *the* neighbor whom a member of the (new) "Israel of God" (Galatians 6:16), according to the instructions of the old covenantal law, must "love . . . as yourself" (Leviticus 19:18; cf. Leviticus 19:34, Luke 10:25-29). The Son of Man, who is to return as judge of the world, will count such an act of love of neighbor as one shown to himself (Matthew 25:40), or alternatively will count a refusal as a rejection of himself (Matthew 25:45), even if (so may one understand Matthew 25:31-46 in the light of Luke 10:29-30) the one in need should be a non-Christian.

Thus, the word of God in Holy Scripture, in the New and the Old Testaments, is fundamentally unified with regard to the required behavior toward strangers, although the New Testament overcomes the national and religious barriers (Samaritans and Jews were arch-enemies for *religious* reasons) still predominantly preserved at least in the Old Testament (Luke 10:29-37).

Endnotes

1. This contribution is based on a hitherto unpublished lecture given by the author on October 17, 1992, at a conference of the Bishop's Academy at Aachen in Krefeld. It was only minimally revised and furnished with footnotes for publication. The treatise is dedicated to Fredrick Holmgren, a foreign colleague who (with his wife, Betty) has become my friend during his many sabbaticals in Freiburg. He can well regard Freiburg im Breisgau almost as his second home. The style of the original lecture has been preserved since the *Festschrift* also has pastoral objectives.

2. A few weeks before the meeting of the academy (August 24-25, 1992), the first riots against foreigners (refugees) took place. Later, in still other locations, terrible acts (arson) against refugees would follow. Indeed, riots against refugees happen worldwide, but such excesses in Germany understandably receive worldwide publicity due to our ignoble recent history (the National Socialist reign).

3. The reader is referred to the following literature on the theme in general and especially regarding Old Testament findings: A. Bertholet, *Die Stellung der Israeliten und der Juden zu den Fremden* (Freiburg im Breisgau: Mohr [Siebeck], 1896); J. Schreiner, "Gastfreundschaft im Zeugnis der Bibel," *TTZ* 89 (1980): 50-60; L. Ruppert, "Der Umgang mit den Volksangehörigen und mit dem Fremden im alttestamentlichen Gottesvolk," in *Und wer ist mein Nächster? Reflexionen über Nächsten-, Bruder- und Feindesliebe*, ed. J. Horstmann (Schwerte: Katholische Akademie, 1982), 1-36; M. Görg, "Fremdsein in und für Israel, *MTZ* 37 (1986): 217-32; J. Schreiner, "Muß ich in der Fremde leben? Eine Frage des alten Israel," in J. Schreiner, *Segen für die Völker. Gesammelte Schriften zur Entstehung und Theologie des Alten Testaments*, ed. E. Zenger (Würzburg: Echter, 1987), 317-30; F. Crüsemann, "Fremdenliebe und Identitätssicherung: Zum Verständnis der 'Fremden'-Gesetze im Alten Testament," *WD N.F.* 19 (1987): 11-24; O. Fuchs, ed., *Die Fremden* (Dusseldorf: Patmos, 1988); B. Land, R. Kampling, "Fremder,"

Neues Bibel-Lexikon [NBL] (Zurich: Benziger, 1991) 1:701-3; Chr. Bultmann, *Der Fremde im antiken Juda*, FRLANT 153 (Göttingen: Vandenhoeck & Ruprecht, 1992); P. G. Müller, "Fremde/r," *Bibeltheologisches Wörterbuch [BThW]*, 4th ed., ed. J. B. Bauer (Cologne: Styria, 1994), 185-88; E. Otto, *Theologische Ethik des Alten Testaments* (Stuttgart: Kohlhammer, 1994), 84 f., 244-48. One can also refer to the article's relevant keywords (such as *gēr, zār, nokrî, tôšāb*) in *Theologisches Handwörterbuch [THAT]*, 2 vols. ed. E. Jenni and C. Westermann (Munich: Chr. Kaiser, 1971/76; ET Peabody, Mass.: Hendrickson, 1997); and *TWAT*, (8 vols., ed. G. J. Botterweck, H. Ringgren, H.-J. Fabry (Stuttgart: Kohlhammer, 1973-95).

4. R. Martin-Achard, "*gūr* als Fremdling weilen," *THAT* 1:409-12, esp. 410.

5. B. Baentsch, "Exodus—Leviticus—Numeri," GHK 1/2 (Göttingen: Vandenhoeck & Ruprecht, 1903), 107.

6. Compare to J. Halbe, *Das Privilegrecht Jahwes, Ex 34, 10-26. Gestalt und Wesen, Herkunft und Wirken in vordeuteronomischer Zeit*, FRLANT 114 (Göttingen: Vandenhoeck & Ruprecht, 1975), 223-25.

7. For more on this, see N. Lohfink, "Bann," *NBL* 1:287 f.

8. Cf. L. Ruppert, "Das Heil der Völker (Heilsuniversalismus) in Deutero- und 'Trito'-Jesaja," *MTZ* 45 (1994): 137-59, 153-55.

9. Cf. J. Schreiner, "Gastfreudschaft im Zeugnis der Bibel," 52 f.; also historically, see M. Görg, "Fremdsein in und für Israel," 220-22.

10. Cf. also N. Lohfink, "Zur Dekalogfassung von Dt 5," *BZ N.F.* 9 (1965): 17-32.

11. Cf. J. Schreiner, "Gastfreudschaft," 50-52; M. Görg, "Fremdsein," 229 f.

12. In addition to the specified articles in *NBL* and *BThW*, see especially R. Kampling, "Fremde und Fremdsein in Aussagen des Neuen Testaments," in O. Fuchs, *Die Fremden*, 215-39.

13. R. Kampling (with reference to Mark 5:17; Luke 9:53) in *NBL* 1:702.

14. According to R. Kampling, "Fremde und Fremdsein," 231, "the least of these my brothers" means "those charged with the gospel." Kampling (332 f.) conjectures in Matthew 25:31-46 "an infusion of early Christian utopia . . . in the sense that through the spread of the gospel and its practice, the world became one in which works of compassion became the expression of life with one another."

15. The discourse, heavily edited by Matthew, is difficult to ascribe to the pre-Easter Jesus. It probably originates in Hellenistic Jewish-Christian circles, so that of course the central thoughts point to Jesus himself (cf. R. Schnackenburg, *Matthäusevangelium* 16,21-28,20, Neue Echter Bibel 1/2 N.T. ([Würzburg: Echter, 1987], 252). According to J. Gnilka, *Matthäusevangelium*, HTKNT 1/2 (Freiburg: Herder, 1988), 367-70, the pericope can be fully ascribed to the evangelist.

16. H. J. Klauck: "It is to be determined that, as in the Jewish synagogues, pagans were admitted to worship as guests" (*1. Korintherbrief*, Neue Echter Bibel N.T. 7 [Würzburg: Echter, 1984], 112).

Parables and the Hebrew Scriptures

KLYNE SNODGRASS

For twenty years Fred Holmgren and I worked together in the biblical field at North Park. Fred was both friend and colleague, and often our conversation turned to a subject of primary interest for both of us, the relation of the two testaments. I am happy to return to this arena and to offer this article to a friend in commemoration of his service at North Park.

The Old Testament Background of Parables

One of Fred's recent publications drew attention to the Old Testament background of the parable of the Pharisee and the Tax Collector in Deuteronomy 26:1-15.[1] Christians—scholars included—have often underestimated the importance of the Old Testament for understanding the New, and this seems especially to be the case with regard to the parables. Usually a distinction is made between the parables of Jesus and those of the rabbis because rabbinic parables serve to elucidate specific texts of the Hebrew Scriptures, whereas Jesus' parables do not. It is true that Jesus' parables are not exegetical tools like the rabbinic parables, *except* for the parable of the Good Samaritan, which comes close to this in explicating the love command from Leviticus 19:18. Jesus' parables are more revelations of the kingdom and its required discipleship. It is also true that Jesus' parables do not usually quote Old Testament texts—*except* for the parable of the Wicked Tenants, which alludes clearly to the vineyard parable of Isaiah 5:1-2 and concludes with the quotation of Psalm 118:22-23.[2] These two exceptions, however, should motivate a closer analysis. As with the parable of the Pharisee and the Tax Collector, some parables seem to be framed on texts from the Hebrew Scriptures: the Good Samaritan on 2 Chronicles 28:8-15,[3] the Lost Sheep (and the Good Shepherd of John 10) on Ezekiel 34, and the Mustard Seed on Ezekiel 17:23. Other possibilities may not be as convincing but merit consideration, as, for example, the Sheep and the Goats framed on Ezekiel 34:17,[4] the Wedding Banquet on Zephaniah 1:7-13,[5] the Sower on the *Shema*[6] or, more likely, on Isaiah 6:9-13,[7] or Lazarus and the Rich Man on Genesis 15 and Isaiah 1.[8]

The influence of the Old Testament on Jesus' teaching in parables cannot be confined to those texts where one can detect allusions to specific texts. The primary influence on Jesus' parables was the parabolic way of thinking evidenced in many Old Testament texts. This may seem obvious at first glance, but, surprisingly, the value of understanding Jesus' parables against the background of the Old Testament has been ignored or undervalued by many. Two examples will suffice to illustrate the problem. David Flusser, a Jewish New Testament scholar who authored a helpful analysis of Jesus' parables in light of their rabbinic counterparts, argues that one will not make much progress in understanding the parables by looking at the Old Testament. He mentions only the story of Nathan's parable to David in 2 Samuel 12:1-7, which he says is not a parable in the actual sense, and he does not even include an index to the Hebrew Scriptures. Flusser is content to see Jesus' parables as derived from the broad sphere of rabbinic parables.[9] In all likelihood, other Jewish teachers were using parables at this time, and it may well be that Jesus drew from a common stock of parables current in his day. The problem, of course, is that no evidence is early enough to verify this. Depending on how one defines "parable," no parables similar to those of Jesus actually appear in Jewish documents earlier than the gospels—except for the Old Testament. Narrative parables do not occur in the Dead Sea Scrolls—at least so far—nor do they appear in the Apocrypha and Pseudepigrapha that pre-date the ministry of Jesus.[10] If we follow Jacob Neusner in saying, "What we cannot show, we do not know," we 'must be much more cautious about merely latching onto rabbinic parables as the key to understanding Jesus.[11] Further, to focus merely on the rabbinic writings ignores the larger question of the relation of the parables of Jesus and the rabbis to similar types of discourse in virtually every culture.[12] From where did the rabbis develop the procedure?

The second example is Bernard Brandon Scott, who, although he views the Hebrew word *mashal*[13] as a background against which to understand New Testament parables, argues that the parable genre is not found in the Hebrew Bible.[14] Contrast Scott with someone like John Drury, who says the Old Testament is full of parables, or Claus Westermann, who identifies numerous texts as parables.[15] Part of the problem is, of course, definition: if we draw a narrow circle defining "parable," not many examples will be found. This is what has happened with Scott. He defines a parable as "a *mashal* that employs a short narrative fiction to reference a symbol." Many *meshalim*[16] occur in the Old Testament, but Scott does not find any short narrative fictions that reference *symbols*, such as the kingdom or the Torah. But why should a parable have to reference a symbol? In fact, Westermann argues that Old Testament parables compare a *process* or an *event* in one arena with that in another.[17] If, contrary to Scott's definition, "parable" is defined as a *mashal* that employs a short narrative fiction to reference reality or one's relation to God, then the Old Testament certainly has parables.

In fact, the problem in parable interpretation has often been definition, and the definitions people have chosen have just as often had a theological agenda. Adolf Jülicher is famous for defining parable as a story with one point of comparison, and then rejecting any account with more than one point of comparison as later allegory from the church.[18] Even now, a century after his work, parable exegesis is still trying to recover from this blunder.[19] Definitions are necessary and also hamper our work. Parable analysis labors between striving for clarity of concept with our definitions and allowing the texts the freedom to shape forms and present accounts that do not necessarily fit our categories. Human language and thinking are remarkably flexible.

To some degree, Christian and Jewish scholarship has been guilty of provincialism and cultural imperialism in studying the parables. Jesus did not merely appear on the scene as the first to speak in parables. To look merely for rabbinic predecessors is myopic. The fact is that parabolic speech is a common human way of thinking, known in virtually all cultures. The Aesopic fables of the Greek world are obviously similar. In fact, Jülicher categorized Jesus' parables as fables.[20] Obviously, differences exist, but one is dealing with the same process of thought. But these stories did not suddenly grow on Greek soil, as the collectors of Aesop's fables were aware, for they themselves point to a Syrian origin.[21] Some scholars suggest influence from Buddhist stories on Aesop's fables and rabbinic parables.[22] The Story of Aḥiḳar, which goes back probably to the seventh century B.C.E., has parabolic forms and had widespread influence in view of the fact that it has been preserved in several languages. Further, Sumerian examples are attested at least to the eighteenth century B.C.E. None of this is to suggest direct dependence by Jesus on any of these precursors; it is only to recognize that parabolic thinking is a common human way of thinking. No evidence exists that anyone prior to Jesus used parables as consistently, creatively, and effectively as he did. Nor has anyone since, but that is not to ignore or detract from the value of others who used the parabolic method, whether it be Aḥiḳar, Epictetus, Blaise Pascal, Søren Kierkegaard, or a host of others in various cultures and times.

Granted that parables derive from a common human way of thinking, with reference to Jesus' parables greater attention must still be given to the Old Testament. Without neglecting later Jewish writings and the culture of the first century, and without diminishing the creativity and uniqueness with which Jesus taught, the one sure, direct influence on him was the Old Testament. If much of his thought and the evidence substantiating his preaching came from the Old Testament, it should occasion no surprise that his method and way of thinking are influenced from there as well. Closer analysis of *mashal* and of Old Testament parabolic forms will offer significant insight for understanding Jesus' parables.

Mashal in the Hebrew Bible

The Hebrew word *mashal*, which the Septuagint translates in most cases with the Greek word *parabolē*, is extremely broad and somewhat problematic. The older Brown, Driver, and Briggs lexicon actually lists three different verbs spelled *mashal*: "to be like," "to use a proverb or parable," and "to rule."[23] Some have attempted to trace all three ideas back to one common word, but most see two distinct and unrelated verbs, coincidentally spelled the same way, one meaning "to be like," which was adapted to refer to proverbial speech, and the second meaning "to rule."[24]

The surprising fact is that, even if one excludes the meaning "to rule" as from an unrelated word, *mashal* still covers a very wide semantic range. The sixteen occurrences of the verb form all fall easily into two categories: seven (all in Psalms, Job, and Isaiah) involve a comparison, such as Psalm 28:1, "I will be like those who go down to the pit"; and nine (eight in Ezekiel and one in Numbers 21:27) refer to speaking parables or proverbs, such as Ezekiel 16:44, "Everyone will quote this proverb." The noun form occurs thirty-nine times, and here the meanings proliferate. The most frequent reference is to a proverb, such as "Is Saul also among the prophets?" (1 Samuel 10:12) or "Out of the wicked comes forth wickedness" (1 Samuel 24:13). The title of the Book of Proverbs is *mišlê Šĕlōmōh*. In Proverbs 1:6, the wise man is able to understand a proverb (*mashal*), a figure, sayings of the wise, and their riddles.[25]

Closely related are several occurrences of the word with the meaning "taunt" or "byword," such as the taunt against the king of Babylon, "How the oppressor has ceased!" (Isaiah 14:4), or the accusing taunt "Woe to him who increases that which is not his" (Habakkuk 2:6).[26] Still closely related is the connotation "a lament," such as in reference to the lament "We are utterly ruined" (Micah 2:4). In Ezekiel 14:8, God's punishment of idolators makes such people a *mashal* and "sign," symbols of the error of their ways. Not so obviously related, however, are the uses of *mashal* to refer to Balaam's oracles (Numbers 23:7)[27] or to the extended discourses of Job (27:1 and 29:1). In Psalm 49:4 [5], 78:2, and Ezekiel 17:2 *mashal* appears in parallelism opposite "riddle." While *mashal* refers to extended discourses in Job and to the prophetic oracles of Balaam, it is *not* used of stories such as we find in the New Testament parables, even where such forms exist. On the other hand, Ezekiel does use it of longer forms: a rather elaborate allegory in 17:2-10 (the Eagle and the Vine), a prophecy using the image of devouring fire in 20:44-49 [21:1-5], and an extended comparison in 24:3-5 (the Cauldron).

Scholars have struggled to find some rationale to explain why such a broad array of meanings can be indicated by one word. Often they end up focusing on the idea of comparison—which is probably correct, but the attempts are not particularly satisfying. Possibly a summary definition is ill-advised; but if one is required, it may suffice to say a *mashal* is any saying to stimulate thought and provide insight.

Just as surprising as the range of meanings for *mashal* is the fact that in the Septuagint *parabolē* is used most of the time to translate all these different nuances.[28] *Parabolē* is not used to translate any other Hebrew word. In fact, in some ways it is surprising that *parabolē* was chosen to cover this range of meaning, for its primary meaning in Greek usage was "comparison," and it was not a particularly common word prior to the end of the first century C.E. For example, Josephus and Philo use *parabolē* only three times each, Plato only twice, and Aristotle seventeen times. Other words such as *ainos* ("tale" or "story," but also "riddle" and "proverb") could have been used to cover the broad range of *mashal*. But, by choosing *parabolē*, the translators of the Septuagint brought into prominence a word that the evangelists would catapult to notoriety.

Before looking specifically at parabolic forms in the Old Testament, we should pause to emphasize that—despite the way translations hide the fact—the same broad range of meaning which *mashal* has in the Old Testament, *parabolē* has in the New. For examples, *parabolē* is used of a proverb in Luke 4:23, a riddle in Mark 3:23 and Luke 6:39,[29] a comparison in Mark 7:17, a similitude in Matthew 13:33, an example story in Luke 12:16-21, a story with two levels of meaning in Luke 19:11-27, an allegory in Matthew 13:3-9,[30] a symbol in Hebrews 9:9, and to convey the idea "figuratively" in Hebrews 11:19. *Parabolē* in the Greek New Testament is a much broader word than "parable" in the English language. Attention to this breadth of meaning could have prevented many of the errors New Testament scholars have made.

Parabolic Forms in the Old Testament

The search for Old Testament precursors to the parables of Jesus understandably looks for stories similar to the best-known parables. Not many examples appear, and disagreement exists as to how many should be included. Birger Gerhardsson identifies only five parables from the Hebrew Scriptures, but also lists ten additional borderline cases.[31] T. W. Manson lists nine parables and two fables,[32] some of which are not in

Gerhardsson's two categories. By contrast, Claus Westermann surveys not just parables, but comparisons, which may be a single word, a sentence, or an extended narrative, only the last of which would be labeled as a parable.[33] Westermann is particularly helpful in forcing the realization that we are dealing with a way of thinking. John Sider also recently emphasized this by underscoring that parables are a form of analogous thinking. They are extended analogies.[34] The important activity for telling parables is analogical thought. If one knows that the word of God is like a seed, the parable of the Sower is a relatively easy step. Or, to take another example, if one has already compared rich Israelite women to the cows of Bashan (Amos 4:1), one could easily extend the analogy to a parable or a similitude.

Westermann also helpfully draws attention to the fact that, for all practical purposes, comparisons (and parables) appear only in certain types of literature. They rarely appear in legal texts and historical narrative, but abound in the prophetic literature, psalms, and proverbs. Comparisons and parables are prevalent in dialogical texts, and especially in confrontational ones. The vast majority of comparisons and parables occur in contexts of judgment and indictment.[35]

Again pause for reflection is merited. One now has insight as to why so few parables appear in the Mishnah: it is primarily legal material.[36] The character of other early Jewish writings is also less conducive to the use of parables. We might have expected more parables in tractate 'Abot in the Mishnah or in the more argumentative Jewish writings, and indeed, some related forms exist, even if they are not the kind of story parables we find with Jesus. The Apocalypse of the Animals in *Enoch* 85-90 is nothing but an extended allegory of the history of the world in the guise of animals, a "zoomorphic" history, in J. T. Milik's words.[37] Second Esdras, which is probably from the end of the first century C.E., has several passages that are close to the gospel parables: 4:28-32 (which is similar to the parable of the Sower), 4:38-43, 7:49-61, and 8:1-3. In any case, the later rabbis seem to have given parables a *new* context. Whereas with the Old Testament and Jesus parables were instruments of confrontation, the later rabbis made them instruments for exegesis.

With regard to Jesus' own preaching, we also have insight as to why he used parables so frequently. Jesus seems consciously to have presented himself in the mode of a prophet announcing an indictment and a crisis for the nation, the context in which parables are especially useful. This may have some relevance in understanding why the Gospel of John does not have story parables, since, even though John has some very confrontational sections, the focus seems to be more on signs and discourses for the life of the believer.

If we seek to isolate the parabolic forms in the Old Testament, several passages are obvious counterparts to the parables of Jesus. Four passages have been identified as juridical parables for the way they force hearers to make judgments on the level of the parable, which end up being self-condemnations in reality:[38] the parable of the Ewe Lamb that Nathan tells David (2 Samuel 12:1-14); the parable of the Widow and the Avengers, which Joab arranges for a wise woman from Tekoa to tell David (2 Samuel 14:1-20); the parable of the Fake Injury, by which an unnamed prophet confronts Ahab (1 Kings 20:35-42); and the parable of the Vineyard (Isaiah 5:1-7), which expresses judgment on the house of Israel and the people of Judah for being so unproductive.[39] Undeniably, the self-condemnations and reversals effected by these stories are reminiscent of the self-condemnations and reversals effected by the parables of Jesus, especially the parable of the Wicked Tenants (Matthew 21:33-45 and parallels).[40] The parable of the Unfruitful Fig Tree (Luke 13:6-9) is very close to the parable of the Vineyard in Isaiah 5.

These Old Testament parables still hold powerful messages for the Church. Nathan's parable to David and the parable of the Vineyard are frequently heard in modern congregations, and rightly so, for all of us too often have to admit our own guilt and our own lack of productivity. The parable from the wise woman of Tekoa, however, receives little attention, which is unfortunate. This parable not only confronts David, but in the process conveys a powerful theological statement that expresses the gospel as much as any New Testament text. In 2 Samuel 14:14 the wise woman of Tekoa says, "We must all die; we are like water spilled on the ground, which cannot be gathered up. But God will not take away a life; he will devise plans so as not to keep an outcast banished forever from his presence" (NRSV). The idea of God thinking up ways to bring back the banished fits very well with the Father who runs out to meet the returning prodigal, and it deserves to be heard in churches as much as the latter.

In addition to these four juridical parables, two fables should be listed, although nothing really like these forms appears in the New Testament. Both Judges 9:7-15 and 2 Kings 14:9-10 recount fables in which trees and plants talk and, in doing so, mirror the political views of the speakers. Plant fables like these are known from other ancient cultures.[41]

All the other story-type parables appear in Ezekiel, which has more use of parabolic forms than any other Old Testament book. At least six passages in Ezekiel are narrations—some would call them allegories[42]—presenting Israel's history in figurative form, and should be listed: 16:1-54, Jerusalem the Prostitute; 17:2-24, the Eagle and the Vine and its explanation;[43] 19:2-9, the Lioness and Her Cubs; 19:10-14, the Transplanted Vine; 23:1-49, the Two Sisters and its explanation; and 24:3-14, the Cauldron and its explanation.[44] New Testament scholarship—prob-

ably rightly—draws no connection between Ezekiel's being addressed as
Son of Man and Jesus' use of Son of Man (which is derived from Daniel
7:13). At the same time, because of Ezekiel's frequent use of parabolic
forms, one can only ponder whether Ezekiel might have had more influence on Jesus than we think. (Note 20:49 [21:5]: "They say of me, 'Is he
not a speaker of parables?'")

Several important features should be noticed about these twelve
Old Testament passages with parables. They do not all follow the same
format, but they do all have interpretations explicitly given. Most of
these explanations follow the parable, but some precede the parable. The
accounts are not general stories, but context specific. They were told for
the purpose of mirroring a specific reality. This has bearing on how one
looks at the New Testament parables. Almost as a matter of course, some
New Testament scholars strike the introductions and conclusions of the
parables of Jesus as stemming from the early church. The truncated forms
often then become enigmatic and susceptible to manipulation in the direction the interpreter wishes. Certainly the evangelists have redacted
and arranged the parables in their larger narrative, and a few of Jesus'
parables are presented to us with minimal indication as to their meaning,
either in the context or by way of interpretation. (See, for example, Matthew 13:33.) But, as is true of nearly all rabbinic parables as well, most of
the parables of Jesus have and need explanations or contextual indicators
that make certain they are understandable. They too are context specific.

We tend to think of parables as simple stories that do not require
explanation, but that is untrue. The degree of explanation required depends on the opacity of the story. Some stories are diaphanous: one can
see through them right from the first, which is what the author intended
(see Ezekiel 23:2-3). Others are uncertain until the author drops the cur-
tain and allows the reality to show through, which is what happens with
Nathan's "You are the man" (2 Samuel 12:7).[45] Parables were told to
stimulate thought and give insight, but the idea that parables are conundra
without precise intent or are susceptible to multiple interpretations, as if
one were discerning abstract art, is a misunderstanding of the nature of
parables. Particularly for parables told in a confrontational setting, it is
almost unthinkable that the meaning would not be made explicit.[46] Who
tells a sharp story and leaves the barb implicit?

These twelve passages, however, do not do justice to the analogi-
cal-parabolic way of thinking in the Old Testament that provides impe-
tus for both Jesus and the rabbis. Both Ezekiel 34:1-31 (an extended narration about the shepherds of Israel and a promise of God as shepherd)
and 37:1-14 (the valley of dry bones) are parabolic. Jeremiah 23:1-4 also
uses imagery of shepherds who scatter the sheep and of God who will

bring his flock back to their folds and protect them.[47] Isaiah 28:23-29 uses a similitude about plowing and sowing to teach about the coming judgment of God. Isaiah 59:16-17 presents God as a warrior putting on his armor to bring salvation. Jeremiah 13:12-14, through a similitude about a wine bottle, depicts the drunkenness and destruction of all the people. The Book of Hosea is largely a parable about God's relation to Israel depicted in the guise of Hosea's relation to his wife. Psalm 80:8-17 describes Israel's history as the story of a vine that was brought out of Egypt, was planted, then was ravaged and burned. Habakkuk 1:13-17 describes the actions of the Babylonians catching people through a similitude of a fisherman who catches fish and then sacrifices to his net. Ecclesiastes 9:14-18 praises wisdom, even if by someone not remembered, by giving a short parable about a poor wise man in a small city beseiged by a powerful king.

Other passages using various analogies might justly be listed,[48] but two other kinds of texts must be included as background to the New Testament and rabbinic parables. *Acted parables* are an important means of communicating a prophetic word. Symbolic acts such as the footwashing, the miracles, the entry into Jerusalem, and the cleansing of the temple are, of course, important in the ministry of Jesus; and some would view them as acted parables, especially in Mark.[49] Whether "acted parable" would be the right label for such acts is debatable; possibly "signs" or "symbolic acts" would be better, for the act and its meaning to some degree both stand on the same plane. With the Old Testament examples, the act and its meaning occupy two clearly distinct planes. What could have been stated as a parable on a figurative level is acted out and then explained on another level in terms of its significance for the life of the people. Jeremiah is probably the best known among those giving acted parables. In 13:1-11, at God's instruction Jeremiah bought a new loincloth, hid it in the river bank, and then returned to find it ruined and profitable for nothing, all mirroring the disobedience of the people. In 18:1-11, the actions of the potter are understood as mirroring the freedom and work of God. In 19:1-13, the breaking of a pot depicts God's coming judgment. In 27:1-28:17, Jeremiah is described as wearing a yoke of bonds and bars to depict the rule of Nebuchadnezzar.

But Jeremiah is not the only one to present acted parables. Isaiah walked about naked and barefoot for three years as a sign against Egypt and Ethiopia (20:2-6). Ezekiel has several acted parables. A series of acts depicts the siege and plight of the city of Jerusalem and the people being taken into exile (see 4:1-5:4; 12:1-20; and 24:15-27). Ezekiel is himself a sign to the people (24:24 and 27). Similarly, Nehemiah stood and shook out the folds of his garment and said, "So may God shake out everyone from house and from property who does not perform this promise"

(Nehemiah 5:13).

The remaining category of texts that demonstrates the analogical thinking of the Old Testament as precursor to New Testament parables is *symbolic visions and dreams*. With visions and dreams, images are shown to a prophet (or someone who needs the prophet's help in interpreting) to depict the reality of the nation's relation to God or an overview of coming events. As with the narrative parables, interpretations are required and accompany the vision. For example, in Jeremiah 24:1-10 two baskets of figs, one good and one bad, mirror those people taken captive into the land of the Chaldeans and those who stay in Judah or go to Egypt. Amos is well known for his series of visions from God: locusts, fire, plumbline, and summer fruit (7:1-9 and 8:1-3). Zechariah 1:7-6:8 is primarily a series of visions and interpretations. The dreams and interpretations in Daniel 2 and 7 depict the succession of human kingdoms and the ultimate kingdom of God. In all these cases the dreams or visions function just like parables. They have two levels of meaning, and interpretation is required to move from the first to the second. No suggestion is intended that these dreams and visions had direct influence on Jesus or the rabbis; rather, they are one instance of an analogical way of thought that is prevalent in certain sections of the Old Testament and is also characteristic of much of Jesus' teaching.

Reflections

In some ways analysis of parables, particularly Old Testament parables, is confusing, and much work remains to be done. We are not dealing with one clearly defined literary genre. By necessity we are dealing both with a way of thinking and with several diverse literary forms. A broad spectrum of analogical thought patterns exists, ranging from comparisons to developed and extended analogical narratives, similitudes, story parables, and acted parables. No profit is gained by trying to collapse all the forms into a few patterns. Analysis of the forms should not only identify the differences in the patterns, but also pay close attention to the different dynamics and components at work in the various accounts. It makes a difference whether God, a prophet, or a plaintiff is the speaker. Of primary significance are the *function* of the parable in its context and the *means* by which this function is achieved.

Jesus did not create the parabolic method; he honed and mastered it. Others no doubt were using parables in first-century Palestine, as even the sayings from John the Baptist attest (for example, Matthew 3:10). One would be surprised if this were not the case, given the popularity of similar forms in the Graeco-Roman world. Still, the only demonstrable influence on Jesus—and surely the primary one—is the Old Testament. From there Jesus drew not only his theology, but his way of thinking and

many of his images. To seek to understand the parables without due attention to the parabolic forms in the Old Testament will result in failure.
All learning moves from the known to the unknown. Parables are
so effective because, among other things, they allow people to see something they already know and understand and then by analogical thinking
move to another plane and gain new understanding about God and the
meaning of discipleship in the kingdom. People still love analogical thinking, and therefore the parabolic method is still a powerful way of teaching. To be effective, this teaching method requires a special skill and
discipline. Stories and analogies do not teach by themselves; they require
interpretation, whether implicit or explicit. Nor are stories inherently
Christian. What makes a story Christian is the theology it mirrors. Pastors and teachers would do well to hone their own parabolic skills; and,
as with Jesus, the parabolic forms and analogical thinking of the Old
Testament are the most effective primers for developing this skill.

Endnotes

1. "The Pharisee and the Tax Collector: Luke 18:9-14 and Deuteronomy 26:1-
15," *Interp* 48 (1994): 252-61. For a similar conclusion based partly on the hypothesis that Luke shaped his travel narrative to Deuteronomy, see Craig A.
Evans, "The Pharisee and the Publican: Luke 18:9-14 and Deuteronomy 26," in
The Gospels and the Scriptures of Israel, ed. Craig A. Evans and W. Richard Stegner
(Sheffield: Sheffield Academic Press, 1994), 342-55.
2. Especially in the accounts of Matthew and Mark; Luke's account is more
abbreviated. This use of the Old Testament cannot be written off as later redactional additions. For a detailed treatment of this parable, see my *The Parable of
the Wicked Tenants* (Tübingen: Mohr-Siebeck, 1983).
3. See F. Scott Spencer, "2 Chronicles 28:5-15 and the Parable of the Good
Samaritan," *WTJ* 46 (1984): 317-49.
4. John Paul Heil, "Ezekiel 34 and the Narrative Strategy of the Shepherd
and the Sheep Metaphor in Matthew," *CBQ* 55 (1993): 698-708, especially 705.
5. See the suggestion by J. Duncan M. Derrett, "The Parable of the Great
Supper," in *The Law in the New Testament* (London: Darton, Longman & Todd,
1970), 126-55.
6. Birger Gerhardsson, "The Parable of the Sower and Its Interpretation,"
NTS 14 (1968): 165-93.
7. John W. Bowker, "Mystery and Parable: Mark iv.1-20," *JTS* 25 (1974): 300-
17.
8. C. H. Cave, "Lazarus and the Lukan Deuteronomy," *NTS* 15 (1969): 319-
25.
9. David Flusser, *Die rabbinischen Gleichnisse und der Gleichniserzähler Jesus*, 1
Teil: *Das Wesen der Gleichnisse* (Bern: Peter Lang, 1981), see especially 17-19
and 146-48.
10. The words *parabolē* and *mashal* occur, and imagery is used to effect comparisons, but nothing like Jesus' narrative parables is found. On Enoch and

2 Esdras, see below, 7.

11. See Jacob Neusner, *Rabbinic Literature and the New Testament: What We Cannot Show, We Do Not Know* (Valley Forge: Trinity Press International, 1994), especially 185-90, which give a scathing critique of Brad Young's *Jesus and his Jewish Parables* (Mahwah, N.J.: Paulist Press, 1989).

12. Flusser, of course, is well aware of the similarities to Greek fables.

13. Throughout this article, this familiar anglicizing of the Hebrew word will be used instead of the more precise transliterated form *māšāl*.

14. Bernard Brandon Scott, *Hear Then the Parable: A Commentary on the Parables of Jesus* (Minneapolis: Fortress, 1989), 7, 63-64.

15. John Drury, *The Parables in the Gospels* (New York: Crossroad, 1985), 8; Claus Westermann, *The Parables of Jesus in the Light of the Old Testament*, trans. and ed. Friedemann W. Golka and Alastair H. B. Logan (Minneapolis: Fortress, 1990).

16. The plural of *mashal*.

17. Westermann, *Parables of Jesus*, 11, 85, 152-54. It is correct that often a process or event is in view, but whether Westermann is correct in excluding all language of pictures or images is debatable.

18. Adolph Jülicher, *Die Gleichnisreden Jesu* (Freiburg i. B.: Akademische Verlagsbuchhandlung von J. C. B. Mohr, 1888-1889), I, 49-73, 77-82, 105-106, and 117-18.

19. Despite the fact that critiques have been offered all along the way. For three quite different critiques, see Madeleine Boucher, *The Mysterious Parable: A Literary Study* (Washington, D.C.: The Catholic Biblical Association of America, 1977), 1-25; Craig L. Blomberg, *Interpreting the Parables* (Downers Grove, Ill.: InterVarsity Press, 1990), 13-69; and David Stern, *Parables in Midrash: Narrative and Exegesis in Rabbinic Literature* (Cambridge, Mass.: Harvard University Press, 1991), 10-12, 191-92.

20. Jülicher, *Gleichnisreden* I, 94-100. See also Mary Ann Beavis, "Parable and Fable," *CBQ* 52 (1990): 473-98; and George W. Coats, "Parable, Fable, and Anecdote," *Interp* 35 (1981): 368-82. For a broader discussion of hellenistic forms, see Klaus Berger, "*Hellenistische Gattungen im Neuen Testament*," *ANRW* 25.2, ed. Wolfgang Haase (Berlin: Walter de Gruyter, 1984), 1031-1432.

21. See the beginning of part two of the collection of Aesop's fables in *Babrius* (*Babrius and Phaedrus, Loeb Classical Edition*, 139) and the introduction to this Loeb volume, xxvii-xxxiv. See also Ronald J. Williams, "The Fable in the Ancient Near East," in *A Stubborn Faith: Papers on Old Testament and Related Subjects Presented to Honor William Andrew Irwin*, ed. Edward C. Hobbs (Dallas: Southern University Press, 1956), 3-26.

22. See Joseph Jacobs, "Aesop's Fables Among the Jews," *The Jewish Encyclopedia*, ed. Isidore Singer (New York: Funk & Wagnalls, 1906), I, 221-22.

23. Francis Brown, S. R. Driver, and Charles A. Briggs, eds., *A Hebrew and English Lexicon of the Old Testament* (Oxford: Clarendon, 1962), 605. The editors may have been influenced by Otto Eissfeldt's *Der Maschal im Alten Testament* (Geißen: Alfred Töpelmann, 1913). See also the discussions by Scott, *Hear Then the Parable*, 8-19; A. S. Herbert, "The 'Parable' (*Māšāl*) in the Old Testament," *SJT*, 7 (1954): 180-96; John Drury, "Origins of Mark's Parables," in *Ways of Reading the Bible*, ed. Michael Wadsworth (Totowa, N.J.: Barnes & Noble, 1981),174-77; and Timothy Polk, "Paradigms, Parables, and Mĕšālîm: On Reading the Māšāl in Scripture," *CBQ* 45 (1983): 564-83.

24. See, for example, Ludwig Koehler and Walter Baumgartner, *The Hebrew and Aramaic Lexicon of the Old Testament* (Leiden: E. J. Brill, 1995), II, 647-48.

25. Cf. the similar thought in Sir. 39:2-3, which uses *parabolē* twice in connection with enigmatic sayings. For other texts in the Hebrew Bible using *mashal* with the sense of "proverb," see Deuteronomy 28:37; 1 Kings 4:32 [5:12]; 9:7; 2 Chronicles 7:20; Job 13:12; Proverbs 10:1; 25:1; 26:7, 9; Ecclesiastes 12:9; Ezekiel 12:22, 23; 18:2, 3.

26. See also Psalms 44:14 [15] and 69:11 [12].

27. See also Numbers 23:18; 24:3, 15, 20, 21, and 23.

28. Other words used in the Septuagint to translate *mashal* include *aphanismon* (byword [literally, "something lost"]), *prooimion* (preamble), *paroimia* (proverb), *isos* (equal), and *thrēnos* (lament).

29. The parallel in Matthew 15:15 about the blind leading the blind seems to understand *parabolē* not about the blind, but with reference to the saying about what enters the stomach.

30. If indeed allegory is a genre, which is debatable. See Boucher, *The Mysterious Parable*, 17-25.

31. Birger Gerhardsson, "The Narrative Meshalim in the Old Testament Books and in the Synoptic Gospels," in *To Touch the Text: Biblical and Related Studies in Honor of Joseph A. Fitzmyer*, ed. Maurya P. Horgan and Paul J. Kobelski (New York: Crossroad, 1989), 291.

32. T. W. Manson, *The Teaching of Jesus* (Cambridge: Cambridge University Press, 1939), 62-63.

33. Westermann, *Parables of Jesus*, 5-151; see 3.

34. John Sider, *Interpreting the Parables: A Hermeneutical Guide to Their Meaning* (Grand Rapids: Zondervan, 1995). See also Roy A. Stewart, "The Parable Form in the Old Testament and the Rabbinic Literature," *EvQ* 36 (1964): 133-47, especially 133.

35. Westermann, *Parables of Jesus*, 2, 20-30, and 150-60. Surprisingly, comparisons do not appear much in the Elijah-Elisha cycle.

36. Scott, *Hear Then the Parable*, 15, admits only one parable from the Mishnah—*m. Sukk.* 2.9—but surely several more merit the label: *m. 'Abot.* 1.3; 2.15 (which is similar to Matthew 9:37-38); 3:17; 3:18 (which is similar to Matthew 7:24-27); 4:16; *m. Nid.* 2.5; 5.7. Note too that, in form, *m. 'Abot* 5.15 is similar to the parable of the Sower.

37. J. T. Milik, *The Books of Enoch* (Oxford: Clarendon Press, 1976), 43. The history of Israel is presented as a history of sheep in chapter 89. Note too that Enoch 1:2-3 identifies this whole work as a parable. Chapters 37-71, the middle portion, are probably from a later date, but are labeled as parables (translated "similitudes") even though they are not what we usually understand as parables. They are closer to the discourses of Job. See the discussion of David Winston Suter, "*Māšāl* in the Similitudes of Enoch," *JBL* 100 (1981): 193-212, in which he understands the similitudes as cosmological and eschatological comparisons. See also Priscilla Patten, "The Form and Function of Parable in Select Apocalyptic Literature and Their Significance for Parables in the Gospel of Mark," *NTS*, 29 (1983): 246-58.

38. For discussions of this genre, see Adrian Graffy, "The Literary Genre of Isaiah 5,1-7" *Bib* 60 (1979): 400-409; and Ulrich Mell, *Die "anderen" Winzer: eine exegetische Studie zur Vollmacht Jesu Christi nach Markus 11,27-12,34* (Tübingen: Mohr-Siebeck, 1994), 82-85.

39. The self-condemnation in Isaiah 5 is implied. Alexander Rofé, "Classes in the Prophetical Stories: Didactic Legenda and Parable," in *Studies in Prophecy* (Leiden: E. J. Brill, 1974), 155-64, identifies 1 Kings 12:33-13:32 and Jonah

both as parables, although he recognizes the difficulties involved. His argument is convincing in neither case. A parable is a story with two levels of meaning, which is not true of either of these two stories, whatever else they are. George M. Landes argues more generally that Jonah is a *mashal* because it contrasts the Ninevites and Jonah. See "Jonah: A Mashal?" in *Israelite Wisdom: Theological and Literary Essays in Honor of Samuel Terrien*, ed. John G. Gammie et al. (Missoula, Mont.: Scholars Press, 1978), 137-58. *Mashal* is a broad category, but whether this is the right label for Jonah is debatable.

40. For other examples, see Matthew 21:28-32; Luke 7:40-47; 18:9-14. However, one should not overemphasize reversal and self-condemnation, for many parables have other purposes and do not use these dynamics.

41. See, for example, the conversation between the tamarisk and the date palm provided by James Pritchard, ed., *Ancient Near Eastern Texts Relating to the Old Testament* (Princeton: Princeton University Press, 1950), 410-11; and Aesop's Fable of the Oak and the Reed (*Babrius*, no. 36).

42. For example, Westermann, *Parables of Jesus*, 81.

43. Cf. also 15:1-8, which is close to being a parable about the vine.

44. On which see Daniel L. Block, "Ezekiel's Boiling Cauldron: A Form-Critical Solution to Ezekiel XXIV 1-14," *VT* XLI (1991): 12-37.

45. Sometimes the explanations contain a mixture of literal and metaphorical speech, such as in Ezekiel 17:22-24.

46. On the necessity of parables being interpreted, see Stern, *Parables in Midrash*, 11-19; Patten, "The Form and Function," 246-58, and Flusser, *Die rabbinischen Gleichnisse*,119-22.

47.This imagery appears often; other obvious examples are Psalm 23, Isaiah 40:11, and Micah 7:14.

48. See the appendix by Sider, *Interpreting the Parables*, listing Old Testament texts with parabolic forms, 251-52.

49. For example, see Patten, "The Form and Function," 256-57.

BIBLIOGRAPHY

Bibliography of the Works of Fredrick Carlson Holmgren

NORMA S. SUTTON

BOOKS

The God Who Cares: A Christian Looks at Judaism. Atlanta: John Knox, 1979.

Israel Alive Again: A Commentary on the Books of Ezra and Nehemiah. International Theological Commentary. Grand Rapids: Eerdmans, 1987.

With Wings as Eagles: Isaiah 40/55, an Interpretation. Chappaqua, N.Y.: Biblical Scholars Press, 1973.

EDITED WORKS

Holmgren, Fredrick Carlson, and George A. F. Knight, eds. International Theological Commentary. Grand Rapids: Eerdmans, 1983- .

Holmgren, Fredrick Carlson, and Herman E. Schaalman, eds. *Preaching Biblical Texts: Expositions by Jewish and Christian Scholars.* Grand Rapids: Eerdmans, 1995.

ARTICLES

"Abraham and Isaac on Mount Moriah: Genesis 22:1-19." *The Covenant Quarterly* 39-40 (August 1981-February 1982): 75-85.

"Before the Temple, the Thornbush: An Exposition of Exodus 2:11-3:12." *Reformed Journal* 33 (March 1983): 9-11.

"Between Text and Sermon: Isaiah 2:1-5," *Interpretation* 51 No. 1 (January 1997): 61-64.

"Both as Servant and Teacher of the Church." *The Covenant Companion.* 74 (July 1985): 11.

"Chiastic Structure in Isaiah 51:1-11."*Vetus Testamentum* 19 (April 1969): 196-201.

"Christian Pietism and Abraham Heschel." In *No Religion Is an Island: Abraham Joshua Heschel and Interreligious Dialogue*, ed. Harold Kasinoiv and Byron L. Sherwin, 135-50. Maryknoll, N.Y.: Orbis Books, 1991.

"The Concept of God as Redeemer in the Old Testament." *The Covenant Quarterly* 19 (May 1961): 9-18.

"Crisis and Response." *The Covenant Quarterly* 30 (February 1972): 3-20.

"Faithful Abraham and the '*amanâ* Covenant: Nehemiah 9,6-10,1." *Zeitschrift für die Alttestamentliche Wissenschaft* 104, no. 2 (1992): 249-54.

"The God of History: Biblical Realism and the Lectionary." In *Remaining for the Future: Working Papers and Addenda*. Vol. 1, *Jews and Christians during and after the Holocaust*, edited by Yehuda Bauer, Alice Eckardt, Franklin H. Littell, Elisabeth Maxwell, Robert Maxwell, and David Patterson, 799-811. Oxford: Pergamon Press, 1989.

"The God of History: Biblical Realism and the Lectionary." *The Covenant Quarterly* 48 (May 1990): 3-18.

"Holding Your Own against God! Genesis 32:22-32 (in the Context of Genesis 31-33)." *Interpretation* 44 (January 1990): 5-17.

"The Holy Spirit." *The Covenant Companion* 62 (April 19, 1968): 8-9.

"Introduction: Free to Listen and Obey." *The Covenant Quarterly* 43 (August 1985): 3-4.

"Israel, the Prophets, and the Book of Jonah: The Rest of the Story: The Formation of the Canon." *Currents in Theology and Mission* 21 (April 1994): 127-32.

"Jews and Christians: The Dark Side of Church History." *The Covenant Quarterly* 35 (February 1977): 3-15.

Lament: "Shepherd and Savior of Israel." *The Covenant Hymnal: A Worshipbook*. (Chicago: Covenant Publications, 1996): 912.

"The Living Word." *The Covenant Companion* 52 (November 1, 1963): 3, 19.

"A New Covenant? For Whom?" *The Ecumenist* 22 (March-April 1984): 38-41.

"A New Covenant? For Whom?" *The Covenant Quarterly* 43 (March 1985): 39-44.

"The Pharisee and the Tax Collector: Luke 18:9-14 and Deuteronomy 26:1-15." *Interpretation* 48 (July 1994): 252-261.

"The Pietistic Tradition and Biblical Criticism." *The Covenant Quarterly* 28 (1970): 49-59.

"Preaching the Gospel without Anti-Judaism." *The Christian Ministry* 26 (May-June 1995): 11-14. Reprint, *Removing Anti-Judaism from the Pulpit*, edited by Howard Clark Kee and Irvin J. Borowsky, 67-74. New York: Continuum; Philadelphia: American Interfaith Institute, 1996.

"Reflections on Jesus and Israel." *The Covenant Companion* 72 (April 1, 1983): 16.

"Remember Me; Remember Them." In *Scripture and Prayer: A Celebration for Carroll Stuhlmueller*, edited by Carolyn Osiek and Donald Senior, 33-45. Wilmington, Del.: Michael Glazier, 1988.

"Some Recent Literature on the Old Testament." *The Covenant Quarterly* 23 (August 1965): 9-18.

"Strange Silence." *The Covenant Companion* 61 (May 1, 1972): 10-11.

"Violence: God's Will on the Edge—Exodus 2:11-25." *Currents in Theology and Mission* 16 (December 1989): 425-29.

"The Way of Torah: Escape from Egypt." In *Preaching Biblical Texts: Expositions by Jewish and Christian Scholars*, edited by Fredrick C. Holmgren and Herman E. Schaalman. Grand Rapids: Eerdmans, 1995.

"What Really Matters." *The Covenant Companion* 73 (October 1984): 30-31.

"Yahweh the Avenger; Isaiah 63:1-6." In *Rhetorical Criticism: Essays in Honor of James Muilenburg*, edited by Jared J. Jackson and Martin Kessler, 133-48. Pittsburgh Theological Monograph Series, 1. Pittsburgh: Pickwick Press, 1974.

REVIEWS

Review of *Das Buch Ezechiel: kap 1:1-20, 44*, by Rudolf Mosis. *Catholic Biblical Quarterly* 42 (April 1980): 247-48.

Review of *Das Buch Nahum: Eine Redaktionskritische Untersuchung*, by Herman Schulz. *Catholic Biblical Quarterly* 36 (July 1974): 431-32.

Review of *The Creative Word: Canon as a Model for Biblical Education*, by Walter Brueggemann. *Reformed Journal* 33 (April 1983): 27-29.

Review of *The Creative Word: Canon as a Model for Biblical Education*, by Walter Brueggemann. *The Covenant Quarterly* 41 (May 1983): 39-41.

Review of *Deuteronomy*, by David F. Payne. *Catholic Biblical Quarterly* 50 (October 1988): 675-76.

Review of *Ezechiel: Der Prophet und das Buch*, by Bernhard Lang. *Catholic Biblical Quarterly* 45 (April 1983): 290-91.

Review of *Faith and Piety in Early Judaism: Texts and Documents*, edited by George W. E. Nickelsburg and Michael E. Stone. *Catholic Biblical Quarterly* 46 (October 1984): 794-96.

Review of *Israel in Exile: A Theological Interpretation*, by Ralph W. Klein. *Theology Today* 37 (April 1980): 144.

Review of *Jeremiah*, by Robert Davidson. *Catholic Biblical Quarterly* 50 (October 1988): 675-76.

Review of *Jews and Christians after the Holocaust*, by Abraham J. Peck. *The Covenant Quarterly* 41 (May 1983): 41-44.

Review of *Jews and Christians in Dialogue: New Testament Foundations*, by John Koenig. *Christian Scholar's Review* 10 (1981): 260-61.

Review of *Judaic Perspectives on Ancient Israel*, ed. Jacob Neusner, Baruch A. Levine, and Ernest S. Frerichs. *Journal of Religion* 69 (January 1989): 137-38.

Review of *The Past, Present, and Future of Biblical Theology*, by James D. Smart. *The Covenant Quarterly* 38 (November 1980): 41-43.

Review of *Problems and Prospects of Old Testament Theology*, by Jesper Høgenhaven. *Reformed Journal* 39 (November 1989): 24-26.

Review of *Sinai and Zion: An Entry into the Jewish Bible*, by Jon D. Levenson. *Catholic Biblical Quarterly* 49 (April 1987): 314-15.

Review of *Theology of the Program of Restoration of Ezekiel 40-48*, by Jon D. Levenson. *Catholic Biblical Quarterly* 40 (April 1978): 248-49.

Review of *To Heaven, with Scribes and Pharisees*, by Lionel Blue. *The Covenant Quarterly* 35 (May 1977): 61-63.